The Urbana Free Library

To renew materials call
217-367-4057

		DATE DUE	

Limbo

Limbo

Blue-Collar Roots, White-Collar Dreams

Alfred Lubrano

WILEY

John Wiley & Sons, Inc.

For general information on our other products and services please contact our Customer Care
Department within the United States at (800) 762-2974, outside the United States at (317)
572-3993 or fax (317) 572-4002.

Wiley also publishes its books in a variety of electronic formats. Some content that appears in
print may not be available in electronic books. For more information about Wiley products,
visit our web site at www.wiley.com.

ISBN 0-471-26376-1

Printed in the United States of America

10 9 8 7 6 5 4 3 2 1

To my parents, for the start.
And to Linda, for everything else that's mattered.

Contents

Introduction

I am two people.

I now live a middle-class life, working at a white-collar newspaper-man's job, but I was born blue collar. I've never quite reconciled the dichotomy. This book is a step toward understanding what people gain and what they leave behind as they move from the working class to the middle class.

To be clear from the start, this is a work of journalism, not sociology—not even "comic sociology," as David Brooks labeled his book *Bobos in Paradise*, an erudite examination of how the educated have become the new elite in America.[1] My goal was to write a book about an existing social class, the white-collar children—first-generation college graduates—of blue-collar parents, and to write one that would be accessible to those without a Ph.D. The little-discussed cultural phenomenon plays itself out in every aspect of our lives—most noticeably in the workplace, but also in our homes and in ourselves.

This book has three components. First there's my personal story: I was a working-class kid from Brooklyn who crossed into the middle class after acquiring a college degree. After a time, it occurred to me that I was becoming a different person from my parents, and I was becoming part of a different class altogether. The things I valued and the choices I made as the white-collar son of blue-collar parents were sometimes at odds with my folks' ideas and instruction on how to live life. When I got into the working world, though, my blue-collar roots started to show, and I felt uneasy among the middle-class-born. The sense that I comprise two people who aren't always compatible never left me. I became curious about whether others felt this way, which led me to identify an overlooked social issue: the emotions involved in social mobility. How does it play in the head and heart to leave family and friends behind and scale the ladder out of the working class? What does it feel like in the new neighborhood of the middle class? And how do people ultimately reconcile the duality within them?

1

Second, I've included a distillation of thought about class and mobility from leading experts, including working-class studies scholars such as Charles Sackrey, Jake Ryan, Michelle Tokarczyk, Michael Zweig, and Sherry Linkon. I also consulted Berkeley mobility guru Michael Hout, class-and-education don Patrick Finn, Brookings Institution economist Isabel Sawhill, and psychologists of class Barbara Jensen and Laurene Finley. In recent years, a working-class studies movement has developed on campuses throughout America. These schools are small and include institutions like Youngstown State University that attract both a faculty and a student body from the working class (Harvard, Yale, and the like are decidedly not among them). Scholars delve into a world that has been overlooked—their lives are not usually reflected in the university syllabus or represented among campus student organizations.

Finally, and most important, the book includes the stories collected from more than 100 interviews I conducted over a nine-month period with people whom I call Straddlers. They were born to blue-collar families and then, like me, moved into the strange new territory of the middle class. They are the first in their families to have graduated from college. As such, they straddle two worlds, many of them not feeling at home in either, living in a kind of American limbo.[2]

My 100 Straddlers range in age from 18 to around 70. White ethnic Protestant or white Anglo-Saxon Protestant (WASP), African-American, Hispanic, and Asian, members of this demographically disparate group express remarkably similar emotions as they tell strikingly similar tales of the seldom-heard, dark side of mobility. Among them are lawyers and doctors, a union organizer, a handful of self-made millionaires, and the head of the National Endowment for the Arts. There is also a clutch of professors. It's a unique group, because in terms of education, they've come the furthest, having earned Ph.D.s in families where parents finished high school, at best. Enjoying some of the best working conditions in America, as Chicago academic Jack Metzgar freely admits, college professors toil in far safer precincts than their blue-collar forebears. The downside is obvious: Rise that far in a single generation and you're liable to feel hopelessly alienated from those who raised you. Professors are the most self-conscious Straddlers, many of them working with middle-class colleagues who don't understand them, all the while teaching mostly middle-class kids how to become the bosses of their parents, siblings, cousins, and childhood friends.

My subjects told their tales with an honest eloquence that moved and humbled me, and that I hope will touch you in the same way. Some no longer speak with their families, so profound are the differences between them. Some struggle constantly with aspects of the middle-class life, its rhythms and priorities intensely foreign to folk born to blue-collar parents.

I've used the elements of story to communicate their experiences—narratives, memories, and anecdotes. For the most part, people allowed me to use their real names. A handful of interviewees spent hours talking with me, only to request in the end that I not include any aspects of their lives, finding their personal stories ultimately too painful and private for public airing. There are a few who agreed to be included only if I used pseudonyms, saying they were uncomfortable telling me things that would get them either fired from their jobs or flogged by their families. Their hidden identities do not make their truths any less real.

As I explained earlier, I've used education as the dividing line between working class and middle class. Any economist or sociologist would tell you that's just part of the story. Along with education, factors such as income, job status, and the amount of authority and control one has at work are generally described in the sociological literature as the major determinants of class. I should also add that my approach is not one of statistical analysis.

Class Definitions

Terminology can get confusing when one is dealing with class. Economists divide white-collar workers into two categories: upper (managers and professionals) and lower (clerks). Blue-collar workers can be catalogued as skilled, unskilled, or farmers. Experts themselves will argue whether there are 16 classes or 9, or 5, or 3. George Orwell said there are but two economic classes, rich and poor, but myriad social classes.[3]

Life itself is untidy, definition-wise. For example, a plumber with an eighth-grade education can command a higher salary than a college professor with more degrees than fingers. The plumber is in an elevated economic class, but is he in a superior social class as well? The permutations are many and . . . well, confusing. So, at the risk of alienating heavy thinkers, I'm streamlining. For my purposes, blue-collar working-class people don't have college degrees and perform manual labor. And white-collar, middle-class people are college educated and work at professional-type jobs. One group works with their hands, the other with their minds.

The term *class* itself is tricky to define. When one human encounters another, scientists tell us, the first things they notice are each other's race and gender. Class is just as indelible a marker in defining who we are, yet because it's not obvious to the beholder, it becomes more slippery to pin down. Any blue-collar kid who works in a bakery can take a trip to the Gap and buy clothes that would make him indistinguishable from a sophomore at Bryn Mawr. For the last 30 years, universities have been awash in the politics of self-awareness, teaching the Holy Trinity of Identity—race, gender, and class. While race and gender have had their decades in the sun, however, class has been obscured and overlooked. It's the "C-word," Straddler-scholar Rebecca Beckingham tells me, the troublesome component of the iron triad. Sawhill says people would rather talk about sex than money, and money before class.

In America, we sing a hymn of equality, one that says that everyone has the same chances to get ahead. But that's not true and never has been. Who your parents are has as much or more to do with where you'll end up in life than any other single factor, social scientists say. Class can hold you back, or limit you. But if you express this, it sounds like whining. We're all supposed to pull ourselves up by our bootstraps in this tough country; those who don't must be too slow, too stupid, or too lazy to move ahead. We're a meritocracy, not an aristocracy, right? Well, the truth is, some of us are simply born to better circumstances and reap the benefits. One could also argue that many middle-class people may not even be aware of the good things bestowed on them— they can't always see their advantages.

When people talk about class, they're referring to nothing less than a culture, with families as the purveyors of that culture. From the moment we're born, our families tell us how to be. You adopt the attitudes held by the people around you, and you learn your place in life. Class is a "cultural network of shared values, meanings and

4

interactions," say Sackrey and Ryan.[4] Each class is a distinctive social existence, a culture that creates a sense of belonging among its members. To borrow a phrase from a different branch of social science, class is an "identity kit," equipped with the proper mask and costume, along with instructions on how to act.[5]

Class is script, map, and guide. It tells us how to talk, how to dress, how to hold ourselves, how to eat, and how to socialize. It affects whom we marry; where we live; the friends we choose; the jobs we have; the vacations we take; the books we read; the movies we see; the restaurants we pick; how we decide to buy houses, carpets, furniture, and cars; where our kids are educated; what we tell our children at the dinner table (conversations about the Middle East, for example, versus the continuing sagas of the broken vacuum cleaner or the half-wit neighbors); whether we even have a dinner table, or a dinnertime. In short, class is nearly everything about you. And it dictates what to expect out of life and what the future should be.

As powerful as it is, though, class is intangible, a metaphor that marks your place in the world. It's invisible and inexact, but it has resonance and deep meaning. It's resilient, having retained shape and structure through the years, sociologists say. I think of class as the dark matter of the universe—hard to see but nevertheless omnipresent, a basic part of everything.

Understanding class helps Straddlers learn who they are. Many Straddlers surprised themselves with their own tears when I interviewed them. They never thought about their lives in terms of class before, and our conversations helped explain a lot—their inability to fit in at work among middle-class colleagues and bosses, for example, as well as the difficulty they've had talking with their parents about topics other than how Uncle Bob is doing since the operation.

My hope is that readers will find pieces of themselves in the experiences of the Straddlers and in mine. I also hope that if they recognize this type of class anxiety, perhaps this book will help by putting a name to a vague sense of not belonging.

By ignoring class distinctions, people may be overlooking important parts of themselves and failing to understand who they really are. They are Straddlers in limbo, still attached to their working-class roots while living a new kind of life in the white-collar world.

1

BRICKLAYER'S SON: THE BIRTH AND CLASH OF VALUES

My father and I were college buddies back in the late 1970s.

While I was in class at Columbia, struggling with the esoterica du jour, he was on a bricklayer's scaffold not far up the street, working on a campus building. Once, we met up on the subway going home—he with his tools, I with my books. We didn't chat much about what went on during the day. My father wasn't interested in Thucydides, and I wasn't up on arches. We shared a *New York Post* and talked about the Mets.

My dad has built lots of places in New York City he can't get into: colleges, condos, office towers. He made his living on the outside. Once the walls were up, a place took on a different feel for him, as though he wasn't welcome anymore. It never bothered my dad, though. For him, earning the dough that helped pay for my entree into a fancy, bricked-in institution was satisfaction enough, a vicarious access.

We didn't know it then, but those days were the start of a branching off—a redefining of what it means to be a workingman in our Italian-American family. Related by blood, we're separated by class, my father and I. Being the white-collar child of a blue-collar parent means being the hinge on the door between two ways of life. With one foot in the working class, the other in the middle class, people like me are Straddlers, at home in neither world, living a limbo life. It's the part of the American Dream you may have never heard about: the costs of social mobility. People pay with their anxiety about their place in life. It's a discomfort many never overcome.

What drove me to leave what I knew? Born blue-collar, I still never felt completely comfortable among the tough guys and anti-intellectual crowd who populated much of my neighborhood in deepest Brooklyn, part of a populous, insular working-class sector of commercial strips, small apartment buildings, and two-family homes. I never did completely fit in among the preppies and suburban royalty of Columbia, either. It's like that for Straddlers, who live with an uneasiness about their dual identity that can be hard to reconcile, no matter how far from the old neighborhood they eventually get. Ultimately, "it is very difficult to escape culturally from the class into which you are born," Paul Fussell's influential book *Class: A Guide through the American Status System*[1] quotes George Orwell as saying. The grip is that tight. That's something Straddlers like me understand. There are parts of me that are proudly, stubbornly working class, despite my love of high tea, raspberry vinaigrette, and National Public Radio. Born with a street brawler's temperament, I possess an Ivy League circuit breaker to keep things in check. Still, I've been accused of having an edge, a chip I've balanced on my shoulder since my days in the old neighborhood.

It was not so smooth jumping from Italian old-world style to U.S. professional in a single generation. Others who were the first in their families to go to college will tell you the same thing: The academy can render you unrecognizable to the very people who launched you into the world. The ideas and values absorbed in college challenge the mom-and-pop orthodoxy that passed for truth for 18 years. Limbo folk may eschew polyester blends for sea-isle cotton, prefer Brie to Kraft slices. They marry outside the neighborhood and raise their kids differently. They might not be in church on Sunday.

When they pick careers (not *jobs* like their parents had, but *careers*), it's often a kind of work their parents never heard of or can't understand. But for the white-collar kids of blue-collar parents, the office is not necessarily a sanctuary. In corporate America, where the rules are based on notions foreign to working-class people, a Straddler can get lost.

Social class counts at the office, even though nobody likes to admit it. Ultimately, corporate norms are based on middle- and upper-class values, business types say. From an early age, middle-class people learn how to get along, using diplomacy, nuance, and politics to grab what they need. It is as though they are following a set of rules laid out in a manual that blue-collar families never have the chance to read.

People born into the middle class to parents with college degrees have lived lives filled with what French sociologist Pierre Bourdieu calls "cultural capital."[2] Growing up in an educated, advantaged environment, they learn about Picasso and Mozart, stock portfolios and crème brûlée. In a home with cultural capital, there are networks: Someone always has an aunt or golfing buddy with the inside track for an internship or some entry-level job. Dinner-table talk could involve what happened that day to Mom and Dad at the law firm, the doctor's office, or the executive suite.

Middle-class kids can grow up with what sociologists describe as a sense of entitlement that will carry them through their lives. This "belongingness" is not just related to having material means; it has to do with learning and possessing confidence in your place in the world. The bourgeois, Bourdieu says, pass on self-certainty like a treasured heirloom, from generation to generation.[3] Such early access and direct exposure to culture in the home is the more organic, "legitimate" means of appropriating cultural capital, Bourdieu tells us.[4] Those of us possessing "ill-gotten culture"—the ones who did not hear Schubert or see a Breughel until freshman year in college, the ones who grew up without knowing a friend whose parents attended college—can learn it, but never as well. Something is always a little off about us, like an engine with imprecise timing.

There's a greater match between middle-class lives and the institutions in which the middle class works and operates—whether they are universities or corporations. Children of the middle and upper classes have been speaking the language of the bosses and supervisors forever. An interesting fact: The number of words spoken in a white-collar household in a day is, on average, three times greater than the number spoken in a blue-collar home (especially the talk between parents and kids), says pioneering working-class studies economist Charles Sackrey, formerly of Bucknell University.

Blue-collar kids are taught by their parents and communities to work hard to achieve, and that merit is rewarded. But no blue-collar parent knows whether such things are true in the middle-class world. Many professionals born to the working class report feeling out of place and outmaneuvered in the office. Soon enough, Straddlers learn that straight talk won't always cut it in shirt-and-tie America, where people rarely say what they mean. Resolving conflicts head-on and speaking your mind don't always work, no matter how educated the Straddler is.

In the working class, people perform jobs in which they are closely supervised and are required to follow orders and instructions. That in turn affects how they socialize their children, social scientists tell us. Children of the working class are brought up in a home in which conformity, obedience, and intolerance for back talk are the norm—the same characteristics that make for a good factory worker. As Massachusetts Straddler Nancy Dean says, "We're raised to do what our mother says, what the teacher says, what the boss says. Just keep your mouth shut. No one cares what you have to say: Don't ask, don't question, do what you're told. Our mothers were all versions of Mrs. This Is My House."

People moving from the working class to the middle class need a strategy, a way to figure out the rules, the food, the language, and the music. "It's a new neighborhood," Sackrey says, "and it has the danger of a new neighborhood. It's unfriendly territory. Upper-class people *do* look down on us. So in your strategy for living, you have to figure out how to make it from one day to the next. It's an endless trek. You can fit in; you can decide to overwhelm and be better than them; you can live in the middle class but refuse to assimilate; or you can stand aside and criticize, and never be part of things.

"But central to the whole thing is language. If you don't talk like them, they won't give you the time of day."

The Uneven Race

Americans have always embraced the notion that this is a land of opportunity, with rags-to-riches possibilities. It's true that there are apples to be picked, but one can argue that not everyone has equal access to the fruit. We begin in different places, with some of us already two laps ahead when the starter's gun goes bang. The family you're born into may well have more influence on your future success than any other single factor, says Brookings Institution economist Isabel Sawhill. To ensure a rosy future, social scientists who study mobility love to say, "Pick your parents well."

If someone gets ahead, our national philosophy goes, it's because they worked harder. Statistics show that there are people who worked just as hard, but were unfortunate enough to have been born on the 2 yard line and not the 42. If your parents are in the upper tier of white-collar folks, there's a 60 percent chance you will be, too, mobility experts say. If, on the other hand, your parents are manual workers, your chances of getting into those clean and well-paying jobs are less than 30 percent, no matter how many hours you put in.[5] Surveys show that two out of three middle- and upper-class high school graduates attended a four-year college, as compared to just one of five from the working and lower classes.[6]

Mobility expert Michael Hout, of the University of California at Berkeley, says that downward mobility has increased 7 percent over the last 30 years, without much increase in upward mobility. He says that roughly 50 percent move up, 40 percent move down, and 10 percent remain immobile. Even if a blue-collar-born person winds up with the same job as someone originating from the middle class—thanks to college scholarships—the middle-class person would not know the journey the working-class person made. That odyssey, some say, makes all the difference in how one ultimately views the world.

Laying the Groundwork

Although they wanted me to climb out of the working class, my parents would have picked a different middle-class life for me. They foresaw a large bank account, a big house down the street from theirs, and a standing date for Sunday macaroni. My father had a tough time accepting my decision to become a mere newspaper reporter, a field that pays a little more than construction does. He long wondered why I hadn't cashed in on that multibrick education and taken on some lawyer-lucrative job. After bricklaying for 30 years, my father promised himself I'd never pile bricks and blocks into walls for a living. He and my mother figured that an education—genie-like and benevolent—would somehow rocket me into the rarefied trajectory of the upwardly mobile and load some serious loot into my pockets. My desire to work at something interesting to me rather than merely profitable was hard to fathom. Here I was breaking blue-collar rule number one: Make as much money as you can, to pay for as good a life as you can get. My father would try to teach me what my goals should be when I was 19, my collar already fading to white. I was the college boy who handed him the wrong wrench on help-around-the-house Saturdays. "You'd better make a lot of money," my dad wryly warned me as we huddled in front of a disassembled dishwasher I had neither the inclination nor the aptitude to fix. "You're gonna need to hire someone to hammer a nail into a wall for you when you get your own house."

My interests had always lain elsewhere. Like a lot of Straddlers, I felt dissatisfied with the neighborhood status quo. That sense of being out of step with the very people you're supposed to be like is the limbo person's first inkling that he or she is bound for other places. For the longest time, though, I tried to fit in. I mean, I chased girls and played ball and lifted weights—the approved pastimes that keep you from getting beaten up in working-class New York. I even had my high school record for consecutive sit-ups (801 in 35 minutes), a bizarre but marginally acceptable athletic accomplishment. It showed toughness, a certain willingness to absorb punishment, which in turn demonstrated manliness. In blue-collar society, proving your manly worth is high achievement. But truly, I never really liked hanging out on the corner, shooting the bull with the fellas. Weeknights, I studied while the guys partied. By the weekend, they were too far advanced for me to truly catch up. I just didn't share their interests—like cars. I never wanted to hunch over the engine of a Mustang, monkey with the pistons, and drain the oil. People think New Yorkers don't drive, but that's just in Manhattan. Car culture was big in Brooklyn, as it is in most of America, and kids lavished attention on their rides. Chrome had to gleam in streetlight on the cruise down 86th Street on Saturday night. (That, by the way, is the very place John Travolta struts at the beginning of *Saturday Night Fever*, the movie that told the story of a few of the guys I went to high school with—people who tried for something better than the neighborhood.) I knew a young woman whose boyfriend gave her whitewalls for her eighteenth birthday, and she squealed as if they were opals. I got my first car when I was 23 and drove it to Ohio to work at my first white-collar job. It broke down often, but I had no inclination to figure out what was wrong and fix it. Somehow, growing up, I was bereft of any curiosity about how things worked—how drywall was put up or how pipes connected—the very real working-class stuff that pre-occupied the lives of most of the people around me. I just didn't care. I read books. That came from my mother, a latchkey child who was never allowed to grow intellectually. She nevertheless became a book-a-week reader and had determined that her sons would follow suit, then advance to the higher education that had been denied her.

My mother was bucking a trend; many working-class people in the 1970s saw little need for college. The guys were encouraged to make money in construction and similar tough fields, while the women were expected to find men and breed. As a result, working-class kids from all ethnic backgrounds reproduce their parents' class standing with an eerie Xeroxity—often more rags-to-rags than rags-to-riches, working-class studies guru Jake Ryan says.

Navigating Social Relationships

Straddlers remember how complicated life in the old neighborhood could get after they realized they weren't really part of the crowd. Their inability to fully fit in made them uncomfortable and rendered them quasi-outcasts.

Back in the day, I couldn't compete for the attention of girls as long as there were dark-haired high school dropouts with steady jobs prowling the neighborhood in cool cars. These guys had pocket money to bestow Marlboros and birthday jewelry; they weren't locked away studying, and they had time to focus on showing girls a good time. In Bensonhurst, I'd be at a bus stop after school, trying to get close to a girl, reaching for whatever charm my heritage would provide. Just when I'd be making progress, one of my fellow *cugines* (cousins) would show up in his new white Cadillac with red-leather interior and a horn that played the first 12 notes to the theme song from *The Godfather*. "Yo, Marie, want a ride?" he'd call out, and away my dark-haired lovely would fly. There I'd be left standing, jerk with a bulging book bag and a bus pass, suddenly alone, waiting for the No. 6 bus and a lonely ride home.

So I didn't fit in. I was smart and got good grades, but I didn't care about Camaros. This earned me the sobriquet of "fag." It was bad to be called this. It had nothing to do with homosexuality. My sin was that I had the brains to pass social studies. It didn't bother me that much. I still got into fights and played guitar in neighborhood bands with my brother, which meant I wasn't a hopeless case. But I felt just as at home in the library as on the concrete basketball court—not something to boast about. My mother bought a blackboard and used it to teach me to read. When I got older, she let me loose in the stacks, hoping I'd find what she did. "Just read," she'd tell me, figuring the books would do the rest—pull me up and pull me away.

There were a lot of good reasons to go. I will always love aspects of blue-collar culture that live on in me—the whatever-it-takes work ethic, the lack of pretense, people's forthright manner—but working-class Brooklyn could be crowded and mean. In our first apartment, in the back of a two-story brick box built 200 feet from the elevated F train, I learned to sleep despite the endless rumble of the train cars and the metal-on-metal screech of the brakes. We lived so close and tight, we could hear arguments and lovemaking, squalling babies, and the disapproving squawks of meddlesome in-laws. Nothing was secret thanks to the thin walls, which showered cheap carpets with plaster chips whenever overwhelmed blue-collar family men would punch them in impotent frustration. There was a surfeit of anger and fear and alcohol. Men's jobs were hard and sapping. Women's afternoons with babies were long and relentless. The dominant themes, as social researcher Lillian Breslow Rubin writes, were struggle and trouble.[7] In my neighborhood, the son of a man we knew stole from his father's restaurant for drug money; an immature teenager joined the Marines during the height of the Vietnam War, compelling his father to go into debt to the local Mafia don, who somehow had the enlistment undone for a hefty fee; a depressed wife weakened and gave in to the blue-eyed pizza man from northern Italy, blowing a hole in her marriage. Survival, as Rubin writes, was a frantic scramble to keep the kids fed and the rent paid. This rough life, she writes, engendered "fatalism, passivity, resignation."[8]

Most fathers collapsed in front of the tube at the end of the day, incapable of anything else. Kids were shushed and ordered to sneak silently past these half-dead grizzlies, whose self-esteem was often undermined by jobs devoid of creativity, freedom, or flexibility. Sometimes after dinner, a few of the men with energy would tinker with their cars, habits left over from younger, better days. It allowed them, as Rubin writes, a sense of mastery not permitted at work, a project to complete without a boss carping about its progress or quality.[9] Of course, wives weren't happy about this withdrawal from the family. And so arguments would start, and hard days would end badly.

People believed the workingman was getting shafted, and they seethed. Perceived societal breaks for minorities made the frustrated white guys of my world crazy. Later, my Marxist professors would say it's how the haves always did it, letting the white and black proles cut each other for crumbs while The Man ate his cutlet in peace. Adults looked the other way when on-the-boil teenagers would beat up strangers—read: black people—unfortunate enough to wander through the neighborhood.

Racism was as common as diaper rash. People would pepper conversations with casual prejudicial judgments, which always made me uncomfortable, because I never understood the source of that anger. The night I saw the movie *Rocky*, a 20-year-old guy jumped from his seat in the theater during the climactic fight scene and screamed racial epithets at the screen. I shrank down in my seat, embarrassed, as many in the movie house applauded his outburst. White Straddlers will say that racism was one of the first things that separated them from their friends. Because they did not share the prejudice, they felt out of rhythm with the neighborhood vibe. Their apparent lack of race animosity made them objects of local suspicion.

I never really recognized class differences in my everyday world when I was very young. Everyone in my neighborhood floated in the same listing boat, tied to the same fate. I remember, though, watching TV and being confused by *The Brady Bunch*—the lawn, the house with two stories, the maid, the backyard fence (that grassy backyard!), and the father with the apparently untaxing job. Our fathers worked, Jack. Real work. Many Straddlers will say that blue-collaring is the more genuine of lives, in greater proximity to primordial manhood. Surely, my father was more resourceful than Mr. Brady. He was provider and protector, concerned only with the basics: food and home, love, and progeny. He's also a generation closer to the heritage, a warmer spot nearer the fire that forged and defined us. Does heat dissipate and light fade farther from the source?

Blue-Collar Values

I idealized my dad as a kind of dawn-rising priest of labor, engaged in holy ritual. Up at five every morning, my father made a religion of responsibility. My brother Christopher, who has two degrees from Columbia and is now an executive with the blue-collar sense to make a great white-collar salary, says he always felt safe when he heard Dad stir before him, "as if Pop were taming the day for us." As he aged, my father was expected to put out as if he were decades younger, slipping on machine-washable vestments of khaki cotton without waking my mother. He'd go into the kitchen and turn on the radio to catch the temperature. Bricklayers have an occupational need to know the weather. And because I am my father's son, I can still recite the five-day forecast at any given moment.

My dad wasn't crazy about the bricklayer's life. He had wanted to be a singer and an actor when he was young, but that was frivolous doodling to his immigrant father, who expected money to be coming in, stoking the stove that kept the hearth fires ablaze. Dreams simply were not energy-efficient. After combat duty in Korea, my dad returned home, learned his father-in-law's trade, and acquiesced to a life of backbreaking routine. He says he can't find the black-and-white publicity glossies he once had made. So many limbo folk witnessed the shelving of their blue-collar parents' dreams. Most, like my dad, made the best of it, although a few disappointed people would grow to resent their own children's chances, some Straddlers say.

As kids, Chris and I joked about our father's would-be singing career, wondering where we all would have been had he become rich and famous. His name is Vincent, but everyone calls him Jimmy. So my brother and I dubbed him "Jimmy Vincent," or "Jimmy V. From Across the Sea," a Jerry Vale type with sharper looks and a better set of pipes. As a young man, my father was tall and slender, with large brown eyes and dark hair. He was careful about his appearance, always concerned with pants pleats, pressed shirt cuffs, and the shine on his shoes.

One of our too-close neighbors once told him they liked it when Dad took a shower because of the inevitable tile-enhanced concert he'd provide. When one of my father's sisters died and Pop stopped singing for a while, the neighbor noticed and asked my father what was wrong.

There was a lot about Brooklyn I felt close to. Much about working-class life is admirable and fine. The trick is to avoid glorifying it without painting life in it too darkly. Sure, we lived with a few *cafones*—what some thought of as the low-class losers (there were classes among the working class, too—a pecking order based on taste, dignity, and intelligence). But the very best of blue-collar culture is something I still celebrate in myself and look for in others I meet. The values are an essential defining factor:

A well-developed work ethic, the kind that gets you up early and keeps you locked in until the job is done, regardless of how odious or personally distasteful the task.

A respect for your parents that is nothing short of religious, something I was amazed to find was not shared among the kids with whom I went to college and graduate school.

The need for close contact with extended family—aunts, uncles, and grandparents—each of whom had the authority to whack you in the back of the head should your behavior call for it.

An open and honest manner devoid of hidden agenda and messy subtext. You say something, you mean it.

Other things, too: loyalty; a sense of solidarity with people you live and work with; an understanding and appreciation of what it takes to get somewhere in a hard world where no one gives you a break; a sense of daring; and a physicality that's honest, basic, and attractive. (When I worked for New York *Newsday*, a disgruntled reader had been stalking me and persistently threatening my life. A colleague suggested I get a "goon" to protect me. An editor answered, "Alfred doesn't need a goon. Alfred is a goon.")

We could, between money troubles and family crises, recognize the good in life. Nobody laughs like blue-collar people, who are unashamed to pound the table in gasping recognition of a pure truth, a glaring absurdity, or a sharp irony. I have seen relatives grab onto each other for

17

support in tear-blurred spasms of guffawing that nearly choke them. It's fun to watch.

Class Distinctions and Clashes

Blue-collar origins implant defining characteristics that will cause conflict throughout a life. Straddlers and social scientists can point to specific differences in manner, style, thought, and approach to life that are class-based. Because there's no exact science to this, much comes from observation and opinion. It's still useful to understand, though, because it demonstrates that people think in terms of class all the time. And while it may be hard for them to define precisely, they know class differences when they see them. Interestingly, among Straddlers, resentments toward the middle class are never far below the surface.

"We working-class people have an appreciation for people no matter what they do," asserts Peter Ciotta, director of communications for a $1.6 billion food company in Buffalo. "And we have to outwork people because we have no connections. We're not going to get invited to the party."

James Neal, a Midwest medical malpractice attorney, who woke up at 4 A.M. on his parents' farm each day and went to school stinking of animals, says he takes special delight in facing off against silver-spoon lawyers and doctors because he believes they're so arrogant. "You just don't find a hell of a lot of arrogant working-class people. And blue-collar people say what they mean. In the end, I avoid people with a sense of entitlement. Until you've had hard times, you're not a complete person. And if you've never had them, well, a whole hunk of you is missing."

Struggle, the working class will tell you, is central to blue-collar life and the chief architect of character. Journalist Samme Chittum, a former college instructor who grew up in small-town Illinois, understands that. "The middle class knows what money bestows on you. Not what it can buy, but what it bestows. It's the intangible things—privilege, privacy, immunity from the vagaries of fortune that people who have to struggle are open to. It would be socially immature to be envious of these people; there are so many others in the world whose stack of poker chips is smaller than mine. But white-collar kids did not have to bust their asses for everything they've got. They came equipped with helium balloons to raise them to a higher stratosphere where things just come to you.

"But if you want a dirty job done, give it to me. I will do the hard job. I'll move 50 pieces of furniture up the stairs, take rocks out of the garden. I will push until the job's done or until I fall over. I don't understand letting others do things for you, or spending your social currency to get favors. I have a scorn for that."

The heritage of struggle, as writer and working-class academic Janet Zandy puts it, develops a built-in collectivity in the working class, a sense of people helping each other—you're not going it alone, and you have buddies to watch your back. It's different in the middle class, Zandy and others argue, where the emphasis is on individual achievement and personal ambition. The middle class, my Straddlers would say, rarely had to pay working-class-type dues and were most likely unaware of the help they got—the cultural capital—to ensure their sinecures in life and business.

If you could get through college without having to work at some outside job or take out loans, for example, that says you did not know privation, and that, in turn, says something about you and your class. If your parents gave you the down payment on your house (Straddlers often hate hearing this one), that tells us something about you as well. Straddlers tend to see the family dynamic as struggle, and they learn to accept it. You never expect things to be easy, and you don't whine when they're not. Nothing is promised, so nothing is expected. "My father's goal for me," says Los Angeles Straddler Jeffrey Orridge, a Mattel executive, "was to be able to eat. Not to drive a Mercedes. Just to eat." The working class is told that anything you get you earn by hard work. "Our family was pain and anguish," says Sacramento Straddler Andrea Todd, a freelance magazine writer and editor. "I saw my dad—a firefighter—sacrifice his well-being to put food on the table. The middle-class girls I knew didn't see that, didn't know that."

While middle-class kids are allowed some say and voice in their upbringing ("David, would you prefer going to Grandma's or to the park?"), working-class kids develop within a strict, authoritarian world ("David, if you don't come with me to Grandma's right now I'll slap your teeth out!") Experts say that children raised in authoritarian homes do less well in school than kids from less regimented middle-class environments. Without meaning to, says Hamilton College sociologist Dennis Gilbert, the parent who stresses obedience over curiosity is championing the values of the working class, and helping to keep their kids in it.[10]

Temple University sociologist Annette Lareau did some interesting work in this area, she tells me. Studying 88 African-American and white children from the Northeast and the Midwest who were between the ages of 8 and 10, Lareau was able to see distinct differences in the way working-class and middle-class kids are raised. In fact, she concludes, the importance of class influence in their upbringing was greater even than that of race.[11]

Class Flash Cards: Perceptions Are as Real as Origins

I asked Straddlers and working-class studies types to list class-based traits to help understand what the classes look like. Some truly believe class in America is akin to a caste system of different values and outlooks. Ultimately, working-class and middle-class cultures are based on different foundations, says Minnesota psychologist Barbara Jensen, herself a Straddler. The core value of the working class is being part of a like-minded group—a family, a union, or a community, which engenders a strong sense of loyalty. The core value of the middle class is achievement by the individual.

The middle class, Jensen says, is solipsistic, seeing nothing but its own culture. That's made easier by the fact that the middle class literally writes our culture. Movies, books, the news media, and television are creations of the middle class. Working-class people see little of themselves in popular culture. (There are exceptions of course: *Working Girl, Norma Rae, Roseanne*. But by and large, Jensen's observation holds true.) As such, the middle class gets to see complex depictions of itself, while working-class people view mostly stereotypes of themselves.

What else? Jensen provided me with class "flash cards," for lack of a better term—quick observations that separate the workers from the managers, the corner boys from the corner-office boys. Obviously, none of these are hard-and-fast rules. They are traits and tendencies gleaned from observation and study, and are by no means scientific:

Working-class people mistrust eggheads, relying more on intuition, common sense, and luck. The middle class is more analytical, depending on cultivated, logical thinking.

In a social setting, the working class may be more apt to show emotion than the middle class. The working class may be tougher, flashier, and louder.

Working-class people are overawed by doctors and lawyers. The middle class knows how to talk to such folks and realizes they are just as fallible and corrupt as the rest of us.

The middle class is burdened with the pressure to outachieve high-achieving parents. Many working-class families are happy if their kids get and keep a job and avoid being seen on *America's Most Wanted*.

The working class will bowl; the middle class will play racquetball. At Columbia, where physical education was a requirement for graduation, they taught us squash and racquetball, trying to tutor future lawyers and leaders on the finer points of business leisure. I played it like a neighborhood kid, diving into the walls and feeling a sense of accomplishment when I nearly separated my shoulder. I was never that good, because I played too blue-collar, too straight-ahead, and never studied the angles and the corner shots. It was nothing like the stickball, stoopball, and handball we played in Brooklyn. In summer softball games, I used to think I could play center field because our cement parks were so small. Then I moved to Ohio and played in lovely suburban fields, watching ball after ball get by me. I couldn't cover the vast territory, green and endless. I switched to first base.

The working class has traditionally expressed a my-country-right-or-wrong patriotic attitude, while the middle class often has questioned government, Jensen says. The obvious example is the Vietnam War era, when working-class kids died in jungles, and middle-class kids protested on campuses.

There's a greater depth of acquiescence among working class people, who tend to feel more powerless: You can't fight city hall. The middle class says you can, and there's more of a constant striving toward self-hood and becoming something else. The working-class man or woman says, "I am what I am." The middle-class person says, "I have to do this [graduate from college, go to business school, pass the bar] to become who I am."

Regarding racism, everyone is guilty. Minority straddlers will say the working class is overt in its prejudices, while the middle class is surreptitious, devious, and hypocritical. Ultimately, writes social critic bell hooks, blacks fear poor and working-class whites more because, historically, they have acted out their hatred in more violent forms.[12]

The working class works at jobs that bite, maim, and wither. The middle class gets to work indoors at desks. This can be stressful, of course, but as Andrew Levison points out in Fussell's book, office buildings don't implode like coal mines, and professors aren't subjected to industrial noises that destroy their hearing.[13]

Finally, Jensen says, the working class sends out Christmas cards that say, "Love, X." The middle class circulates Christmas newsletters, with proud news of Timmy's adventures in the fourth grade.

Obviously, people are more than just class. We all embody interlocking cultures—ethnicities, races, and genders. We possess different skills and inclinations. Still, imprecise as many of the flash cards are, they do reflect people's perceptions.[14]

In Brooklyn, I used to notice people eyeing each other across the class divide. Older, ethnic working-class women in housedresses would sit on their stoops on summer evenings and watch the single, yuppie women trudge home from Manhattan offices at 8 P.M., carrying their small, Korean-grocer salads in white plastic bags. The old women would laugh, then shake their heads at what they saw as the empty, ascetic lives devoid of children, real food, and steady men. The yuppies, I'm sure, had their own thoughts about overweight, middle-aged women with limited horizons, bad clothes, and inattentive husbands.

Smaller class-based skirmishes go on daily in offices, with janitors, secretaries, and maintenance people on one side, and CEOs, executives, and tech people on the other. It happens everywhere; it happens every day. The perceptions we all have of the other side can have a greater impact than reality.

F Train: Lifeline from the Past to the Future

When we were young, my mother took Chris and me into Manhattan on special days. I think she wanted to show us there was grace in this world. We visited museums, Radio City Music Hall, and the top of the

Empire State Building. I remember climbing the metal stairs to the F
train and noticing the train direction signs: "To City" and "From City."
Though Brooklyn was as much a part of New York as Manhattan, sign
makers understood the sociological divide provided by the East River,
the sense that Brooklyn wasn't the real New York. If people in my neighborhood said, "I'm going to the city," everyone knew what they meant.
They were headed to Manhattan, the place with the water-beading high
gloss, the island polished clean by money. They were traveling from the
borough of workers to the borough of work. Straddlers told me they
lived for such moments in their own lives: a trip out of the drab hometown to some Oz of light and rich circumstance. These forays provided
knowledge and hope of something better.

The silvery train car with orange seats smelled like sweat, perfume,
and urine—a Brooklyn potpourri. We rode past tight houses made dingy
by train soot. We felt special as we viewed the narrow streets from
above, as though we were not part of them—at least not today. At the
Smith and 9th Street station, the F train arced high into the air, and
suddenly you could see the harbor and the Statue of Liberty. Vistas
shifted as the train lurched forward. We got a glimpse of the skyline,
spiky and shining, across the water, beyond the airless gray grid of
Brooklyn. The world suddenly opened up, and we were aware of a new
kind of geography, a new way things could look. When we got to our
stop, we squeezed out of the car and climbed out of the subway. That
moment when you slowly rise out of the train hole onto a Manhattan
street is something that still excites me even now, so many rides later.
Your senses acclimate in stages. First you hear the traffic, denser and
more intense than in Brooklyn. Then you smell roasting chestnuts and
bus exhaust. Finally, as you reach the sidewalk, you see the buildings,
outsized and overwhelming, and you think the sign makers were right
about the "To City" thing, because this is nothing like home.

Manhattan had wealth. Women wore furs; limos choked the streets.
As a working-class person, you could partake of it in bits and enjoy its
plenitude at the edges: Eat soup at Lord & Taylor without necessarily
buying clothes, then light a candle at St. Patrick's Cathedral, gawking
at the opulence in both places. My mother taught us to find a hotel if we
needed a bathroom, and I'd feign bladder emergencies just to see
Manhattan's grand lobbies.

Sometimes, we'd simply look at the buildings on which my father and grandfather had worked. My grandfather was Ellis Island, Class of 1914. As a kid, he boxed and performed gymnastics on piles of horse manure dumped by the city in empty lots. Once, he lifted his junior high school principal and hung him on a clothes hook in a classroom wardrobe. "Guy deserved it," my grandfather said, and we believed him. He was handsome, with his mustache, thick hair, and eye twinkle. George Clooney looks so much like him in the movie *O Brother, Where Art Thou?* that my mother cried when she saw it. Now when the urge strikes, I can go to New York and see his handiwork—run my hands over the bricks that line the Brooklyn-Queens Expressway or any one of dozens of places that look like buildings to you but are monuments to me. He saw New York as two things: the deepwater port of possibility where you could make enough money to buy a place for your wife and raise your three daughters, and the lunatic town where punks sprayed graffiti over his bricks. He died when crack was big, and the city's rene-gade feel had soured him. Several Straddlers told me about a blue-collar elder who impressed them as much as my grandfather did me. These tough-guy old-timers possessed a characteristic—strength, or dignity, or willfulness—that Straddlers tried to emulate in their own lives. While working-class machismo doesn't always serve a Straddler well, sometimes just the knowledge that they share genes with people of courage can help a limbo man or woman through the hard days and nights.

I liked knowing my grandfather's DNA was coiled down inside me somewhere. He was decent, responsible, and tough. Tough is good, I told myself. Taking what you want is good.

We wanted so much. When I got older, I would schlep to Manhattan with my friends whenever I could, drawn by its transcendent promise. We wondered whether Manhattan girls kissed differently, talked differ-ently, or smelled nicer. We yearned to connect with the city's central cir-cuit, to splice into the main wiring and vibrate with the energy and buzz of the crazy place. As kids, Straddlers were naturally drawn to the kinetic doings outside the same old circle they would soon dismiss as dull and predictable. Hungering for something more, they thrust them-selves into shimmering middle- and upper-class spaces, eyeing new experience like pacing young tigers eager to pounce. There we'd be outside clubs, the dreaded bridge-and-tunnel boys from disfavored area codes, wearing disastrous clothes—stonewashed jeans and Converse sneakers. Doormen knew to exclude us, and they did so without a second thought. We were the help—the stockboys and the busboys, the guys from nowhere, left out in the cold in Members Only jackets. You could find my clueless kind outside places like Studio 54 or Limelight, an old church-turned-nightclub that had a decadent Mardi Gras/cabaret vibe. Kenny Kenny, the fabulous drag-queen doorman in a plaid green Vivienne Westwood dress, polished Army boots, and Kabuki makeup, oversaw the midnight encampment of wannabes that gathered even in the coldest weather: giggling 20-year-old men wearing tight skirts beneath their coats; unsmiling young women adhering to a strict black-only dress code; easy-smiling Hugo Boss hunks, angst-free and existentially secure, used to taking life's beaches like sharp-dressed Marines. Then there'd be guys like us, passed over for inspection in favor of preppies and outlanders from the Midwest or wherever, who have traditionally flocked to the city to begin careers.

E.B. White once wrote that there are three New Yorks: the city of commuters, whom he disdained as locusts who feasted on what the city offered, then left before it got too late in the evening; the city of natives like me, who, he said, took the town too much for granted; and the city of people born elsewhere in the country, the group upon which he showered favor. He said they were the special ones, the talented newcomers who gave New York its passion and artistry.[15]

I just thought of them as supercompetitive types, the people voted most likely to kidney-stab you with a cafeteria spoon to get ahead. We noticed that a disproportionate number came from the middle and upper classes, because no matter how lowly a job they toiled at, they always seemed to have money to spend at night. Trust-fund drunkards, they were the fools who staggered to their feet in bars at 2 A.M. when the jukebox played Sinatra's "New York, New York." It was the outsiders' anthem, the song they sang to themselves to remind one another that they had left Missouri or wherever behind and were now making it in the Apple. Well, these ersatz New Yorkers took our places on the dance floor, took our women, and took our seat at the table. That's what we told ourselves, anyway, as we worked ourselves into a low-boiling class rage. Once a Straddler wandered beyond the neighborhood to see what the world could offer, it was not unusual for the person to grow resentful of people perceived to be enjoying all of life's goodies. We wanted what they possessed—their polish, their worldliness, and the apparent control they had over their lives.

This was the basis for my beef with Caroline Kennedy. When I decided in high school that I wanted to be a reporter, I applied to be a copyboy at the New York *Daily News*, the spirited, blue-collar tabloid that talked tough and spoke to my people. My father would read the *Daily News* out loud to us over breakfast on Saturday mornings. He and my mother would laugh at the latest outrages of politicians and assorted city scoundrels. Here, I figured, they'd give the workingman a break. When I was 18, I wrote a nice letter to the editors about my father and the breakfast table and his loyalty to his union. They told me, sorry, they weren't hiring copyboys. Then I read a few days later that the editors had given a copyboy's job to Caroline Kennedy, who I am sure is a lovely person. But still. So it's like that? I said to myself. The workingman's newspaper was populated by starry-eyed, class-conscious folk just like at the *New York Times?* Years later, when I was interviewing for a reporting job at the *Daily News*, I made a point of mentioning the Kennedy story to the editor. I told him, "You guys owe me." The editor, whose father had been a cop, must have appreciated my attitude, because he hired me. One Straddler recognized another. He saw his own class journey mirrored in mine and figured I was worth a chance. Many Straddlers say they treasured any such connection to a fellow traveler in the workplace, because it made them feel less alone.

Dreams of Escape

It was a close call, the blue-collar life. I got my first job at 16, working as a stockboy for Leo's Discounts after school. Leo was a no-nonsense, working-class Jewish guy, an ex-boxer and a relative of Jerry Stiller. His daughter was always trying to break into show business via the family connection. Bald and muscled, Leo told me how you could irritate a fighter's ears by constantly sliding the laces of your boxing gloves across them. My job was boring: storing 100-box deliveries in a dark, filthy basement and filling the shelves with toothpaste, disposable diapers, and deodorant. For some reason, Leo placed all the feminine products up high on the shelves. Embarrassed women would have to ask me (I was nearly my adult 6-foot-3) to reach up for them. A few of them were just a little older than me, already saddled with kids. They were dark and beautiful neighborhood women, older versions of the girls who'd abandon me at bus stops. This is what happens, I told myself, after a few rides in the car. Entire lives could be mapped and plotted with relative accuracy, beginning with the moment they slid next to a guy in a Lincoln with leather seats: marriage, Pampers from Leo's, endless Sundays with the in-laws, and boredom and joyless toil for a lot of years. That scared me. Suddenly, I could see what my parents were talking about—how college was important. "Otherwise," my father would say, "I got a shovel in the garage waiting for you." Only today can I appreciate the true significance of what he was saying; my father was telling me not to be like him. How hard that must have been to carry in his head. By telling their kids to go to college and rise above them, working-class fathers offer their lives not as role models to emulate—as middle-class parents can—but as mistakes to avoid, say social commentators Richard Sennett and Jonathan Cobb.[16] My father held himself out as a negative object lesson. If you don't do your homework, ace the test, and apply to college, you'll wind up laying bricks. You'll wind up being just like me. What does that make a father feel like, to have to instruct his son not to be like the old man?

When I was about to graduate from high school, Leo pulled me aside and asked me whether I wanted to learn the business. His starstruck daughter sure didn't. He was offering me a blue-collar future, something what would have been considered a decent existence for a neighborhood kid like me. I projected my life into it, stuffed inside a 900-square-foot store over a basement filled with rats and cans of Lysol, forever fetching tampons—then eventually adult diapers—for customers who'd be aging along with me, tied to the insular, isolated neighborhood. It was sweet that he asked. But I gotta go to college, I told him.

It's always interesting to hear how Straddlers describe their backgrounds. Some sentimentalize it; some remember it with contempt. The truth is, Jake Ryan says, you wouldn't be class-mobile and ready to hop the first bus into White-Collar World if you were all that happy with your original circumstances. On some level, I'd believed it was wrong to want to go. The tug of turf is strong, and anyone who thought of life beyond neighborhood borders was seen as arrogant. "He thinks who he is," is how the guys put it. What makes you so special? Limited homeboy that I was, I'd only applied to schools in New York City. Why abandon the family? I reasoned. I was accepted by Columbia, but our college advisor thought that it might be too tough a school. "Why not send him to Brooklyn College?" he asked my mother during a parent-teacher conference. "It's easier."

"Is your daughter going to Brooklyn?" my mother asked him.

"Well, no," he said.

All I knew was that Columbia was expensive. New York University, itself a pricey though less prestigious private college in Greenwich Village, had offered me a full, four-year scholarship. Columbia sent me a scholarship package as well, contingent on my maintaining a B-plus average, but they weren't giving me as much cash. I told my parents I'd go to NYU to save us money, but my mother blanched. When I was in fourth grade, I'd gone to Columbia for a class presentation, and she'd fallen in love with the stone and ivy. "Go to Columbia," she said. "We'll figure out the money."

It wasn't easy. Recession had damaged the construction industry, making jobs scarce for men like my father. Lots of Straddlers told stories about hard times. Some said they feel guilty as adults, working through their middle-class days with an ease of worry their parents never knew.

Like a lot of tough, blue-collar women, my mother got a job when the economy went south. She went to work in a nearby high school and became part of what I dubbed The Club, a tight circle of blue-collar women who worked as support personnel—the lunch ladies, the school aides, and the attendance mavens. At school, the women would speak of their own precocious sons and daughters with pride and befuddlement. They'd commiserate, watching as each other's kids moved from acne through divorce, the entire life continuum analyzed in the hallways and offices of a building brimming with other people's children. School administrations came and went, but the women's first loyalty was to the kids.

Once during a race riot, the women of The Club waded into the chaos to calm things. Gym teachers were bleeding and deans were getting banged around. But my mother touched the kids on their arms, saying, "It's okay," and they began to unclench. The women were a different color, from a different place. But they were mothers comforting children. That's all the kids needed to understand.

During the Vietnam War, my mother and her friend Reenie chased away an Army recruiter who'd come to meet with students. They were relentless, and the guy figured it wasn't worth it and left. Another time, my mom and Reenie screamed at drug dealers who had set up shop in front of the school. Probably armed and generally impervious to intimidation, the young men didn't know what to do. But mothers were yelling at them. So they got in their fancy car and drove off.

When she was a child, my mother was the double Dutch jump rope champ of her block. I picture a taut little girl counting to herself, then hurling herself into the whir of churning ropes, knowing instinctively when to leap and when to land—never tangled, never tripped. At night, when her body aches, I'm sure she hears the ropes slapping concrete, reminding her that she once had promise and dreams of her own. She never had the chance to fulfill them. But she'd stay awake figuring how her two sons would. Straddlers' parents have such plans for their kids. With strong hopes but scant information, many push their progeny toward the vague realm of Something Better —the glorious middle class. Imbued with these dreams, Straddlers lurch awkwardly out of sheltering enclaves into unknown realms. On their sometimes troubled way, they become educated, and awaken to class differences between the past and their would-be future. Priorities shift. Some values change, while some remain constant. Unlike many they meet in the new, white-collar world, these people are hybrids. That duality is their strength and their struggle, and will comfort and vex them throughout their days.

2

CRAWLING OUT OF THE BLACK HOLE: THE PAIN OF TRANSITION

Like a lot of blue-collar parents, mine looked at the world with the hard stare of workers who know what a 5 A.M. winter Monday feels like. It had to be 28 degrees, with the temperature rising, for my father to work. I used to think that was a humane condition insisted upon by the brick-layer's union to protect the health of the men. The truth is, mortar freezes below 28 degrees, making it impossible to lay brick and block. Once he determined the temperature, my father would sometimes have to literally crawl out of bed, his back wrecked from lifting. One morning I saw his face, twisted and gaunt, in the precise second when his sense of responsibility overtook the pain. He was trying to button his shirt. He turned away, unwilling to let me see him. "Go to school," he said to me, "and you won't have to do this." I owe him so much for that moment. So many Straddlers could not have attended college and climbed out of the working class without the support of family. That encouragement to become an educated person eases the blue-collar's eventual transition into the white-collar world.

ut not every father dreams of the day his kid walks across a stage to grab his diploma. Not every mother looks forward to hearing her baby channel some professor yammering on about Aristotle or the Japanese parliament. For some families, college is seen as a waste of time and money, a hideout where lazy—or at least misguided—progeny burrow to retreat from the real work of life. "I told my mother I wanted to go to college to learn," says Barbara Jensen, the Minnesota Straddler and psychologist who studies the blue-collar journey to the middle class. "She said to me, 'We're not gonna pay for anything if you're just going there to learn.' 'Learn' was a dirty word. I was so shocked. So I just worked and went to school, paying for it myself, first as a waitress, then as a cook." The attitude, sometimes, is that there is no place in the blue-collar world for the luxury of higher education. In a world where life is stripped to its utilitarian essence—where every move has to be about survival and money coming in—going to college is criminally self-indulgent.

Sometimes, parents' anticollegiate feelings can't be simply explained as tuition sticker shock. Deeper, decidedly nonpaternal motives can compel the folks—such as the fear that junior's education will facilitate an economic and intellectual ascendence over the old man, which will lead the kid to lord his highfalutin book learning over everyone. "No, Dad, I told you: Roosevelt really was in a wheelchair while he was president." In the movie *An Officer and a Gentleman*, the Richard Gere character, a lost young man with a college degree, presents his boozehound father, a low-level Navy man, with his plan to attend officer-training school. Rather than congratulate his son, the father derides him, asking why he'd want to become part of the military ruling class he's learned to hate. Stung, the kid shoots back that maybe Dad is really worried he'll have to salute his son one day. Some working-class parents feel they might lose their standing at home as the ultimate authority should they have to recognize the superior knowledge of a child, or hear about the kid's trip to Europe or his grasp of what's really going on in China.

Worse still, an educated kid could morph into Them, the boss-type people many working-class folk have learned to despise throughout their clock-punching lives. To have a child jump from worker to middle-class manager in a generation would be an outright betrayal for some working-class people. Besides, wasn't it another group of Them, in the guise of intrusive social workers in the 1910s and 1920s, who lifted the lids of cooking pots in tenement kitchens and criticized our grandparents' diets, instructing them to put more meat in with the potatoes, or the tomato sauce, or the pierogies, even though they couldn't afford it? It was always Us against Them, through strikes and layoffs and years of meager pay. How can a kid of mine cross over that deeply etched line? Besides, college and the kind of jobs it leads to aren't real work—they're merely paper-pushing.

Beyond this, there's the sense that the kids might move out of reach somehow. If children can simply educate themselves away, where will the parent fit in their new world? Would your kid still watch the game with you if he's running with that shirt-and-tie crowd? Or would he become ashamed of you and invent excuses to avoid Sunday dinner? Kids could become strangers, just like that. So why let it happen in the first place? Stress the status quo; don't push the bold beyond. Of course, holding back your kids can backfire, making them into the very thing you don't want them to be. Patrick Finn, the Buffalo education expert (and Straddler), says that his mother didn't want him to go to college because she feared he'd become an atheist and a communist. "So," he says, "I went to college and became an atheist and communist so as not to disappoint her."

Some sociologists argue that while rags to riches is the first law of mobility—and the American myth we like to tell ourselves—there is simultaneously a strong rags-to-rags dynamic at work. Often, families will exert a hefty tug on their kids: If this working-class life was good enough for us, they preach, it's good enough for you, too.

"Donna" (not her real name), a journalist who works for a national magazine, says her mother's only plans for her were to sell cosmetics in a department store until she got married. "My mother is of a culture that believes girls aren't worth educating," she says. As for Donna's father, he said that people from his background are just not equipped to matriculate. Resigned to his blue-collar status, Donna's father's belief was "Why reach for the sky when you can be happy on earth?" Donna says, "My dad was trying to save me from disappointment. The daughter of peasant stock shouldn't strive to be in the ruling class, he thought." The lack of support for college engendered a bitterness in Donna—who eventually did graduate from college after a lot of unaided effort. "If I had had parents who backed me," she says, "I could've owned my own company by now. I was always struggling against my parents."

That's what happens in what I call *black-hole families.* Black holes are dense, dark stars whose gravitational pull is so great that no light can escape. The universe burns with constellations of dull stars. If you're part of such a family, you have a choice: You can succumb to parental fiat and stay true blue collar, your light forever dim, or you can buck the folks and pay a price for your incandescence.

Fighting Your Family: Dot's Story

Bucking is what Dot Newton chose to do in order to make her own transition.

Easygoing and 40 years old, Dot makes her living in predominantly African-American and Latino North Philadelphia as a social worker helping the elderly. Once in a while, she'll organize "graduation" ceremonies for seniors. They haven't actually completed course work anywhere, but they get a certificate for having lived life. People cry as they accept their "diplomas," and relatives applaud. It was Dot's idea.

To her, even a pretend degree is better than nothing. God knows, getting her own was a struggle.

"My mother didn't encourage education," says Dot, a heavyset woman with kind, dark eyes. "But if she had encouraged me just a little, all she had to do was name it. If I had thought that my mother even wanted me to be a doctor, all she had to do was name it, I'm telling you. If she said it, I could have done it, because it would have been important to her. But education wasn't important, wasn't really stressed in our home. My mother was about survival. You didn't talk to her about dreams."

The area around Dot's neighborhood is not exactly what you would think of as a dream incubator. With around 40 percent of families below the poverty line, parts of North Philly are among the poorest places in America, according to U.S. Census figures. It is a quicksand of pathologies made dangerous by drug-related crime. Graffiti, regarded by many of the residents there as the shorthand of chaos, covers nearly every inanimate object on the street. Drive by at moderate speed and the tagging looks like a single, unending word. Pit bulls owned by drug dealers strut and growl on sidewalks. Sometimes you'll see ostriches, standing dumb-eyed in their own waste, behind a Cyclone fence—dealers use their kicking skills as defense against thieves. There used to be work here, but now the factories are cold, their boarded-up windows looking like eyes punched shut in a street brawl. Meanwhile, white drug buyers in Infinitis roll through to shop for product in the open-air market, keeping the money coming in.

This was the kind of world in which Dot's divorced mother "Jane" (not her real name) raised six children. And she'd already known tough times before migrating to Philly from South Carolina. When she was a child down South, Jane found her younger sister lying sick in the house, so she ran to a doctor—a white doctor. "You're on the wrong side of the line," the doctor sniffed, refusing to treat a black child. By the time Jane got to a black doctor, it was too late. Her sister had died of a burst appendix.

The incident taught Dot's mother that you make your own way in this life. The lesson is simple: Get a job and understand that you can't depend on anyone else for your survival. At one point, Jane had three jobs she reported to each day, at three different cleaners, pressing shirts. She'd leave for work at 5 A.M. and return home at 1 A.M.

Jane rarely had time to celebrate the precocious gifts her daughter was starting to demonstrate. Once, an English teacher told Dot that she had the writing ability to pursue journalism. Such work would require college, but the teachers assured Dot she had the intellectual goods. She giddily shared the revelation with her mother.

"All you need to do is 9-to-5 work, and to be at church on Sunday," Dot remembers Jane saying. "You don't need college."

"You make me feel like I'm not smart," Dot said. "You don't know who I am."

"You're a black female," Dot says Jane told her. "What do you think you're gonna get in this world?"

In truth, Dot's mom had all sorts of fears about college: She was afraid her daughter would find some man, get pregnant at school, and embarrass her at church. "She was determined I would not get pregnant on her watch," Dot says. The mother worried, too, that her daughter would grow away from her. Even as a teenager, Dot was acting like she knew it all, a great source of irritation for the mother. Jane was from the South and said "y'all." Dot would correct her, and her mother would snap back, "Don't you think I know that?" At times, mother and daughter would really get into it.

By the age of 13, Dot realized she had a gifted voice, and her gospel songs at church were making her well-known in the community. Recognizing her daughter's talent, Jane one day presented Dot with a $79 tape recorder. "I fell in love with her," Dot says. "She pressed shirts for three cents a shirt and bought that. It was unbelievable to me."

But true to the pattern, things became unpleasant when the idea of Dot furthering herself came up. One night, Dot had phoned *Problem Exchange*, a midnight call-in radio program. In the course of conversation, she had told the host that she could sing, and he asked her to prove it. Dot did "Amazing Grace" with her powerful, Mahaliah Jackson–like voice, the kind that listeners can feel vibrate in their sternums.

The radio host was so impressed, he promised he'd get some hotshot to listen to Dot. Sure enough, a representative from a record company phoned Dot soon after, offering an audition in New York. But Jane wasn't having it. "She said she didn't even know how to get to New York," Dot remembers. "And she didn't know who would feed the other kids if we went."

That was that.

By 15, Dot Newton was coming undone. Her mother was remarried to a man Dot didn't like. She was also flunking classes for the first time. She prayed for guidance. "That was the time of a miracle in my life," Dot says. One day, Dot was offered a work-study job through school at the Philadelphia Naval Yard. There she met Gladys, an older, light-skinned African American with green eyes. "You think I'm a white woman, don't you?" is how Gladys greeted Dot, Dot remembers. "Girl, I'm from North Philadelphia."

Things Dot couldn't say to her mother, she could tell Gladys, who spoke openly about all matters. "She became my co-mother," Dot says. "She talked to me about my future. She told me I had a lot to offer in life." At Gladys's suggestion, Dot wrote Jane a letter, showing her mother her heart. She told her about all these thoughts she had inside, these dreams that knocked from within her head and kept her awake at night.

"It was a two-page letter, and to me, it was eloquent without being disrespectful," Dot says. "I thought she would read it and finally find out who I was. I put it on her bed."

Jane tore it up without reading it. She was livid and told Dot writing a letter was a cowardly thing to do. "She said if I had something to say, I should tell it to her face," Dot recalls.

Dot tears up when she recalls that day. "It was one of the most hurtful moments in my life."

Still, Gladys was not going to let her charge fail, and with her encouragement, Dot embarked on a precollege course of studies in high school. In her senior year, Dot was offered a partial journalism scholarship to the University of Pittsburgh. All she needed was for her mother to attend a financial aid meeting and sign some paperwork.

But Jane refused, saying she had to get to a church meeting, Dot says. Then Jane's husband joined in, telling Jane that if she allowed Dot to attend college, she would get pregnant, Dot remembers. All college talk ended after that.

Though higher education seemed ridiculous, Jane still wanted to reward her daughter for the hard work of graduating from high school. She and her ex-husband combined to make a $1,000 down payment on a Chevy Vega. They also sprang for the insurance.

Dot moved out of the house when she was 18, finding an apartment with a cousin. She got a job as a microfiche researcher and began patching together a college education, a couple of credits at a time.

Dot remembers a heated fight when she confronted her mother about Jane's allegiance to her husband over her daughter. "I've lost my life because of him, because he said I shouldn't go to college, and you listened," she told her mother.

"I probably should have said it a long time before," Dot remembers. "Whatever I was going to be from then on was because of me. My mother gave me some powerful stuff, some good stuff. She's really caring and giving. The things I inherited from my mother I'll always cherish. But we're made up of a lot of characteristics."

Dot got her B.A., and at 38, she was working toward a master's degree when a psychology professor assigned a project: Write an autobiography, and talk to your parents about your childhood. Really open things up.

Oh, Lord, Dot said to herself.

Jane had been against the idea of college to begin with. A master's degree was worse. And here was her daughter coming with this psychology stuff. Most working-class African Americans don't believe in psychology, Dot says. They think it's hogwash, a white thing. The conversation started, and the subject of college came up. Jane listened and, to Dot's surprise, said that what her daughter was telling her was lying heavy on her heart. She said she had actually prayed on it.

"God said to me if somebody is hurt by you, you need to get it right," Dot remembers her mother saying. "I didn't know I was hurting you by saying you can't go to college. You only get one chance at raising a child and you don't always know the things you're doing. With six kids, if this one wanted college, and that one wanted college, there was no way to pay for it. If I was hurting you, I'm sorry. I didn't know. And I am proud of you, of what you became."

That's what Dot needed to hear: a life-changing benediction that validated her. "I needed confirmation that she was satisfied with me. That I was the kind of daughter she wanted. I had to show her the work ethic was there, but that I took a different path, went to college, and it was okay.

"Her acceptance was what I was looking for. The apology began to erode the bad memories. This respect was the final cure-all."

Never Educate Women

It was never important for girls to go to college—that's what families around us said. "Why waste your money that way?" the cheese guy on 18th Avenue in Brooklyn asked a family friend. "They're gonna get married anyway, have kids, cook the Sunday gravy. What, you need college for that?" For a lot of the girls in my neighborhood, and women born to blue-collar families everywhere, no one expected very much. You were born, then you blossomed in high school, hit the clubs, and got your man by the time you were 21 or 22, settling in for the long haul. If you wanted to break out of the status quo, the cultural hurdles you had to vault were enormous. When I hear stories about women who freed themselves from that black-hole grip, I know they traveled much further than I ever had to.

Maria Fosco is the perfect example. Nowadays, Maria, 40, is the director of administration of the Calandra Italian-American Institute in New York City. Her job is to foster higher education among Italian Americans. She likes helping kids—especially young women who feel less valued. But, she remembers, her own struggle to make the blue-to-white transition was Herculean. "I couldn't believe you had to be politically savvy with your own parents to get to college, but I did," she says, remembering some very hard years back in Astoria, Queens. "You can't be a screaming teenager and get what you want."

Maria's father, Antonio, was old school, an immigrant from Italy. Unlike many Italians who immigrated to New York City, he arrived in the mid-twentieth century, not during the early years of ship steerage and Ellis Island. I found in my interviews that it's not uncommon for immigrant parents—fathers especially—to prevent their daughters from attaining college degrees or to present some conflict on the matter. "Young women in immigrant families have a difficult time," notes Joe Scelsa, vice president of Queens College of the City of New York. "That first generation is tough to get educated. Some parents believe the adage that if you educate daughters, you lose them." Sociologists are seeing that same trend now among Latinos new to America. It's explained as a desire to keep other students' hands off their baby girls in far-off dormitories and a need to maintain the traditions instilled in the daughters. "You can be a success without spending time with books" is what Veronica De Vivar, a Sacramento pharmaceutical executive, says she was told by her Mexican immigrant father. "His big concern was that if you spent too much time in school, you wouldn't get married. But maybe he was intimidated by having his eldest daughter want college. I don't know."

Maria's father was an interesting case. She says he didn't want his girls to be educated beyond high school, but he boasted to all the relatives that his daughters would be going to college someday. "He had it planned," Maria says. "He wanted to show off his smart, American children by talking college. But when the time came, he would have said we didn't want to study and had decided not to go."

A New York City "sandhog," Antonio worked on Water Tunnel Number Three, a dark and dangerous underground project designed to run water from the Catskill Mountains upstate to a thirsty city. Lots of men have died on that job. Facing serious injury at work, Antonio wasn't about to deal with disharmony at home. Maria recalls being kept close to Astoria by her excavator father, tied to the house in Queens that was originally a brick-oven bread bakery. She looked around and saw her future as one of what she called "the *cuginette* girls," the little cousins, destined to marry a neighborhood guy and see nothing of the world. Her own image of a limited, uneducated life gnawed at her: baby talk with the girls in the ugly, concrete park and an exhausted husband uninterested in child rearing. The biggest event in life would be the occasional movie at the local theater. No, thank you.

Predominantly German, Irish, and Italian when Maria was growing up, Astoria (which is now mostly Greek) is one of those places tourist guidebooks refer to as part of the mosaic of "teeming" neighborhoods that give the city its color and vibrance. When Maria was growing up, Astoria had crowded, bustling avenues filled with small stores and fruit stands, as well as long, narrow side streets crammed with apartment buildings and one- and two-family houses.

Geographically, it's close to Manhattan, but for all their cultural differences, neighborhoods like Astoria could as well have been in Cleveland back then. Immigrants will leave behind family and friends in their home countries to make the brave journey to America, crossing the ocean and swallowing anxieties, steadying themselves through customs, then walking out into a tough, indifferent country hard by the curb at Kennedy airport—only to dig themselves into neighborhoods like Astoria and rarely venture out.

"You do the big move," Maria says, "traumatize yourself and your family, then get to America and crawl into a little shell." Families then try to pass that same cramped sense of community on to their kids. "You make sure your kids never leave the block," adds Maria. What Antonio was trying to do was re-create his Italian village in Queens, Maria says. He would eventually buy two more houses on his block in addition to the original one he purchased, with the full expectation that his three daughters would stick around and live in them. None did; each woman sold her house.

Antonio did not have a car because he was afraid to drive. Only one family on the block that Maria knew of ever went on a vacation.

Antonio saw no need to leave town for any reason. Anything you wanted, you had it right there in Astoria.

"A lot of people in the neighborhood didn't realize there's another kind of life out there," she says. "If you're not told this inside your home, you may not know." The best you can get is a limited life, a neat reproduction of the previous generation, with just a few changes. So Maria secretly applied to colleges in the city. She figured that trying to get to a place like the University of Virginia would just be pressing her luck. When she was accepted by Queens College, they sent a postcard in the mail.

"What did you do?" Maria's mother exploded when the card came. "Your father's in the garage. He wants to talk to you."

Shaking, Maria walked out back to the former carriage house that was the garage to make a case for a future on her terms. As long as she lives, she will never forget the look on the old man's face. This was a betrayal, a disgrace. She thought he would kill her. "How dare you do this without telling me?" he said.

"I thought you told all the relatives we'd go to college," Maria said, trying to turn the tables. She says her dad glared and grumped, then didn't speak to Maria for 30 straight days.

"I don't know," says Maria. "You got the sense they were afraid you'd be smarter than them, or that you'd pick up and go." That's what happened with someone the family knew. She went off to Spain to get a master's degree, and it was regarded as though she had committed murder. The woman returned and never recovered from the full-on clan scorn. "At age 54, she became the good little daughter again, a teacher, living close to home," Maria says.

Here was a strange dichotomy that many Italians and other immigrants lived. They needed America for its opportunity, but despised it for its perceived weaknesses—its promiscuity, its multiculturalism, and its lack of recognizable tradition.

Imagine the pressure on a young woman in those circumstances. "It took courage to do what you wanted," she says. "You had to look long and hard into the future and say to yourself, 'It's either me or them. Either I'm going to make something out of my life or I'm going to wither away.' You have to take every ounce of strength you have to defy them, but—and this is important—never insult them."

41

Many Straddlers said they wound up in permanent warfare with parents who objected to their collegiate aspirations. But Maria quietly set out on a remarkable campaign to defy her father without allowing him to lose face. She'd yield to Antonio when he called her away from her desk to watch television, knowing she had hours of reading yet to do. She got home for dinner by 5 P.M., no matter how hard it was to arrange. Yet through it all, she studied and progressed.

Over the years, Antonio softened, and actually planned Maria's graduation party down to the flowers. He was supposed to have an angiogram on the day of the graduation, but decided to skip it. At the ceremony, he suffered what the family would later learn was a heart attack. Yet he insisted on carrying on. He attended the lunch, and died eight days later.

Reflecting on her life and her eventual career as what she calls a "professional Italian," she realizes that she's doing a job her father would have wanted her to have. "It's only now just dawned on me," she says. "This is my penance for going to college. I guess this was the deal I made, without knowing it: You let me go to college, and I'll do what you want me to do for a living."

The Fight for Light

People from black-hole families remember the college talks with their parents, the times they tried to stand up and allow some light to shine. For some of them, wanting to become educated was tantamount to treason against the family. These moments of declaration were quite difficult to plan and execute. Shaking youngsters would appear before parents who still retained the power of gods. Fighting for identity, the would-be Straddlers laid out arguments that had been painstakingly set down on reams of stationery, or scratched out in school notebooks, then practiced in front of mirrors. When the time came to present themselves—vulnerable but resolute—the transitioning people spoke their hearts and hoped for understanding.

At 6 P.M. on a Chicago evening 40 years ago, Mary Lou Finn (scholar Patrick's niece) told her father she wanted to be a nurse. There were nine people in the family, grandma included, and most everyone had already eaten and drifted off. Earnest Mary Lou, then a seventh-grader, was sitting across from her parents at the huge 12-seat table, trying to tell her plumber father what she thought she might do with her life.

"I want to be a nurse, Dad," she said.

The answer was immediate and unequivocal.

"That's not possible," she remembers her father, now dead, saying, "because you'd have to go to college for that. And you're not going to college."

Mary Lou said that her father continued to stare at her after she made her amazing pronouncement, "looking at me like I had two heads." Then she said that perhaps she'd join the Navy. "All the women there are sluts," she remembers him saying. "You'll do some kind of work in the city." The father was interested in Mary Lou kicking in for rent and keeping the family going until she married and moved. Laying out bucks to educate his daughter was nothing he ever planned on. At 13, Mary Lou could say little. But she knew this would not be the final answer for her. "At that point, I just accepted it," she says. "In the back of my mind I thought I'd eventually do whatever I wanted to. But at that age, I had no means of doing what I wanted."

Cut to seven years later. The family was sitting around that same table. Mary Lou was working as a secretary for a downtown Chicago agricultural chemical company, feeling restless and unfulfilled. A cousin who was close to Mary Lou's age was about to graduate from college with a degree in library science. Mary Lou made a joke, something like, who would want to work in a library all her life?

"Well," Mary Lou says her dad chimed in, "she was always smarter than you."

Cutlery clattered onto dishes and Mary Lou's mother, long silent on the college question, got into her husband's face. "She is not smarter," Mary Lou's mother spat angrily, "she had the chance to go to college."

"I thought my mother was going to kill my dad right then," Mary Lou remembers. "He's been dead now for 30 years, and she still will say how angry she was. She resented my father for not trying to find another way for us. She felt he was shortsighted in thinking our lives should be just like hers."

The father thought that his daughter would work for the city or the plumber's union, where he had some buddies to look out for her. For him, college was a danger, a thing he could not supervise or understand.

Mary Lou, now 53, eventually educated herself and works in public relations. But the memory of the day her father bragged about the librarian cousin still stings.

"Oh, that hurts even today," she says. "It's painful to think your father, who didn't want you to go to college, thinks someone else is smarter because they did."

Things wound up being easier for Michael Moronczyk. When he had his college talk with his father, he was older and better prepared to handle the counterarguments. Michael, now a 24-year-old advertising executive in Detroit, knew he'd have a rough time convincing his father, Tim, to help him pay for college six years ago. Michael's older sister, a bartender, had tried community college, and it hadn't worked out. "She conned her mom into paying for classes before she signed up," says Tim, a line worker at a Ford Motor Company plant. "Then she decided to drop some classes. We got reimbursed for one, but not the other. She took the class and flunked it. So let's put it this way. I didn't pay for any more of her college."

Tim, who is 53, says he never really saw college as a help to the children of his friends. "They go to school, then graduate, and I see them working for a little over minimum wage at bad jobs." No tyrant, Tim simply didn't believe it made sense to spend $10,000 or so a year and be $40,000 in the hole at graduation, when you could stay home and make $30,000 a year doing something in the automotive industry.

A savvy third child, Michael had heard all his father's anticollege arguments already. "My parents had talked my brother out of college," Michael says. "He's a tree trimmer for Detroit Edison. And then there was the thing with my sister. But they didn't address it the right way. They didn't convince my father that, look, I need this for my future."

Like Maria Fosco, Michael understood that getting into college would be a finesse job. "My dad tends to take a standpoint and he really believes in it," Michael says. "You need to come up with a good argument to get him to believe otherwise. I'm not smarter than my siblings, but I am more focused. And I learned a lot from their mistakes with my father."

Tim had some money that Michael could use for tuition. The trick was to get him to open his mind; his checkbook would follow. Michael had already been accepted by Northwood University in Midland, Michigan, on a partial lacrosse scholarship. Tim had a question: "Did he want to go to college to play lacrosse or to learn? I had to kick in $6,000 to $8,000 a year. That's an awful lot of money for a guy just going to play lacrosse, know what I mean? I was questioning his motives."

Father and son had been circling the issue for months. Then came the conversation. It was at the kitchen table after supper one night in June. Mom—who was mostly silent on the subject, except to tell Michael what Tim was thinking from time to time—was there, too. For reasons Michael still can't explain, that night would be the night he'd press Tim.

"I started by telling my dad I thought it was better to go to college and concentrate just on getting my education instead of trying to do it by working full-time and making school secondary. Without his help, I was facing the possibility of never finishing college. I had to stress to him I'd be getting into the working world better prepared." Tim says he doesn't remember the conversation. That makes Michael smile. "He was being particularly stubborn that night." To get through, Michael tried using a little imagery. "Dad," he said, "when you get an idea in your head, you put it on one side of a wall and no matter how good somebody else's idea is, it's on the other side of the wall, and it can't get through."

There was no rancor as they talked. No one raised his voice, although what was at stake was tremendous: A young man was arguing for his life in a Michigan kitchen with a guy 30 years older who thought he knew better. Michael changed tack, going into his good-boy history, his clean-life record of having stayed out of trouble in troubled Detroit. Then he talked precedent. "I want to be the first in the family to go to school, Dad," he said. "And I won't let you down. I'll make you proud."

At this point, Tim's demeanor shifted. At first, he'd looked stony and resolute. But now he softened, and Michael detected a different emotion. "He started looking at me like he was unsure, like he was scared almost. Like he was kind of thinking, right at that moment, 'What if you fail?'"

They went back and forth. Michael kept telling himself, "I know my dad loves me, I know my dad loves me. But, oh, he's stubborn."

Finally, Michael said it out loud: "Dad, you're stubborn. And I'm not a kid anymore. I need to do this for me. This is what's best for me."

That did it. After 30 minutes, Tim quietly looked at his son and said, "Okay, you're right. This is what you need to do."

"All three of us broke into tears," Michael says. "As storybook as it sounds, we all ended in a hug, the three of us crying. After that day, I became pretty much the only one who could stand up to my dad in the family."

Once Michael was in college, Tim did that "my son's a college boy" routine very well. Michael made the dean's list every term but one, and when he did, a community paper would publish his name. One day, Michael learned that Tim had been posting the listings in the Ford lunchroom. "Our relationship changed," Michael says. "He was real happy I'd done it."

"What can I say?" Tim says today, a little sly, a little repentant. "I questioned him, but Mikey did me proud."

Not all black-hole families resolve their problems so amicably. Some Straddlers say that the day they announced their college plans was the last day they spoke to their parents for a while. Still, people agree that no matter how painful the transition was, they cannot imagine not having gone through it. Standing up to their parents afforded Straddlers the important knowledge that they could handle a tough situation. But as long as they live, they may find few moments harder than the time they crawled out of the black hole to save their own lives, and to see what they could become.

3

THE SHOCK OF EDUCATION: HOW COLLEGE CORRUPTS

College is where the Great Change begins. People start to question the blue-collar take on the world. Status dissonance, the sociologists call it. Questions arise: Are the guys accurate in saying people from such-and-such a race are really so bad? Was Mom right when she said nice girls don't put out? Suddenly, college opens up a world of ideas—a life of the mind—abstract and intangible. The core blue-collar values and goals—loyalty to family and friends, making money, marrying, and procreating—are supplanted by stuff you never talked about at home: personal fulfillment, societal obligation, the pursuit of knowledge for knowledge's sake, and on and on. One world opens and widens; another shrinks.

There's an excitement and a sadness to that. The child, say Sennett and Cobb, is deserting his past, betraying the parents he is rising above, an unavoidable result when you're trying to accomplish more with your life than merely earning a paycheck.[1] So much will change between parent and child, and between peers, in the college years. "Every bit of learning takes you further from your parents," says Southwest Texas State University history professor Gregg Andrews, himself a Straddler. "I say this to all my freshmen to start preparing them." The best predictor of whether you're going to have problems with your family is the distance between your education and your parents', Jake Ryan says. You may soon find yourself with nothing to talk to your folks or friends about.

This is the dark part of the American story, the kind of thing we work to hide. Mobility means discomfort, because so much has to change; one can't allow for the satisfactions of stasis: You prick yourself and move, digging spurs into your own hide to get going, forcing yourself to forget the comforts of the barn. In this country, we speak grandly of this metamorphosis, never stopping to consider that for many class travelers with passports stamped for new territory, the trip is nothing less than a bridge burning.

Fighting Self-Doubt

When Columbia plucked me out of working-class Brooklyn, I was sure they had made a mistake, and I remained convinced of that throughout most of my time there. My high school was a gigantic (4,500 students) factory; we literally had gridlock in the halls between classes, kids belly to back between history and English class. A teacher once told me that if every one of the reliable corps of truant students actually decided to show up to class one day, the school could not hold us all. (We were unofficially nicknamed "the Italian Army." When our football guys played nearby New Utrecht, which boasted an equivalent ethnic demographic, kids dubbed the game the "Lasagna Bowl.") Lafayette High School roiled with restless boys and girls on their way to jobs in their parents' unions or to secretaries' desks. How could you move from that to an elite college?

At night, at home, the difference in the Columbia experiences my father and I were having was becoming more evident. The family still came together for dinner, despite our disparate days. We talked about general stuff, and I learned to self-censor. I'd seen how ideas could be upsetting, especially when wielded by a smarmy freshman who barely knew what he was talking about. No one wanted to hear how the world worked from some kid who was first learning to use his brain; it was as unsettling as riding in a car with a new driver. When he taught a course on Marx, Sackrey said he used to tell his students just before Thanksgiving break not to talk about "this stuff at the dinner table" or they'd mess up the holiday. Me mimicking my professors' thoughts on race, on people's struggle for equality, or on politics didn't add to the conviviality of the one nice hour in our day. So I learned to shut up.

After dinner, my father would flip on the TV in the living room. My mom would grab a book and join him. And I'd go looking for a quiet spot to study. In his autobiography, *Hunger of Memory: The Education of Richard Rodriguez*, the brilliant Mexican-American Straddler, writer, and PBS commentator invokes British social scientist Richard Hoggart's "scholarship boys," finding pieces of himself in them. Working-class kids trying to advance in life, the scholarship boys learned to withdraw from the warm noise of the gathered family to isolate themselves with their books.[2] (Read primarily as a memoir of ethnicity and—most famously—an anti–affirmative action tract, the book is more genuinely a dissertation on class. At a sidewalk café in San Francisco, Rodriguez himself tells me how often his book is miscatalogued.) Up from the immigrant working class, Rodriguez says in our interview, the scholarship boy finds himself moving between two antithetical places: home and school. With the family, there is intimacy and emotion. At school, one learns to live with "lonely reason." Home life is in the now, Rodriguez says; school life exists on an altogether different plane, calm and reflective, with an eye toward the future.

The scholarship boy must learn to distance himself from the family circle in order to succeed academically, Rodriguez tells me. By doing this, he slowly loses his family. There's a brutality to education, he says, a rough and terrible disconnect. Rodriguez says he despised his parents' "shabbiness," their inability to speak English. "I hated that they didn't know what I was learning," he says. He thought of D.H. Lawrence's *Sons and Lovers*, and of Paul Morel, the coal miner's son. Lawrence is a model for Rodriguez, in a way. Rodriguez remembers the scene in which the son watches his father pick up his schoolbooks, his rough hands fingering the volumes that are the instruments separating the two men. Books were establishing a disharmony between the classroom and Rodriguez's house. Preoccupation with language and reading is an effeminacy not easily understood by workers. "It sears your soul to finally decide to talk like your teacher and not your father," Rodriguez says. "I'm not talking about anything less than the grammar of the heart."

Myself, I studied in the kitchen near the dishwasher because its white noise drowned out the television. As long as the wash cycle ran, I could not hear Mr. T and the A-Team win the day. I did not begrudge my father his one indulgence; there wasn't much else that could relax him. He was not a drinker. TV drained away the tumult and hazard of his Columbia day. My own room was too close to the living room. My brother's small room was too crowded for both of us to study in. You never went in your parents' bedroom without them in it, inviting you. When the dishes were clean and the kitchen again too quiet to beat back the living room noise, I'd go downstairs to my grandparents' apartment. If they were both watching the same TV show on the first floor, then the basement was free. Here was profound and almost disquieting silence. I could hear the house's systems rumble and shake: water whooshing through pipes, the oil burner powering on and off, and the refrigerator humming with a loud efficiency. Down in the immaculate redwood-paneled kitchen/living room, which sometimes still smelled of the sausages and peppers my grandfather may have made that night (my grandparents cooked and ate in their basement, something that never seemed unusual to us), I was 90 minutes from my school and two floors below my family in a new place, underscoring my distance from anything known, heightening my sense of isolation—my limbo status. I read Homer, Shakespeare, and Molière down there. I wrote a paper on landscape imagery in Dante's *Inferno*. In my self-pitying, melodramatic teenager's mind, I thought I had been banished to a new, lonely rung of hell that Dante hadn't contemplated.

By 11 P.M., I'd go back upstairs. My mother would be in bed, my father asleep on his chair. I'd turn off the TV, which awakened my dad. He'd walk off to bed, and I'd study for a couple more hours. His alarm would go off before 5 A.M., and he'd already be at Columbia by the time I woke up at 6:30. That's how our Ivy League days ended and began. When my father was done with Columbia, he moved on to another job site. When I was done with Columbia, I was someone else. I'd say I got the better deal. But then, my father would tell you, that was always the plan.

Up from the Corner

In *Hunger of Memory*, Rodriguez writes that guys who show a love of books are violating the macho code of their blue-collar upbringing.[3] Ideas weaken the way things are, calling accepted culture into question. What's mysterious to Straddlers is why they were the ones who paid attention in school while everyone else was tuning out. What made them different? Why did Salinger speak to them and not to the rest of the kids in class? One thing limbo folk understand, regardless of generation, is that they were among a small minority of peers who stood out, stood up, and walked away. One of them was Dennis George.

Up and down the streets of narrow row houses in South Philly, people share walls and world views. On a warm summer night back in June 1969, Dennis gathered with his friends on the corner at 10th and Wharton like he always did, like they always did. The guys cut on each other, sang, and lied about girls—the usual. But if you want to know the truth, Dennis thought that there was a sameness creeping into the routine, a disappointing sense that if you weren't careful, every night from now until you're dead could smell and feel this exact way.

Dennis was 17, fit and tough. He'd been accepted to Penn State University, and this was his last summer before college. He felt bad, even slightly disloyal to the guys in his gang. Most of them would be staying put, working in construction, getting into their fathers' trade unions—things like that. Dennis didn't understand why, but he needed more. That night, he was already feeling different from the fellas. Then, too, there was that guy—Dennis can't remember his name today—who had gone to college. A corner boy like them, he started growing his hair long, putting down the war in Vietnam, and banging on Nixon. Amazing. What he was saying was unusual and provocative. "He was one of the most progressive-thinking guys," said Dennis, now a lawyer sitting with gleaming cuff links in his Center City Philadelphia office, from which he can eyeball the glorious wedding-cake flourishes of city hall. Most of the guys would argue with the college oracle and call him a wimp. But Dennis listened. It was important, because it was the first time he'd heard contrary stuff coming from a boy who hung out. Plus the guy read. "I remember knowing two or three guys like him who actually read books on a summer day. It fascinated me. I would read, too, and write vocabulary words I didn't know in the backs of books. I still don't know why I was different. What makes somebody who grows up in the same neighborhood as everyone else want to do something different? I don't know." Dennis used to ask his mother, a homemaker, but she had no answer, except to say, "You're very bright, just like your father." Maybe it was that one week he worked in a tailor's shop when he was 15. God, it was hard, boring work. Dennis had made a promise to himself that there was no way he'd do that for the rest of his life.

To Dennis, it was like there was this script written by God knows who that everybody in the neighborhood had to follow. It told you how to be, how to act, and how to think: which Philadelphia Eagle to idolize, what Jersey shore beach to hang at, what kind of car to use as trysting bait for girls, and what job you killed yourself doing. There was a uniformity to it, like the bricks in all the walls in South Philly. Bricked and mortared into a place like that, what chance did you have to break out? Well, Dennis was starting to question the gospel as the corner boys preached it, and he was already poised to take a new direction.

Anyway, this one night, everybody was just standing around when the word came down that the girlfriend of one of the guys was seen stepping out with a guy from another corner. Very *West Side Story*, Dennis remembered thinking, except, of course, his boy was Italian, the girl was Italian, and the guy from the other corner was Italian. Dennis was having a hard time trying to figure out what was at stake here, except maybe the usual thing: turf and territory. Still, for perhaps the first time, it sounded a little stupid.

"I remember saying, 'What's the big deal?,' but the guys who still had short hair and shaved everyday, who still had the old bebop Philly style—these guys led the charge, saying, 'We can't take this crap. We gotta honor the corner and honor our friend.'"

Dennis had been in a few of these dumb rumbles before. Maybe there was a bat or belt buckle, but usually guys just threw from the shoulder. "Generally, these things would end with the toughest guy from each side going at it in a fair fight. Our guy was Carl. He's dead now, from drugs of all things. But he was our designated animal." Into a Chevy Caprice and somebody's Ford junker hopped Carl, Dennis, and the boys, gunning it for about 10 or 20 blocks. Dennis didn't want to go but believed he had to. "I didn't want to send them out to war alone. It was still death before dishonor for me. That was the value we had in the neighborhood: You took care of your own."

So Dennis and the guys pulled up to the jerk's corner, saw a few boys hanging out—the jerk himself not being among them—then jumped out of the cars and gave chase anyway. Down the tight streets and alleys they ran, whooping and cursing, adrenalized and alive for the first time that day—maybe for the first time in a while. Dennis, though, remained immune to the blood thrall. In fact, his small doubts blossomed into a reasoned anxiety, even as he halfheartedly gave chase. "It just struck me that it didn't make sense. It was so idiotic, chasing people through their own neighborhood. And for what?" It being a hot night, lots of adults were out. They saw what was happening, and now grown men, who had once been boys who had defended these streets, mobilized as they might have years ago and started chasing Dennis and his crew. Tough-guy hunters became retreating prey just like that, as the neighborhood rose ugly against them. "There goes my whole future," Dennis began thinking as he ran back to the Chevy. "I'm 17 years old, with everything in front of me, the first one in my family accepted to college, and one of just five guys from the neighborhood going to college. And it's all going to end with a bat to my head or a crowbar across my brain. This is so nuts." He began running faster, and experienced an on-the-fly epiphany born of two fears—the immediate peril of a beating in the gutter and the deeper worry that he could never outrun the blue-collar realities of this airless place.

"That was the instant I grew up. I never thought before that a night could ruin your whole life. I told myself that this has got to change."

So Dennis got to college and went all-the-way hippie: ripped jeans, white-boy Afro, beard, and wire-rim glasses. The vegetarian thing didn't go down too well with the family. (Blue-collar parents get very upset once you take meat off the menu; it's just too odd for them and suggests a repudiation of long-held values and all those expensive, hard-earned home-cooked meals.) But Dennis was reveling in it. The great change was beginning. Core blue-collar values and goals were augmented by notions Dennis had never had before. He thought about the environment. And the war. New ideas crammed the head he'd managed to save that June night. In two short years, he was very different from the 10th and Wharton boys, and something his parents had never seen before. He was new—to himself and to them.

Radicalized and political, Dennis became president of the student government, and in 1971, the winter of his sophomore year, he was asked to give a speech at the dedication ceremonies for a new campus building for the university. Deans, professors, and even the university president showed up. The school invited his parents, who dressed up and walked into the place proud, only to be told the auditorium was too full and that they had to view it via closed-circuit TV in an adjacent room. They smiled and, a little intimidated, obligingly moved to the other spot. Their Dennis delivered a give-peace-a-chance, flower-child oratory without acrimony, a paean to the antiwar movement that served as an explanation to his elders of what was on his generation's mind: "You look at us, your children, and think we are trying to tear it all down. But we want to build it up and save it." Like that.

Dennis got a standing ovation. The faculty loved it and crowded around him. His dad, a Lebanese cabdriver and professional gambler who was generally at ease with people, led his mom in from the other room to join in the congratulations. If Dennis could change any moment in his life, it would be that one, the very second his mother and father stood by him after making their way through the crowd.

"Mom and Dad, why don't you sit down, and I'll be right with you," is what he said to them. His father's face fell and his mother looked down. Sure, sure, they mumbled, suddenly in a hurry to leave. They both did as their son told them and walked away from the growing knot of well-wishers.

Remembering the day, Dennis tries to understand himself. He was thinking—what? Well, a number of little things, really. His parents said "youse" a lot. They were South Philly and he was, in just a short time, something else, built up by the books and broadened by scholarship. They might have said something to embarrass him, you know? After all, this was his new world, and no one needed to be reminded of his blue-collar past.

"Schmuck" is what Dennis calls himself now. "As a parent now myself, I've been to my son's plays. It's greater than any accomplishment you could have on your own. I've won major jury trials, but the proudest moments have been with my kids. After your son stars in a play, and people come up to you and say how wonderful he is, it's the greatest." Now Dennis understands what he took from his mom and dad. "If there's one thing in my life I regret, it's that moment. If I could have done it again, they would have been in the front row. My parents were more intelligent than most of those professors, anyway. It should have been one of the proudest moments of their lives. And instead, I shunned them." Dennis never discussed the day with his parents. He just tried to make it up to them over the years, one kindness at a time.

Macbeth and Other Foolishness

Middle-class kids are groomed for another life. They understand, says Patrick Finn, why reading *Macbeth* in high school could be important years down the road. Working-class kids see no such connection, understand no future life for which digesting Shakespeare might be of value. Very much in the now, working-class people are concerned with immediate needs. And bookish kids are seen as weak.

Various education studies have shown that schools help reinforce class. Teachers treat the working class and the well-to-do differently, this work demonstrates, with the blue-collar kids getting less attention and respect. It's no secret, education experts insist, that schools in poorer areas tend to employ teachers who are less well-trained. In these schools, the curriculum is test-based and uncreative. Children are taught, essentially, to obey and fill in blanks. By fourth grade, many of the children are bored and alienated; nothing in school connects to their culture. Beyond that, many working-class children are resistant to schooling and uncooperative with teachers, experts say. They feel pressure from other working-class friends to not participate and are told that being educated is effeminate and irrelevant. Educators have long understood that minority children have these problems, says Finn. But they rarely understand or see that working-class white kids have similar difficulties. "So we're missing a whole bunch of people getting screwed by the education systems," he says.

In our conversations, Finn explains that language is a key to class. In a working-class home where conformity is the norm, all opinions are dictated by group consensus, by what the class says is so. There's one way to do everything, there's one way to look at the world. Since all opinions are shared, there's never a need to explain thought and behavior. You talk less. Language in such a home, Finn says, is implicit.

Things are different in a middle-class home. There, parents are more willing to take the time to explain to little Janey why it's not such a good idea to pour chocolate sauce on the dog. If Janey challenges a rule of the house, she's spoken to like an adult, or at least not like a plebe at some military school. (Working-class homes are, in fact, very much like the military, with parents barking orders, Straddlers tell me. It's that conformity thing again.) There is a variety of opinions in middle-class homes, which are more collaborative than conformist, Finn says. Middle-class people have a multiviewed take on the world. In such a home, where one needs to express numerous ideas and opinions, language is by necessity explicit.

When it's time to go to school, the trouble starts. The language of school—of the teachers and the books—is explicit. A child from a working-class home is at a huge disadvantage, Finn says, because he's used to a narrower world of expression and a smaller vocabulary of thought. It's little wonder that kids from working-class homes have lower reading scores and do less well on SATs than middle-class kids, Finn says.

In high school, my parents got me a tutor for the math part of the SATs, to bolster a lackluster PSAT score. That sort of thing happens all the time in middle-class neighborhoods. But we were setting precedent among our kind. Most kids I knew from the community were not taking the SATs, let alone worrying about their scores. If you're from the middle class, you do not feel out of place preparing for college. Parents and peers help groom you, encourage you, and delight in your progress. Of course, when you get to freshman year, the adjustments can be hard on anyone, middle-class and working-class kids alike. But imagine going through freshman orientation if your parents are ambivalent—or hostile—about your being there, and your friends aren't clear about what you're doing.

It was like that for my friend Rita Giordano, 45, also a journalist, also from Brooklyn. Her world, like mine, was populated by people who thought going from 60th to 65th Streets was a long journey. So when Rita took sojourns into Greenwich Village by herself on Saturday mornings as a teenager, she made sure not to tell any of her friends. It was too oddball to have to explain. And she'd always come back in time to go shopping with everyone. She couldn't figure out why she responded to the artsy vibe of the Village; she was just aware that there were things going on beyond the neighborhood. When it came time for college, she picked Syracuse University because it was far away, a new world to explore. That bothered her friends, and she'd have to explain herself to them on trips back home. "What do you do up there?" they asked her. "Don't you get homesick?" Suddenly, things felt awkward among childhood friends who had always been able to talk. "It was confusing to come home and see people thinking that you're not doing what they're doing, which meant you're rejecting them," said Rita, a diminutive, sensitive woman with large, brown eyes. " 'Don't they see it's still me?' I wondered. I started feeling like, how do I coexist in these two worlds, college and home? I mean, I could talk to my girlfriends about what color gowns their bridesmaids would wear at their fantasy weddings. But things like ambition and existential questions about where you fit in the world and how you make your mark—we just didn't go there."

And to make matters more complicated, there was a guy. Rita's decision to go to Syracuse didn't sit well with the boyfriend who was probably always going to remain working class. "In true Brooklyn fashion, he and his friends decided one night they were going to drive 400 miles to Syracuse to bring me back, or whatever. But on the way up, they totaled the car and my boyfriend broke his leg. He never got up there, and after that, the idea of him bringing me to my senses dissipated."

Another Straddler, Loretta Stec, had a similar problem with a blue-collar lover left behind. Loretta, a slender 39-year-old English professor at San Francisco State University with delicate features and brown hair, needed to leave the commotion of drugs and friends' abortions and the repressed religious world of Perth Amboy, New Jersey, for the calm life of the mind offered by Boston College. The only problem was Barry. When Loretta was 17, she and Barry, an older construction worker, would ride motorcycles in toxic waste dumps. He was wild and fine— what every working-class girl would want. But Loretta knew life had to get better than Perth Amboy, so she went off to Boston. Barry and she still got together, though. They even worked on the same taping crew at a construction site during the summer between Loretta's freshman and sophomore years. But the differences between them were growing. All the guys on the job—Barry included—thought it was weird that Loretta would read the *New York Times* during lunch breaks. "What's with that chick?" people asked.

By the time Loretta returned to Boston for her second year, she knew she was in a far different place than Barry. The working class was not for her. Hanging around with this guy and doing construction for-ever—it sounded awful. "I was upwardly mobile, and I was not going to work on a construction crew anymore," Loretta says. She tried to break it off, but Barry roared up I-95 in a borrowed car to change her mind. Loretta lived in an old Victorian with middle-class roommates who had never met anyone like Barry. When he showed up with a barking Doberman in tow, she recalled he was screaming like Stanley Kowalski in *A Streetcar Named Desire* that he wanted Loretta back. The women became terrified. Loretta was able to calm first Barry, then her room-mates. Afterward, the couple went to listen to some music. In a little place on campus, a guitar trio started performing a Rolling Stones song. Suddenly, Barry turned to Loretta and began scream-singing about wild horses not being able to drag him from her, really loud, trying to get her to see his resolve. "People were wondering who was this guy, what's his deal?" Loretta says. "It pointed out the clash between my new world and the old. You don't do stuff like that. It was embarrassing, upsetting, and confusing. I didn't want to hurt him. But I knew it wasn't going to work for me." They walked around campus, fighting about things com-ing to an end. At some point, she recalls, Barry noticed that a college student with a nicer car than his—Loretta can't remember exactly what it was—had parked behind his car, blocking him. Already ramped up, Barry had a fit and smashed a headlight of the fancy machine with a rock. There Loretta was, 100 feet from her campus Victorian, newly ensconced in a clean world of erudition and scholarship, far from the violence and swamps of central Jersey. Her bad-boy beau, once so appealing, was raving and breathing hard, trying to pull her away from the books, back down the turnpike to the working class.

"That was really the end of it," Loretta says. "I couldn't have a guy around who was going to act like that. He was wild and crazy and I was trying to make my way." Barry relented, and left Loretta alone. They lost touch, and Loretta later learned that Barry had died, the cause of death unknown to her. It was such a shock.

Unpredictable Alchemy

For a lot of working-class parents, the idea of educating their kids is not necessarily tied to the idea that the child will become a different person.

Sure, the folks can see the potential financial benefit—if you earn a degree, you can get a good job and command a higher salary. To lots of blue-collar moms and dads, college is simply a crowbar to pry money out of some corporation so the kid can have a better deal in life. But blue-collar parents can't know how college can change someone. They can't know that college isn't just a tool you work with; it works on you. And the alchemy is unpredictable and often disturbing for people who couldn't possibly be prepared for the molecular-level metamorphosis they will behold in their son or daughter. College makes one understand there is no single way to look at things. That can be an unwanted revelation in a blue-collar place, where the rules are pretty much cast in concrete, and the primary colors are black and white.

bell hooks writes that her parents worried when she went to Stanford University because they feared she would not hold onto their ways and beliefs. College would just interfere with the basics. The proper life, hooks's parents believed, was centered on family and God, with the rare good day thrown in. There is value in the day-to-dayness of it, and little need for "fancy ideas."[4] Straddler Andrea Todd, a Sacramento freelance editor and writer, says her firefighter father had a term for such fancy ideas: "Berkeley crap." Both Andrea and her sister graduated from the school, and their father believed college afforded the women license to maneuver through the world without worrying about consequence. Once, Andrea got a bunch of parking tickets from the school and didn't pay them. The car got towed by campus cops and when she recovered it, she talked the police down from a bill of $400 to $200. "That's Berkeley crap," her father said. "You should have paid it all."

It was precisely the fancy ideas of the academy that got "Michael" into trouble with both God and family. Michael, a middle-aged businessman in the Northeast, grew up in the coal mining town of Moundsville, West Virginia. His father was a coal miner, then a truck driver. His mother was a homemaker at first, then worked in an insurance office after Michael's father became an invalid.

Generations of young men had gone into the mines, just like Michael's father. But there was a darkness in the black honeycombs that Michael knew he could never abide for eight hours out of every day. The sunless, cramped dampness was its own kind of wilderness, beneath the everyday lives of friends and kin, buried under fields, roads, and cemeteries. Coal dust invaded miners' orifices, darkening and slowly sickening their lungs. It made for a troubling symmetry: The miners were in the earth, and the earth was in the miners. Buried in the shapeless gloom somewhere between hell and the decomposing dead, miners balanced the risk of disease and cave-in with decent wages. The good money seduced a lot of people. But Michael thought there should be more to life than stuffing yourself into an ancient seam of slick blackness each day. As he considered his options, he became a barber, and prayed on what to do next.

Michael always had been extremely religious. He and his family belonged to a fundamentalist Christian religion that held to a strict, literal interpretation of the Bible. Michael was so steeped in the church that he became an occasional preacher and Sunday school teacher. Even in high school, Michael was so taken by the Lord that he would deliver fiery sermons to an appreciative congregation that believed itself lucky to have such a young and gifted holy man in their midst. That pleased his mother. "Religion was her whole world," Michael says.

Michael had an interest in a girl in town who attended night classes at a local college, and he started tagging along on a whim. Scholarship seemed interesting, so he stuck with it. His father thought it was crazy, wondering why anyone needed college. But Michael was hooked, and he would go on to get a Ph.D. in the sciences and an MBA.

After a time, he realized that education was changing him. Already considered liberal compared to his peers—friends thought he was odd for arguing that the N-word was offensive—Michael's science studies were interfering with his religious beliefs. "Science made me search for the truth in things more," Michael says. "And it almost became my new religion. I had been taking all these courses that argued for evolution, a direct challenge to my religion, which said the world was created in seven days."

People started noticing that Michael's sermons were becoming less fervent, less intense somehow. They could no longer feel the Holy Ghost stir in them as he talked, couldn't lock into the preacher's cascading rhythms like before. Now, Michael's philosophy texts that questioned God's existence were taking up increasing space in his head. "I was wrestling, always wrestling."

Around that time, the church had been experimenting with a new Bible, a more liberal text written in today's vernacular. Michael liked and supported the new edition, but much of the deeply conservative congregation rebelled. Then, during a high school Bible class that he taught, Michael started questioning reality and consciousness, trying to get the kids to think, asking them, "How do we know this life is real and not just a dream?" The adults heard about it and went crazy. "They thought I was somebody from Mars, even though I'd grown up right there with them. It was very clear people started thinking of me as an outlyer, moving in a more and more liberal direction."

Michael's family, especially his devout mother, was disappointed. But science and philosophy had kicked up an absolute crisis of faith within Michael. "I was struggling to stay with my family and friends because that was my roots. I was trying to find a way, even with this new intellectual awareness."

Michael quit preaching and moved away to attend graduate school. His mother visited him and accompanied him one Sunday to his new church, a nondenominational place where people played guitar during services. No one played guitar in the home church. As soon as she heard the music, Michael's mother burst out crying. Rather than confront him, though, she screamed at Michael's wife. His mother thought it was the woman, not college, that had turned her son. "That was the last straw. I said, 'I quit and I can't take it,' and I never went to any church again. It hasn't been easy for me. I worked very hard to keep my beliefs and not lose my family. But I became educated. And there's no religion in my life now."

Altering religion and custom can cause quite the family ruckus. My parents were displeased with our choice not to have a priest at our wedding. Neither Linda nor I is religious. My folks aren't particularly devout Catholics, either. But, like a lot of people, they want that cleric around for the rites of passage—baptisms, weddings, and funerals. I said it would have been hypocritical of me to participate in a wedding Mass. This is precisely the kind of thing you learn in college: consistency in thinking, avoiding intellectual hypocrisy when you can. Because religion could not stand up to my own scrutiny, I could no longer let it be part of my life. College makes agnostics of lots of people. We had our wedding at the Columbia chapel, officiated by the nice judge who had presided over a sodomy trial I had covered a year before at a previous newspaper job. The family really loved that. We were going to have our reception at a zydeco nightclub until my father saw the place and noticed the pool table in front. It didn't seem proper to him. The *New York Times* indicated it was interested in a possible story about our wedding in the Sunday "Vows" section, because they thought our party choice was so bohemian and idiosyncratic. To keep peace, we opted for a Greenwich Village carriage house, dragging the zydeco band with us. The *Times* did not attend.

One of my oldest friends, Marianne Costantinou, a college buddy who attended Columbia's sister school, Barnard, had her own class warfare with her parents over tradition at her wedding. "It was the biggest proof to me there really was this middle class versus working class thing," she tells me. Marianne's parents are Greek immigrants who live in Queens. They have made their livelihoods dealing with the Manhattan well-to-do. Her mother altered their suits at Bloomingdale's; her father served them food and drinks at the Polo Lounge. Nixon used to be a customer. Dark, sultry Marianne was marrying tall, patrician-slender Marty, a great guy from middle-class, well-educated parents. Everyone was happy about the match. An Ivy League graduate and newly minted member of the middle class, Marianne also wanted her wedding to be the kind you read about in the *Times* (Marianne actually worked there)—elegant, whimsical, upper-middle-class-ish, and sophisticated. She did not want a veil. She did not want a train on her dress. She did not want ethnic music—maybe just a flute and a harp. But most of all, she did not want to dole out *bou-bou nieres* to her guests. These are Greek wedding favors, usually a piece of crystal—an ashtray or a paperweight—with a ribbon that includes the names of the husband and wife. White, sugar-coated almonds were also involved in the package. To Marianne, this was hideous. "It was without class, and to be without class was to be totally blue collar," Marianne believes. She put her foot down. And family warfare broke out.

"Oh my God, what a disgrace," Marianne says her father shouted in Greek. "They'll all think I'm cheap."

"Under no circumstances will I do it," Marianne said. "But I'll give in on the veil, the train, and the Greek music. You can have those."

"Okay," her father said. "No *bou-bou nieres*," Marianne recalls.

The wedding day came. Marianne and her family were piling into the limo to take them from her parents' place to the church.

"My God," Marianne says her father exclaimed. "The stove, I left the gas oven on." He ran back into the house, and reemerged with two huge boxes that he threw in the trunk. Marianne did not speak to him during the entire wedding, except to say, "If you give them out, I'll throw them against the wall."

Marianne thought that was that. People danced to the lively Greek songs in the spacious Westchester County wedding hall. It was fun. Marianne was mellowing, until she spied her father in the parking lot. He'd been sneaking the favors to guests near their cars, pressing them into their hands as they left.

"Of course, my parents won the class skirmish," Marianne says. "And all my friends who were there from the *Times* loved it, because they viewed the whole Greek wedding as a Margaret Mead experience. They had gone overseas and come across a pygmy tribe with interesting customs. And I felt I was viewed as an aborigine."

Don't Think You're Any Better Than Us

It's not unusual for Straddlers to spar with or feel slighted by family because they've become educated. You don't hear about it because it's not the kind of thing people like to admit. The stories we've come to know about social mobility in America start with misty-eyed parents at colorful graduation ceremonies. A young person is being propelled out of the ghetto, the ethnic enclave, or the map-dot-tiny farming community. It's a time to rejoice. No one mentions the ambivalence—and, sometimes, antipathy—of relatives on hand to watch the launch. "I remember," says Donna, the national-magazine journalist, "my relatives throwing $5 graduation presents in envelopes at me—literally throwing them. 'Now you think you're better than we are,' one of my aunts said. My relatives were so resentful that I graduated. When I have nightmares to this day, it's of the trailer we lived in, that depressed, rural area and the people who were suffocating me."

Like Donna, Nancy Dean, the 46-year-old Massachusetts medical researcher, recalls being roundly attacked by aunts who lashed out at her after college graduation for having left her mother and gone off on her own, breaking the family pattern. Some of the pique, Nancy says, stemmed from her setting herself up as an independent woman who would not be living at home and kicking in money. "It was very revolutionary in an Irish blue-collar family that you did not stay at home and help out around the house." Nancy was a teacher at first, and she recalls that all her pipe-fitter father had to say upon her graduation was that all teachers are jerks and she would fit right in.

On her first weekend home from college, Barbara Peters, 53, a Long Island sociologist, was warned by her blue-collar Wisconsin family, "Don't get too big for your britches. You think you're so smart 'cause you're in college." That meant, Barbara says, that you should just come back and act like us. When she had final exams, her parents were moving and demanded that she return to help. She didn't and they held it against her.

That was the sort of static Anthony Lukas absorbed when he attended college. From working-class Philadelphia, Lukas, a 38-year-old advertising executive, says his college experience did not go down well at home. It didn't help matters that Anthony was already something of an unusual character in his neighborhood. Once when he was 7, he was forced to accompany his bookkeeper mother as she did some furniture shopping. As she wondered what to buy, Anthony just started telling her what pieces and fabrics worked well together. It was a gift he didn't know he possessed. "I wanted to stay within primary colors and didn't want to stray from the design of the house. There was oak woodwork everywhere and it seemed absurd to me to put modern furniture in. I tried to go with a more classic design, with the modern features she was looking for." Flabbergasted, his mother took his advice. The neighbors who visited loved Anthony's taste so much, they asked his mom if they could borrow the design wunderkind for their own furniture forays. So Anthony wound up decorating nearly the entire block.

The other parents never squealed about this to their own kids; Anthony would have been beaten up. Luckily for a boy growing up in a blue-collar world, he acquired a tough reputation as a hockey player. He also had been experiencing some problems. There were curfew violations and shoplifting charges and fights. He flunked out of high school. So his dad was inclined to be tough with the boy.

His mother's brother, who worked in the advertising business, took a liking to Anthony and had him up to his North Jersey house for a summer. One day, Anthony watched a print ice cream ad being shot in

Manhattan. It took 8½ hours to photograph a single scoop of vanilla. A woman who wielded surgical instruments to sculpt the ice cream was being paid $5,000 for a day's work. Instantly convinced that the ad game was for him, Anthony knew that he needed college to get there. He got his GED, was accepted into a college, and started the transformation. Dad, a welder, didn't like it.

In blue-collar homes, there's rarely such a thing as a civil argument. Working-class people have two speeds: silence and rage. It's the middle class that debates things, able to conduct an argument without becoming emotional; working-class people yell. Anthony, the college man, decided he would break the screaming pattern and try reasoning with his dad. He'd wanted to go down the Jersey shore one day, and his father was against the idea. "I tried to dispute my father's position in a logical manner—why I should be able to go to the shore. I questioned him. And then he hit me. That was the predominant form of communication in our house."

Anthony had tried using precise reason, just as one of his professors might. But his father was angry with his son's hyperarticulation, the way he came off sounding high-handed. "You can get away with that stuff in Jersey [with his ad-exec uncle], but not here. What you learned in school and up in Jersey means squat here. You think you're better than us now," Anthony remembers his father saying.

Anthony says his father was probably jealous that his son was going somewhere he could not. "There was something worldly about how I spoke, what I spoke about, and how I questioned him, that he didn't like." You don't question the patriarch in an authoritarian, blue-collar household. And this logical reasoning stuff just does not fly. As a result, the bad feeling has remained intact as an unmelted ice cube through the years. "There's really no relationship with my family other than the formal stuff—you get together at holidays and say the things you're supposed to say. They have no idea what I do and if I bring it up, their eyes roll into the backs of their heads. I don't know if they're proud of me or not."

The problem Anthony had with the way he talked to his father is something Straddlers everywhere remember experiencing. Often, language itself is a problem. After a while, maybe all the talk that's left is family gossip. Barbara Jensen, the Minnesota shrink who, along with scholar Jack Metzgar, calls Straddlers "crossover people," says that college changes the way people speak, and they are in turn ridiculed by their own families for it. "The pernicious side effect of being mobile," she says, "is that you can lose your family this way." Families can become mocking and resentful of crossovers, Jensen says, creating a mesh of psychological knots. The double bind in which crossovers are placed forces them to choose between staying connected and loyal to the family and getting ahead in life, she says, adding, "It's fraternity versus ability."

Indeed, says Gillian Richardson, a 47-year-old, British-born college writing professor in Buffalo, her Ph.D. made her "the freak of the family. I was the first person in the entire history of the family to go to college, let alone get a doctorate." After Gillian would speak, her sister would complain to their mother, "Mom, make her stop talking smart." Uncomfortable with Gillian's erudite manner, the family let her know how odd she seemed. And whenever Gillian tried discussing what she did, no one got it. "I explained the doctoral process a million times to them and I never got through. I got to the point where I stopped discussing it. They are the people closest to me in life, and they treat me differently." While many academics hide their working-class roots from middle-class colleagues, Gillian has had the opposite problem. She learned to conceal her intellect around her family. "As soon as I brought up college, or my work, my mother literally changed the subject. I think she doesn't want me to think I'm better than she is. She was out of school by the time she was 14, and I think she just feels insecure." As accomplished as Gillian is, she can never communicate to her family how she feels. "I don't feel like I'm any better than anybody else. So I hide myself because I don't want them to feel less. All I am is educated. That's all. My background is the same as theirs."

Like Gillian, Cheryl Shell—a civilian who works for the Army in Washington state—has trouble with her doctorate, her mother, and the English language. "Your parents want you to improve yourself and get educated," the 51-year-old says, "but then they're ambivalent about the result. They don't like it, but I can't help using my vocabulary. I try not to criticize them for reading the *National Enquirer* and watching Jerry Springer."

One Easter, Loretta Stec remembers, she made a surprise visit to the family from college, anticipating their delight upon seeing her. She walked through the door, and her working-class cousins were there. Still thrilled by the newness of college, Loretta launched into an animated recitation of all she had seen. "I was so full of my experiences and wanted to talk about what I was doing. And I remember so clearly my mother and my cousin sitting there, talking about pork chop recipes. That was for me a moment of profound alienation. I had stopped eating meat. I had never even cooked a pork chop. I was having all these incredible experiences they were not. And I felt this incredible gap. In some ways, it's not closed up. They still don't understand."

A limbo friend of mine tells me she purposely loses at Scrabble with her mother, allowing the woman to invent words. My pal also has stopped correctly answering her mom's questions—such as Why is the sky blue? The mother gets this odd look on her face whenever the daughter explains anything that complex with precision. But even if Straddlers learn to subsume their educated selves and tone down the use of $12 words, they still can't win. Larry Gabriel, editor of a United Auto Workers magazine in Detroit, says that after he received his B.A., he retained his African-American neighborhood-guy manner so he would not sound like a snob to his older, uneducated brother. Instinctively believing it was right, Larry would address his tough, streetwise brother in familiar vernacular. But the older brother finally got his own B.A. because it had bugged him that his siblings were educated and he was not. After graduation, the older brother phoned Larry to set him straight. "I have a degree now," Larry's brother said. "Talk to me and use big words." It was a heartbreaking discovery: "It made me realize that he felt I had been talking down to him all those years. It was very emotional for me. I wasn't aware of it until that very moment." Tragically, Larry's older brother died a few days after that conversation. "I never really had the opportunity to apologize to him for that."

Ultimately, Richard Rodriguez writes, prepare for education to divide a family. It did his, especially after he curtailed speaking Spanish at home and started being embarrassed by his immigrant parents' lack of education.[5]

Things were never so dramatic in my house during my college years. In fact, one day I invited my mother to sit in on my cultural anthropology and modern U.S. history classes at school. The woman deemed unfit for college by her family was taking the measure of herself among the Columbia scholars. I knew she was asking herself whether she could do it, whether she could flourish there. In history class, my professor was trying to make a point about trusting intuition in historical research, trusting what you feel in your bones about something. I remember he'd made eye contact with my mother when he said that, maybe thinking that this older woman—whoever she was—would understand that we can learn from experience as well as from books. That night at dinner, my mother glowed, talking about the day with my father. It was as if she had passed some aptitude test she'd given herself. She never said it out loud. But I think she thought she could have found a place for herself there, had she been given the chance to go.

What We Owe

All conflicted Straddlers will have a day when they have to decide, very simply, what they owe their families and what they owe themselves. There will always be separation issues when any child, regardless of class, leaves the family to go to college, says Laurene Finley, a Philadelphia psychologist who treats the white-collar children of blue-collar parents. But such issues are exacerbated when a person enters another culture. Finley says, "How do you keep your family and yourself when you're in two worlds?" The trick, she says, is to be facile in both realms. Obviously, that's hard. You can make it up and out, but the family is trying to draw you back. Finley says this can be especially true in the black community.

A wonderful thing about African-American families, Finley says, is how everyone in the extended family stays close. But there are costs for those who make it out into the middle class while other kin languish behind. "A friend who's a college department chair is responsible for nieces, nephews, and aunts—their financial, emotional, and physical needs," Finley says. "You have an unevenness of accomplishment in these extended families. You may have a doctor here and a garbage collector there and a welfare person over there. And they look at you as the one whom the opportunity structure let out. So you have to reach back, maybe open your home to them. And sometimes there's stress, and a physical and emotional cost for the person who gets educated and rises above."

Beyond this, black middle-class Americans say they have to deal with being labeled "bourgies," short for *bourgeois.* Appearing in the PBS documentary, *People Like Us: Social Class in America*, a group of Straddler African Americans say that blacks have an especially difficult time becoming upwardly mobile because working-class people from their families and their neighborhoods see them as traitors of a kind, joining the ranks of the white, dominant culture.[6]

In the final analysis, Finley says, for your own health, whether you're African American, white, Latino, Asian, or anything else, the important questions you wind up asking yourself are "What do I owe others?" and "What do I owe myself?"

For Rebecca Beckingham, the wrenching answer reverberates throughout her life. To survive, she had to choose herself over her family, a decision that changed everything. Now there are only stiff and stilted interactions and polite chitchat on the rare occasions the family gets together. But for Rebecca, that's better than the wasted life that might have been.

We talk on a warm, rainy night in New York City, at a Starbucks near her apartment on Manhattan's Upper East Side. She'd been sheepish about suggesting the place, not knowing whether I would approve of a yuppie hangout to discuss class. I told her I don't drink coffee, so I didn't care where we went, and I have nothing against Starbucks. Small and thin, with a voice that sounds much younger than her 31 years, Rebecca's sophisticated urban look of green velour top, beige pants, and up-to-the-moment-stylish, brown, rectangular glasses belies her rural background on a dairy farm in Cherry Valley, in upstate New York. Her current life steeped in academia, Rebecca is a part-time social work professor and is studying to be a psychotherapist.

All anyone ever expected of Rebecca was that she would take care of the farm and her parents. She was discouraged from becoming involved with sports or any other extracurricular activities at school; they would have interfered with farm chores. Rebecca loved horses, and her father saw that as the hook: If she stayed and helped in the dairy business, he would parcel out some of the farm to her and her animals. None of her siblings seemed interested. "When I was younger, horses were my highest aspiration." Most people in Cherry Valley became carpenters or auto mechanics or farmers. When Rebecca projected herself into the future, she saw nothing there. "I was unhappy, and I needed some escape." Rebecca started doing cocaine and other drugs. Life was a mess.

Then in high school, she began dating a boy from a middle-class family. The romance didn't last, but Rebecca's relationship with the family did. The parents were elementary school teachers. The sister—who became Rebecca's best friend—was an Ivy League student. "Just looking around, being in their presence, was all I needed to get myself in gear and get to college. It just came to me by being exposed to that life—the clothes, the sophisticated kinds of magazines, the kind of food they ate."

Rebecca soon grew embarrassed by her family. She never wanted her boyfriend's family to meet hers. "I was embarrassed by their speech patterns, the car, the way the house was organized, what they talked about, what they didn't talk about, and, eventually, what they did for a living. There's a stigma for anyone who ever grew up on a farm: stupid country bumpkin, synonymous with anti-intellectualism and low IQ."

After enrolling in a small college, Rebecca grew more distant from her family. "The strange thing about getting an education and piercing a class level higher than your parents' is you gain a better lifestyle, money, status, but you lose your family." Rebecca says her parents didn't understand how much work was involved in college, especially for someone who had to overcome the shortcomings of an inferior high school. The family expected Rebecca to still pitch in on the farm. The chasm between them grew. Her insecurity as a student and aspiring academic was also growing. She was feeling more ashamed and increasingly angry that she didn't get what she needed educationally and otherwise from her family.

After graduation, Rebecca took the unusual step of enrolling in Tel Aviv University in Israel. She wanted the distance, and the Middle East fascinated her. She thought it was a good time to go. Soon after, her mother suddenly fell ill, and Rebecca was called back to the farm. The youngest of six kids and the only child in the family who was unmarried, Rebecca, who was then 24, was expected to show up and take care of things. So she did. "They didn't perceive education as enough of a commitment for me to not go back and help out."

Rebecca's mother, who had suffered a systemic infection and collapsed lungs, was soon on the mend. But Rebecca was back on the farm she thought she had said good-bye to long ago. For her, it was an inconceivable turn of events. Bivouacked in her old room, staring at the same walls through which her adolescent eyes had bored holes, Rebecca felt like she was losing her independence and the just-beginning life she'd worked hard to get. An awful panic welled inside.

She tried talking to her father, asking him what plans he'd made for the future, for the time Rebecca would leave and resume her life. He never had an answer. In the meantime, she milked the cows and took care of the house. "I don't do 4 A.M., so we were seven o'clock milkers. Seven o'clock, A.M. and P.M. We were up at the barn until 11 every night." Rebecca felt trapped. College had opened up new avenues and suggested paths her life could take in which she would never have envisioned shoveling cow manure. Now it was all slipping away. "My father refused, absolutely refused, to talk about how to deal with things without me. My mother was healing, but there was nothing said about me going back to school. He just expected me to stay."

It was hard to buck the working-class culture, the sense of obligation to the family. Rebecca was very close to giving in, just doing and saying everything that was expected of her: running a dairy farm instead of figuring out who she was. At least she would be thought of as a good daughter. Wasn't that enough?

Unable to stay and afraid to leave, Rebecca sought out her former boyfriend's family, with whom she'd stayed in close touch throughout college. The young man's mother had become a kind of foster mother to Rebecca since she was 17. Rebecca sat crying at the older woman's kitchen table one night, despairing over what to do. "There were lots of beers and tears and cigarettes," Rebecca says. In the late hours, the answer came. The middle-class woman's solution blew Rebecca away.

"It's the parents' job to raise a child," she told Rebecca. "You don't owe them anything. You can opt out of the family."

Wow, Rebecca said. Opt out?

She began to form a plan. Well, not a plan exactly, but an escape. She would leave, just go. At 24 years old, Rebecca Beckingham would run away from home. "I knew I was having a bit of a breakdown. I was feeling unhappy and there was no way out. If I didn't run, I knew I'd be stuck there forever."

On the day she decided to do it, she milked the cows as usual in the morning. When her father was out spreading manure in a field, Rebecca grabbed a piece of luggage and started packing. "I didn't want to do it

when Dad was there. It was too painful, and I didn't have the courage."
She would leave no note. A sister-in-law was in the house and could not
understand why Rebecca was shaking and throwing clothes into a bag.
The woman said nothing as Rebecca's boyfriend's brother showed up
with a car. His sister had offered Rebecca the $1,100 she needed to get
back to Israel. Rebecca grabbed Monty, her Jack Russell terrier, and
rode off.

Was she betraying her family or saving her life?

"I think it was really one of the most courageous things I've ever
done," she says today, already on her second cup of Starbucks. "But I
still used to feel terribly guilty about it. My family still feels I was disloyal to them." She's seen them just a few times in the last seven years.
It's a polite, distant relationship. The incident, as Rebecca calls it, is not
discussed. Recently, one of her brothers visited her in New York and
they passed Pace College, where Rebecca had once taught.

"I worked there, you know," Rebecca said.

"Really?" her brother said. "Were you a secretary?"

"I taught the courses. I was the professor. This is who I am."

"Oh," her brother said. "I didn't know."

Finding your way through the transition into the middle class
requires that you redefine yourself, conquering self-doubt and sometimes even the family and past you love.

4

CULTURE CONFLICTS: FIRST ENCOUNTERS WITH THE UPPER CLASSES

On my first day of classes at Columbia, I got off the No. 1 train at 116th Street and Broadway and walked into a classroom filled with sockless young men. Shoes, no socks. I had never seen that before. I also noticed the guys were wearing wrinkled dress shirts—Brooks Brothers, I would later learn, with some L.L. Bean tossed in. Sloppy khakis completed the picture. The seemingly superficial aspects of the new culture required an education all their own.

There I was among the graduated preppies, my shirt ironed, my pants creased, and my socks on. I never felt so out of place, so dumbly lost. These guys seemed confident, cocky even. It appeared as if they all knew each other—or at least knew the secret handshake. They'd light up Camels and opine on everything, from the Yankees to politics in India. They gave me the impression that they were older somehow. Smarter, too—worldly in a way I had never seen. I'd thought that by dint of my being born a New Yorker I'd automatically be seen as sophisticated. But I fell terribly short in holding my own.

To my astonishment, the Barnard women from across Broadway

would respond to these guys, who might be shunned back in my neighborhood. It was, I should say here, a symptom of my blue-collar background that I didn't know that women did not like being addressed as girls. Brooklyn was full of girls only. When I dated someone from Barnard, I'd tell my father I was seeing a woman. "A girl," he'd correct. " 'Woman' sounds like your takin' out your grandmother."

Anyway, these pasty, slight fellas—all of them, it seemed, 5-foot-7 and sandy-haired, and who would have seemed effeminate and prissy on 20th Avenue in Brooklyn—were getting play and attention from a bevy of smart, good-looking women. I'd stand there with perfect posture, my abs still aching from those 801 sit-ups, a graduate of my high school's weight-lifting class, wondering when the females were going to wise up and notice the wonder that was me. But clearly something else was going on; there was apparently more to being a man than anything I'd picked up in Brooklyn. These Barnard women were drawn to the assuredness of the preppies—the attitude that the streets of Manhattan had been laid out for them, that the professors worked for them. Unlike me (and my mom), they were unawed by the buildings and expanse. It was as though the granite and marble were a birthright. Success was preordained; they didn't have doubts. They were the people for whom Columbia was erected.

At the end of the day, I would leave them all and go down in the subway to begin a trip to a world that was starting to feel smaller. From the 116th Street station down Broadway to the 59th Street station, there were students, musicians, and professors on the No. 1 train. At 59th, where I changed for the D or A train, businesspeople began to clog the cars. By the time I switched to the F train at West 4th Street, then rumbled onto the elevated tracks into deepest Brooklyn, I was riding with office clerks, maybe a few gung-ho Wall Streeters, the Hasidim, and some high school kids, all of us staring at the thighs of overperfumed secretaries who crossed and uncrossed their legs under Bufferin ads.

The world had altered by train triage, a rolling winnowing from Columbia to Brooklyn. I'd get off at my stop, then walk in the dark past the shuttered salumerias and past apartment buildings whose lobbies smelled like cabbage and onions. I could not find 1 in 100 people whom I could talk to about my day—about the sockless boys, about Chaucer, or about the growing realization that there was a world of people with self-esteem and feelings of entitlement we never knew existed. On Broadway, I felt stupid. Back in the neighborhood, they thought I was a snob. One freshman Monday, I asked a Barnard woman what she'd done over the weekend. She smiled, thinking about staying up until 3 A.M. with her boyfriend, reading *Moby Dick* together by candlelight with a Bible nearby, looking up religious allusions in the text and drinking wine. "And what did you do?" she asked. Call me Clueless, I felt like saying. I had spent the weekend in Brooklyn.

I'd foolishly decided to commute to school, to save money and to stay close to home. Straddlers I've met since shared the same idea: that you don't break up the family; you orbit close to your kind. That was a blue-collar blunder. Middle-class parents instruct their kids that living on campus is a vital part of the college experience; I had no way of knowing that. In order to smoothe the transition to the middle class, it would have been easier to immerse myself completely in the new world.

By second semester, I tried to get a room on campus, but by that time, the school was too crowded to house New York students who at least had places to stay. A dean helpfully suggested I check into the YMCA to learn the important lesson of living life on my own. Except for a semester during my junior year, when I finagled a room in a nearly empty graduate dorm, I commuted every day to Columbia—three trains up, three trains back, three hours total every day. Anthony Trollope wrote a novel during his train commute to work. That meant he probably found a seat; I wasn't always that lucky.

Meanwhile, guys up in the Columbia dorms were bonding, I knew—meeting great women and having casual but important sexual liaisons. A few were probably even soul-mating with special someones. I could only press my nose against that window of opportunity, open to them, of finding like-minded lovers. Even if people weren't discovering girlfriends and future wives, I just knew that the men were forming friendships that would flourish, tight and infrangible, for a lifetime. A critical aspect of immersion in the middle class would have been to find peers among the new class, relationships to solidify the transition.

My fellow students would learn Columbia lore from wise upperclassmen—things about my school that I still don't know today. There would be bull sessions on the great books, on what a person owes society, on who could drink the most beer. Soon after graduation, they'd be getting each other jobs and stock tips, then internships for each others' children. I'd fantasize about being part of this dynamic group of young scholars who'd invite me back to their Connecticut homes, where their sisters would flirt with me and their fathers would say upper-class stuff to me— such as that they "like the cut of my jib." They'd boil lobsters on the beach and take me sailing on Long Island Sound. Someone would say their grandfather once taught Einstein how to hoist the fore-royal studding sail in a storm, and laugh about what a klutz he was. And in a late-night exchange, the fellas would offer me top-shelf liquor and a benediction, telling me that I was damned all right for a low-class, Guido-punk-loser of absolutely no standing. Or something like that. These days, if I were to go to any of my class reunions, it would be to meet people for the first time. Commuters are ghost students, and nobody remembers them.

As it was, I tried to make the best of circumstances, looking to make friends on the trains. But it's rare that anyone will talk to you on a crowded subway car. Once, I was able to strike up a conversation with a woman and wound up getting her phone number. I called her a couple of days later and she answered in a giggling panic, saying her friends had told her she was crazy to give her number to a stranger on the subway.

Work-Study

One of the most obvious ways in which blue-collar students are separated from their white-collar peers is that they have to earn money while going to school. Because money was tight to nonexistent, I had to find work to keep my college enterprise afloat. Lots of Straddlers worked their way through school. (And many took heavier course loads each semester to finish up more quickly and pay less tuition.) My menial job in the law school library started at 9 A.M. I grew to resent the well-off kids who simply fell out of bed and ran to class, unencumbered by commutes and the pressing need for tuition and book money. They'd be playing tennis, or flag football on the Columbia lawns, or flinging Frisbees (What was that all about, by the way? We threw balls), while I was shelving books. It made me peevish at first, I must confess. But blue-collar people know how to adjust. Nothing gets handed to you in this life. You work for your own happiness.

As it happened, I wasn't crazy about many of the law students, known for having the second-highest rate of book theft on campus, right behind the medical students. They made it so we had to search everyone's bag, even the professors'. (My big claim to fame during those years was that I once had to root through the briefcase of Professor Ruth Bader Ginsburg, many years before her ascendance to the U.S. Supreme Court.) Budding Baileys would read assigned material from books, then razor-blade the pages out so that no one else in their class could see them. The vast majority were spoiled, entitled, competitive middle- and upper-class kids, perpetuating minor attorney atrocities then, in antici-pation of larger ones to come. I got a few of them back, though—part of my ongoing campaign of class warfare. One strict library rule was that students who were writing papers could keep research books in their study carrels for 24 hours only. The librarian—a prickly Straddler her-self who despised law students more than I did—would send me to col-lect books that had been parked too long. I did it with glee, taking special delight in first removing the bookmarks the students had placed in the hoarded volumes. Then I'd shelve them. When the students found out, they'd be livid and would run to the front desk of the library to complain. I especially liked fielding the "How dare you's?" and the "Do you know who I am's?" I'd simply get all 6-foot-3 and Brooklyn on them. They backed down fast, and I got the impression that they weren't used to anyone saying no to them. Ever.

Always the Governor

Talk to Straddlers and they will tell you that there was a moment, a spe-cific place and time, when the difference between the class into which they were born and the ones above it was made clear to them. It could have happened in childhood, when they first met up with the kids of the town doctor, let's say, in fourth grade. Perhaps the moment of reckon-ing came in high school, when the Straddler visited the home of a friend whose dad was a lawyer. Boston book editor Joe Terry, for example, remembered being stunned when his carpenter father brought him into the 5,000-square-foot house of some rich guy in East Hampton, Long

Island, for whom he was working. Joe could not understand why someone's vacant summer house was warm in the dead of winter. Turns out they heated it all season long, just so the pipes wouldn't burst. Joe never knew that kind of wealth before; his father had struggled to keep the lights in their own home on.

For many Straddlers, enlightenment about the upper crust would not come until years later, among well-born colleagues who looked like peers on the organizational chart but were, in fact, leagues ahead. More often, though, the culture shock registered in college—especially if the person attended an elite school. Suddenly, the Straddler from some backwater high school was surrounded by people who knew how to ski and drove fleets of daddy-bought BMWs and Mercedes.

"Every day of my undergraduate life," says poet Dana Gioia, a working-class kid from Southern California who graduated with degrees from both Stanford and Harvard universities, "I saw something to remind me of how different I was. Someone's grandfather was always the governor of Arizona."

Winner of the American Book Award and head of the National Endowment for the Arts, Dana once was a vice president of General Foods in White Plains, New York, overseeing an operation that brought in $750 million in annual revenues. That's before he became a professional working-class intellectual. Dana's 1991 essay "Can Poetry Matter?" touched off a worldwide debate about poetry's place in modern life and made him famous among the literati. In 1984, *Esquire* included Dana on a list of people under 40 who were "changing the nation." Along with his writing and editing, Dana regularly explains America to the British in essays on BBC radio.

Dana's Mexican/Native-American mother, Dorothy, was a telephone operator and his Sicilian father, Michael, was a cabdriver and chauffeur for a Beverly Hills real-estate millionaire. They had eloped to Tijuana because his maternal grandmother had disapproved of the marriage. One of Dana's great-grandfathers was born in Chihuahua and died in a barroom gunfight in Lost Cabin, Wyoming. All Dana's relatives came splashing into America, either by crossing the Rio Grande by foot or by crossing the Atlantic in steerage. They settled in working-class Hawthorne, California, home of the Beach Boys, along with "Okies, Mexicans, and 100 Italians," Dana likes to say. Most of the men worked in nearby airplane factories. "We were poor but the good weather was free," Dana says.

He grew up in a triplex among relatives; the neighboring triplex was crammed with family, too. The view across the street included lines of garbage cans from a Chinese restaurant, along with a mortuary and a liquor store. Dana was raised by a clan, kept close to old ways, and was made to understand the dignities and deprivations of the blue-collar life. It has stayed with him. "Both my poetry, which is meticulously wrought but accessible, and my literary politics—enlightened democratic—come out of my core identity." He saw his grandparents every day of his first 18 years of life, right up until he went to college. Neither particularly Mexican- nor Italian-looking, Dana, 53, has large, expressive eyes and the easy attractiveness of an athletic Californian in middle management. With a deep, resonant voice, he can be disarmingly self-deprecating and mildly self-promoting at the same time. The man has charm.

For as long as he can remember, Dana says, his parents had always disapproved of rich people (which Dana claims he is most definitely not, despite the fancy corporate job he once held and his dazzling white, book-filled home in Santa Rosa). The rich, Dana's father told him, have no morals, and family means nothing to them. As a result, their children turn out badly. People with too much money get drunk, get divorced, and don't pay the medical bills when their parents get sick, Michael preached. His proximity to the high and mighty offered object lessons. During the Kennedy administration, Dana's dad did some driving for the U.S. State Department. "He couldn't believe all the whores that were bought," Dana says. Michael shook his head in disgust as he wound up stopping at nightclub after nightclub, fulfilling the floozy quotas of the insatiable knights of Camelot.

The father's religion was family and hard work. The only way a man could earn respect was by living that religion every day, young Dana was told. A successful person made his own way and earned what he needed. He never forgot where he came from and who his people were. No black-hole dad, Michael actually built up a library of college guides as his son grew. Somehow finding time during his 72-hour work weeks, the elder Gioia pored over the books he'd store in a cupboard at home. He became convinced Stanford was the best place for his kid.

After 12 years of Catholic school, Michael Gioia's boy would attend the palm-lined enclave where the rich people he so despised educated their children. It was ironic, of course, but Michael figured the school offered the best chance for his son to become a scholar.

Dana says he was both impressed and repulsed by his rich classmates. "I was the only white guy in my dorm whose parents had not gone to college," he says. "Our class differences became quite obvious to me." Dana was thrown in with the kids whose parents ran and owned America. "There's hardly a major corporate figure in the United States whose kids I did not meet in Stanford and then at Harvard: the Bechtels, the Rothschilds, the Woolworths—people like this. Face it, the rich send their kids to Stanford and Harvard." In Dana's freshman dorm there was a Coors and a Du Pont. He dated a woman whose father was an executive of one of America's largest banks. One guy who'd gone to prep school at Exeter showed Dana a closet filled with sports coats, a sight he'd never seen. "You have to understand how odd it was for someone like me to hear people say their grandfathers were surgeons."

During vacations, classmates would go off to ski in Colorado or the Sierra Nevada, while Dana would return to the Los Angeles area to work. It never occurred to him that somebody his age would be taking a vacation. He took sales jobs even during Christmas and Easter breaks. Everybody else would return to school tanned or full of skiing stories.

Dana was starting to think that education meant more to him than it did to the flamboyant good-time kids who didn't seem to take school seriously. "I cared more about culture than these rich people did. To them, they could take the books and the education for granted. For me, it was the meat of life." An enduring image of that time that Dana still carries with him is that of a classmate, in the fall of 1969, driving off to an antiwar rally in a Lamborghini his father had given him. "Everybody was a radical except me," said the son of conservative Michael and Dorothy. "That Lamborghini thing really cracked me up."

It is, Straddlers will tell you, during the unguarded moments on campus that class differences smack you in the forehead. At the University of California at Davis, Cheryl Shell remembers that the class was reading Jane Austen. She had become disgusted with the balls and social occasions that are part of the characters' milieu, but not Cheryl's.

"God," Cheryl said aloud in class, "if I read another description of a ball gown I'm gonna go crazy."

Everyone was shocked. The professor looked at Cheryl and said, "Are you, by any chance, from working-class parents?"

Wham, right between the eyes. Cheryl hadn't seen that one coming. "It was a revelation," she recalls. "I remember saying to myself, 'Oh, so that's what this is.' To me, all that gown stuff was unimportant. But to the upper-class students, Jane was a goddess and all this made sense to them." Cheryl had been embarrassed by what the professor said, but he hadn't meant to be unkind. He was simply picking up on something Cheryl hadn't been able to see. Having taught other working-class students, he'd been more attuned to it. Hating Jane Austen, or at least not finding her relevant, was a class-based attitude.

"It made me think about all the students who had been given bad grades and rejected by teachers because they had a different way of looking at the world, having come from the working class. And literature is such a middle-class thing to do. You almost have to have come from money to pursue and understand it. So I got out of it and joined the Army."

Cashmere Living

Psychologist Barbara Jensen calls these well-off folk that Straddlers view as Martians the "cashmere kids." Inspiring simultaneous envy and enmity in crossover types, the bourgeois elite embody much of what many of us are striving for and so much of what seems phony and ostentatious, given our humble backgrounds. First encounters are always jarring—sometimes off-putting.

"It's like you went to a country church all your life," says Barbara Peters, the Wisconsin-born Straddler and sociologist, "and suddenly you must attend a grand cathedral—and you're supposed to know how to act when you get there. We're in awe, and we figure it's good because of all the stained-glass windows." College life is lived in a middle-class space with middle-class rules. People from the working class must change themselves—or, at least, important parts of themselves—to fit. A problem arises: At the same time they are feeling like imposters who don't belong in the Valhalla of the cashmere-ians, Straddlers can become resentful that they are the ones who must change. In this multicultural, I-accept-who-you-are, I-acknowledge-your-right-to-exist world, class is one of the few things people will try to make you alter and try to teach you how not to be. African Americans aren't expected to blanch Caucasian when they deal with the white world. Yet working-class people, steeped in their own culture and standards, must leave that identity behind and live as middle-class people in a middle-class world. We must be saved from our state of original sin, says writer Valerie Miner.[1]

Of course, for many of us, the goal *is* the middle class—specifically, a more comfortable life of less backbreaking work and greater reward than our parents knew. But we don't want to have to totally reject who we are and where we came from to become educated and live in nicer houses. There is, then, unease in the transition, because Straddlers are making a difficult journey. That trip is invisible to the middle class, who don't have to cross class lines to become educated.

Straddlers, though, are simply supposed to assimilate. They rarely find a working-class person's association on campus, as they would a Latino Club or any other kind of group. No one wants to hear about what you've given up to join the middle class. You still agonize about what was lost? Tough. The middle class doesn't care. After all, you volunteered to leave your background behind. You must change who you are, then spend a long time becoming someone else. And it's all supposed to be invisible and seamless, without any carping on Oprah.

A few Straddlers reported being accepted by heavily endowed, big-time colleges and then rejecting them in favor of smaller, less prestigious schools, simply because they dreaded having to deal with classmates from ritzy upbringings.

Things went differently for Signe Kastberg, who chose the boutique school that accepted her. A 47-year-old counselor and psychotherapist in Ithaca, New York, Signe is the daughter of a cook and a waitress. She grew up in Schuylerville, New York, a blue-collar mill town where kids spent summers swimming in the PCB-laden Hudson River. Elementary school teachers were considered the rich people in town. Knowing Signe's poor background, high school counselors didn't encourage her to go far. Hers was not a college-type family, she was told. Annoyed at the box arbitrarily built around her, Signe went to college anyway, to a state school. She transferred to Skidmore after an impressed member of the English lit faculty took her aside one day and asked an important question: What the hell are you doing here?

So off to the fancy school she went. "And I got the I-totally-don't-belong-here experience. I was a poor kid in among the rich ones. There was this big disjuncture. It's as if you were to look at a poster depicting the entire universe, and it had a little dot saying, 'You are here,' and the dot would be so far out on the outer rim of the galaxy that you would simply not feel like you were part of it."

At Skidmore, Signe had her state school attire with her: jeans, sweatshirt, and sneakers. But literally 95 percent of the women at Skidmore were wearing Saks Fifth Avenue couture. Signe would be standing in the bursar's office, trying to cash her $28 work-study check, when she'd overhear the most incredible things.

"Oh," one young woman dripping with jewelry and swathed in soft wools said, "I forgot to cash the $500 check Daddy sent me. I saw this quilt in town for $200. I'll go get that later." Signe couldn't conceive of it—the exorbitance, the freedom to spend. The family house had only recently gotten running water, and you still had to be careful that the well wouldn't run dry.

The differences in background pretty much made friendships impossible. "Quite a large population of the women came from New York City or Long Island, but they might as well have come from Mars," Signe said. Aware of an attitude being darted her way, Signe says her classmates practiced a covert discrimination. That was fine with her. "I had a boyfriend back home. I stuck with my own crowd."

When she won a Fulbright Scholarship and went on to study at Harvard, Signe felt no easier. A wine-and-cheese reception became a minor disaster. "I didn't know what to ask for, how to deal with appetizers. Then two faculty advisors asked me to dinner. I didn't know what forks to use, what drink to order, how to handle stuff. So whenever it came up in the future, I would just avoid going. I didn't know how to behave and I didn't want to make a fool of myself over just the simple stuff."

The idea of choosing the right fork in a fancy place has always tripped up Straddlers, and it's amazing how many describe trepidation about cutlery. (At a working-class studies workshop I attended at the

State University of New York at Stony Brook, professors at dinner stared in mock horror at the formal place settings and joked about their congenital inability to choose the proper implement.) Lobster has been another bugaboo. Peter Ciotta, the Buffalo public relations executive, says a college friend's parents took him to Windows on the World, the restaurant that once topped the World Trade Center. Everyone ordered lobster, and Peter, the son of an immigrant autoworker, had never partaken of such a feast. "I didn't know what to do with the tail and the shell." Lobsters became symbolic of the upper crust he'd first encountered in the dorms at the University of Notre Dame. "The differences between their background and mine became clear when I was reading a *Wall Street Journal* one day and the father of a dorm mate was right there in a story on the front page."

Along with forks and shellfish, the whole beer-versus-wine thing could be a problem, too. North Dakota anthropologist Tom Fricke remembers his first soiree as a young faculty member at the University of Michigan.

"What would you like to drink?" asked the host as he cracked open bottles of chablis and filled tall, stemmed glasses.

"I'd like a beer," said Tom, a plain plainsman from Bismark who'd attended his share of keggers in cornfields back home.

"Oh, I think we might be able to find you one somewhere," the host said. (Was that a smirk on his face?) "Would you like a glass?"

"No, the can will be fine."

Tom says he knew right then, knew it as surely as if it were written in calligraphic letters on some framed, fancy piece of parchment somewhere—some anti-diploma—that he would never, ever get tenure.

Another time, he found himself sitting around a table of faculty members and a clutch of visiting professors. For some reason, the host was asking people what their grandfathers did, or had done, for a living. Typical white-collar, reflected-glory kind of thing. "I could feel a bad moment coming on," Tom says. The retro-resumes started being recited.

"My grandfather was a stockbroker," some colleague said.

"Actually, mine was a diplomat," another chimed in.

On it went, a round-robin of graybeard achievements. These weren't even people's fathers they were boasting about. God knows what *those* men did. This was three generations of accomplishment Tom was stacked against—men standing on the shoulders of men standing on shoulders. Back and back it went, lines and legacies of books and culture, middle-class comfort and bourgeois ease.

Tom had two choices: One grandfather had been a brakeman on the railroad; the other was a farmer who'd lost his land and was, at that time, filling candy machines in Bismark.

"I thought they'd respond to the saga of diversity, of how the family progressed," he says. "So I told them about both men."

Thud. "Oh, it stopped the game. It was a big conversation stopper. And nobody came back with a comment. Class is not talked about in America. And I had a tremendously different class experience than they did."

To deal with the impossible gap between themselves and their classmates and colleagues, many college Straddlers simply withdrew. "You didn't brand yourself as having a blue-collar background because it didn't feel safe," Signe adds. "You feel like you'll be rejected or looked down upon. When I talked to other people like me, the word 'chameleon' comes to mind." Shading herself to the foreign color of her new surroundings, Signe thought a lot about Ginger Rogers—doing everything the middle-class Freds did, but backward and in heels. "You have to be smarter, adapt quickly, and fit in. That's the key. Even though all the time you're fighting this imposter syndrome." If people knew who Signe really was, they would have drummed her out of school, she believed. That's why you watch your vocabulary and maybe dress up your wardrobe a little if you can. If not Saks, at least lose the sneakers. Don't let the obvious stuff trip you up. And figure out the forks.

Ultimately, a certain sense of the absurd creeps in. Signe had a Straddler friend who survived Barbara Jensen's cashmere kids, only to become a professor teaching the kids' kids in the Ivy League. It was incredible: This woman, who could never afford to travel, found herself teaching students whose fathers owned airlines.

It was like that for Samme Chittum, the former journalism teacher at NYU and Columbia from tiny Findlay, Illinois, who would marvel at the scions of privilege to whom she lectured in her classrooms. Her semesters with them triggered memories of her initial class culture shock years before. Forty-seven and a self-described "authentic mutt," Samme is a tall, slender woman with dark hair and eyes and a backslapping, put-you-at-ease manner. She is the daughter of a "man's man," James, a former Navy demolitions expert who made his living as a tool-and-die maker. Her mother, Ida, wrote 12 children's books, some of which were favorably reviewed. Neither she nor Samme's dad, both of whom are now dead, attended school beyond the eighth grade. Tall, handsome, athletic, and smart, James had a taste for beer and the occasional fist-fight. He'd take his daughter with him to the bars. "Serious drinkers don't go to bars at night," Samme says. "They're there in the daytime. I spent a lot of time with him in bars and pool halls. I wasn't a girly girl, and my dad didn't prepare me to be one. I was not delicate and pretty like my sisters. I entered the world of men. He gave me a pocketknife and took me golfing and shooting. We were simpatico like that. We had a wavelength, and we got along well." The family lived among ditchdiggers and hard union men who always seemed to be on strike. The Chittums' old wooden house had no central heat, and Samme was frequently cold. In the freezing night, she endured the added indignity of the stench of soybeans bubbling in huge industrial cookers nearby.

None of this was preparation enough for graduate school in New York City. "That's when I had my mind blown away by people in class with trust funds. There were people with money and social pedigrees that I didn't know existed. And I saw how much it mattered to them." She met the first person she ever knew with taste, she says—a southern, liberal Jewish woman with a highly developed social conscience. She used to pay for the schooling of poor children she'd met in Jamaica. Straddlers' families weren't usually big charity givers, barely having enough themselves. Samme's friend collected rugs, paintings, and antiques, and taught her about the great comfort of high-thread-count cotton sheets. "It simply opened my eyes." Others at school were not so kind. "The world of the WASP, the inner sanctum—it was the first time I became aware there was a world that would exclude me." These were the kids of adventurous, risk-taking entrepreneurs. She was a conservative, small-town, blue-collar kid. "All these people used to think big. But I was modest and afraid to overreach myself. That's blue-collar." In this new world, people's well-off backgrounds propelled them to softer berths in life and opened doors that would stay closed to Samme. "They had the connections. And I didn't."

You can't hide your class from others. They just know. Obviously, it's not an immediate recognition, like gender and race. Class, Australian scholar Kathryn Hegarty notes, is not written on the body. But after a few cafeteria encounters or dorm room talks, people had you pegged. Once they knew you were working class, says Barbara Peters, middle-class college peers excluded you from the structures that could move you ahead, like fraternities and sororities. "You take your class with you wherever you go. All these privileged kids had the same way of talking—what their parents did, the skiing, the vacations. And everywhere we looked, we were getting class messages. We'd come to see that things you knew weren't as valued by people whose parents went to college."

For some it was worse. In various writings, bell hooks explains that she was "invalidated" by college because the new world forced its own reality on her, squeezing out what she previously knew. She believed she was an object of ridicule by student elites—even by the bourgeois blacks, who knew about as much about her working-class world as bourgeois whites did.[2] Straddlers felt like intruders invading citadels of "the white supremacists," as one struggling Straddler puts it. These fortunate sons and daughters seemed to have come kicking into the world with 400 piano lessons under their belts and much of the Western canon already committed to memory. There are legions of people out there who will tell you this was what college was like for them. "Immigrants to the realm of thought," philosopher Robert Nozick called us, according to writer Chris Overall. "It was not a level academic playing field," Overall concludes.[3]

Knowing that classmates had already read many of the books on the college syllabus when they were back in prep school was a troubling realization. Knowing that they were already jaded about travel was irksome, too. "I'm so glad Daddy's not taking us to Europe again for spring break," my wife actually overheard a classmate saying. "We're trying South America this year." School chums' talk of gambling in Monte Carlo or sailing the Caribbean made us all feel smaller. A friend of mine complained that she believed that the privileged probably shipped their darlings all over the world just to give them something to talk about in college entrance essays. How can you hang out with people whose parents read them *The History of the Peloponnesian War* to help them sleep?

Naturally enough, many people tried. Many succeeded, I'm sure. But not everyone could pull it off. For as long as he could remember, Paul Groncki wanted to be part of a fraternity, a house full of like-minded guys who looked out for one another and had fun. But, says Paul, 53, a former Wall Street economist with a Ph.D., he never felt as though he were good enough for the middle-class fraternities at the University of Albany. He truly wanted to join but knew he was not class compatible with the other guys, whose fathers were doctors and lawyers, not blue-collar men in charge of the tool bin at General Electric in Schenectady, New York, as his dad was. Middle-class dads worked in hushed places—clean, quiet offices with carpets and decent coffee. Our fathers worked in noisy pits and banging factories. Their damaged ears absorbed metal-on-metal discord, the riot of overheated machines.

"Nobody came to me and asked me to join any fraternities," Paul says, laughing as he speaks. I wasn't sure whether he was trying to cover up old wounds or was really over the hurt. Talking with the guys at school, Paul had been honest about his background, and that simply didn't suit. Besides, everyone knew that he worked 30 hours a week at a nearby grocery store. Frat boys didn't toil like that. Paul would be putting on his work smock in the dorm while everyone else was getting dressed to go out. That gave him away. "You try to convince yourself that you're glad you're not involved in a fraternity. But a voice in the back of your head says you're a failure, you're not good enough to be among them. It was hard knowing something was going on that you could never be a part of."

Life on campus is layered and complex. Straddlers quickly learn there are parties going on to which they are not invited. Susan Borrego, the associate dean of students at Cal Tech University, understood in graduate school that others were taking advantage of unpaid internships and semesters abroad. "But how could you do that if you had to work?" In class, Susan could go toe-to-toe with peers on papers and projects. But she couldn't navigate the system, couldn't figure out how to shmooze the professors and work on their research. Many Straddlers reported thinking that professors would volunteer their services as mentors, to help young charges through. I know I thought that. When does the mentor find his ment-ee? People like me don't realize that, in most cases, the student has to make that first move.

"We were all just so clueless," says Gillian Richardson, the Buffalo writing teacher. "White-collar people just have the know-how, from their backgrounds, to get fellowships and other assistance on campus we didn't have." Because it's part of their family consciousness, second- and third-generation college students know how to manage their time, how to figure out what to focus on, and how to work their way through. Literature professor Patricia Clark Smith writes that she'd wind up going to campus parties wondering whether there was anyone there who was like her and "wasn't born knowing how to do this."[4]

It's not as if middle-class kids don't have issues in school, Straddlers and experts say. There are problems of self-esteem; there's drug abuse; there are adjustments that must be made. But middle-class students are doing something their parents did, something for which their parents could prepare and coach them. College is not such a leap from reality as the family knows it. However, it takes gutsy resolve for first-generation college kids to get there and stay there. "It's a different sense of things for working-class kids in college," Michelle Tokarczyk tells me. A Straddler herself, she teaches English at Goucher College in Baltimore. "While middle-class students may be nervous about getting into the college of their choice, they don't doubt that ultimately they can do college work. Working-class students may not be sure they can do that kind of work at all." After all, they most likely didn't attend a prep school or a particularly good high school.

Myself, I lived in absolute fear that Columbia would tell me that it was all a mistake and that the admission would be rescinded. Even when I was getting good grades, I thought that my A's weren't the same as other people's. False and fluky, my modest successes could not stand up to scrutiny. I was amazed to hear other Straddlers express the same worries. Most of the time in college, Rebecca Beckingham, the upstate New York farm girl who ran away from home at 24, lived with a fraudulent feeling that the admissions office had messed up. "I literally thought I was gonna get kicked out," she says.

So did Christine Lunardini, who feared the Princeton deans would form a posse and run her out of town. "They were going to find me out at any moment, I thought," says Christine, 61, director of development at St. Michael's Academy, an all-girls Catholic high school in Manhattan. With a father who didn't get beyond sixth grade and a mother who didn't finish high school, Christine suffered what she and other Straddlers kept calling "imposter syndrome." It was hard to believe in yourself when you got into close proximity to the kings and queens of Jersey. Most Princeton people Christine knew were supremely self-confident. After a while, she learned that these contented souls were not necessarily any smarter. "It's just the sense that good things could be expected, that they had this sense of entitlement and they all expected their lives would work out perfectly. It was a legacy from their parents." Things would unfold in a way that was almost preordained. They were the children of college graduates, exactly where they were supposed to be.

Once, a fellow student had decided to answer only two of the four questions on a written exam. Christine and her chums thought he'd done something extraordinarily stupid, but the guy simply said the professor would allow it because he was the son of someone important. "And darned if that didn't happen," Christine says. "The professor accepted it and passed him. While the rest of us scrambled to write these questions in the time allotted, this person just had the confidence that he didn't have to, and that whatever he said to explain himself, people would listen."

While Straddlers sometimes feel like pretenders on campus, they are quick to spot ersatz working-class folk trying to get down with the little people. Social commentator Barbara Ehrenreich, herself the daughter of a copper miner, writes how she has sympathy for the parents of middle-class "blue-collar wannabes," who looked to "proletarianize" themselves by going to work for a time in factories during the 1970s.[5] My wife was infuriated by a college boyfriend of means who used to say he sometimes wished he had been poor to learn whether he could have made it through life unaided by papa's pile of dead presidents. He would have paired nicely with the rich girl who told Linda in their Smith College dormitory that she should get financial aid, too, because daddy was getting squeezed, what with the boat and the country house and the mortgage. (She, by the way, was pals with the woman who lived on a former plantation and told my wife, "You know, not all people used to beat their slaves. My family didn't.")

"Tina," a student at a northwestern college, remembered wasting time in Colorado with some privileged college kids who liked to play at being poor. They would follow the Grateful Dead in the days before

Jerry Garcia's death, selling vegetable burritos to the audience. Naive, Tina liked the peace-love-dope vibe and hung around with them. "I wasn't aware at first that a lot of kids were trust-fund babies with family vacation homes in Vail," she says. "I had taken social activism seriously and was doing some protesting in those days. But these late-capitalism hippies were only privileged people slumming."

Yonna Carroll (no relation to my wife, also named Carroll) lived with similar folk in Evergreen State College in Olympia, Washington. She called the would-be hippies "trust-afarians"—dreadlocked, white trust-fund kids from the East Coast paying that expensive out-of-state tuition rate. Yonna's mother had lived a poor, hippie-ish existence before she became a captain on the Washington state ferries. She had flipped burgers, worked the "slime line" in fish canneries, picked apples, and was on and off welfare. Without money, Yonna recalls, she and her mother lived variously in the back of a truck, in a teepee, and in a barn. Now 32 and a union organizer in New York City, Yonna remembers being miffed at the Evergreen wannabes. "I had seen the real life of what it was to be a hippie and I was not enamored of it. Yet they were embracing this culture. Also, it's disgusting to see people dress like they're poor when they're not. It's hard to stomach, these kids and their Saabs. I really didn't connect with the children of well-to-do families. I wasn't comfortable with their sense of entitlement. They were just snooty."

To make some money, Yonna took a job cleaning the dorms at the end of the school year, after the students had cleared out. "I got to see how they lived and got grossed out by them even further." Careless with the belongings that Mom and Dad had provided, the students left behind stuff Yonna could really use, like kitchen knives and can openers. Worse still were the rich foreign students who took summer courses at Evergreen. Their parents paid for maid service, and Yonna had to clean up after people who were used to treating housekeepers with shabby disrespect. More than once, a male student would suddenly appear out of the bathroom, wearing only a towel, as Yonna was leaning over his bed, clearing off food from the night before that was sticking to the sheets. She had to fend off the jerks, then get out fast, carrying bedding laden with grease and chicken bones as she retreated. "The whole thing was so disgusting."

Intimidation and Defiance

One guy in college intimidated me. In our brief interactions, he was always kind and friendly, and we never exchanged a cross word. I barely knew him, to tell you the truth. But his presence, his bearing, so impressed me. He is from a monied, philanthropic family whose name people would recognize and celebrate for its longtime support of the arts and eclectic achievement. The differences between us humbled me, kicking off a sleep-robbing anxiety that made me miserable for a short while. "Tom" was an editor on the college paper, which I worked for the one semester I lived on campus. The guy was also in a couple of my classes, including the one and only journalism-related class that was taught on the undergraduate level at my school. It was a seminar run by the late Fred Friendly, former head of CBS News. Friendly would invite all his big-time journalism pals to talk to us about the news business. One day he brought an editor at *Time* magazine. When it came time for questions, Tom—who already had a reputation as a fearless campus journalist, taking on deans and speaking his mind—ripped the editor. My self-assured classmate savaged *Time*'s approach to news reporting and its writing style in a passionate diatribe. Finally, Tom unloosed the most denigrating insult of all: "Your magazine is just television. It's nothing more than television." Friendly quickly shut Tom down and made sure we moved on to other topics.

My reaction came in stages. First, I was floored that a young man my age would have the self-confidence to get up on his hind legs and bark at an older person like that, let alone some big-deal editor. Second, he sustained an argument without losing his temper, something I'd never seen before. Later that day on the train ride home, my awe turned into a kind of depression, as I realized something important: I could never do what Tom did. I might have the same thought that he did, might even react to an idea in the same way. But I was unable to believe that what I had to say was worthwhile enough to sustain a monologue in front of intelligent others. Nor could I trust myself saying it. I'd start out stuttering, then wind up yelling, reason overtaken by frustration, overtaken by anger. Tom spoke better than I did. My vocabulary was comparable, but anxiety choked off the flow of words. His sentences flowed seamlessly; mine stopped and started like rusting clunkers on the highway. I felt inferior. Throughout the semester after the *Time* incident, Tom continued to speak out in class, while I remained silent. Ideas would flare in my head, things that might have been relevant to the discussion, or even insightful. But I never said anything.

Working-class kids are not empowered by their parents. Blue-collar households stress order, obedience, and discipline. No one is worrying whether junior is self-actualizing as he sits over there in the corner, just as long as he's not bothering anybody. Middle- and upper-class people like Tom were encouraged to express themselves early. They were permitted to hang out with the grown-ups and chat, if not as equals, then certainly as little people with something to say. I ran my Tom story by Art Shostak, the Drexel University professor who studies class. Though Tom and I both attended Columbia, Shostak analyzes, we did not attend the same Columbia. In fact, they were dramatically different places. "You were never on the same plane as he," Shostak tells me. "For example, you didn't bring the same cultural capital to the reading as he did." Though we read many of the same books, they resonated differently in our heads. More than likely, Tom had many more experiences to which he could relate the reading. Prior to Columbia, he had accumulated more varied reference points from things his parents told him or things he was exposed to as a young man in a family of resources—foreign countries, perhaps, different foods, alternate ways of thinking, and a comforting sense that his was the right and proper way. "Your favorite book would probably not be his," Shostak says. "And if it was, each of you would give different interpretations. There are profound differences between you, because of class." Maybe it's not surprising that while I'm a mere newspaper reporter, Tom is now the publisher of an influential magazine. I know he's extremely smart and deserves his success; but his background didn't hurt him.

Not every Straddler was as easily defeated as I. A few fought back. Weary of feeling like the downtrodden in the halls of the middle class, these intrepid types became reverse snobs. At Syracuse University, Rita Giordano and a few friends would laugh about the New York City girls whose parents would pay for them to fly to Manhattan once a month to get their hair cut. "We had more to us," Rita tells me. "We were city kids, not silver-spoon kids, and we were making it on our own. We had lower-class chauvinism, and we weren't spoiled rich kids who always got bailed out of trouble. I was never sad I wasn't rich."

Like Rita, Mo Wortman carried on with a sense of working-class superiority. Mo, 51, is a gynecologic surgeon who performs abortions in Rochester. The son of blue-collar Holocaust survivors from Brooklyn, Mo is a tough man living in hard times. The last time I saw him, he was strapping on a gun over his surgical scrubs, ready to defend himself and his family from snipers. It was fall, and fall has been known as the killing season in western New York near the Canadian border, where abortion providers have been attacked in recent years. The shootings are thought to be loosely tied to Remembrance Day—November 11, the Canadian Veterans Day—as a way to commemorate what antiabortion activists call "the dead children lost to abortion." On October 23, 1998, ob-gyn Barnett Slepian was shot dead in his kitchen. He had been the primary abortion provider in nearby Buffalo's only abortion clinic. Very few can live on the edge like this. For a while after Slepian's murder, Mo avoided turning on the lights in his home at night. His wife, Rebecca, rushed around the house, throwing blankets over the windows. Muscular, with a shaved head and large hands, Mo was a shot-putter and a brawler when he was younger. When he built his clinic, he didn't hide it in a hospital corridor. It's a handsome place, with cathedral ceilings and oak floors. Mo calls it an "in-your-face facility"—architecture as political defiance. It has $14,000 in security enhancements, including bullet-proof glass and steel-reinforced concrete. Only a working-class guy, Mo believes, could handle the bull's-eye life of a medical target. Nobody can intimidate Mo Wortman.

So, when he was in medical school at Rochester, the culture shock registered on his Richter scale. He just didn't allow it to shake his core. Classmates got Corvette Stingrays from their parents if they made good grades. One-third of the class had parents who were doctors. And all their mothers, it seemed, were psychiatrists. The students were more reserved, better at keeping their opinions under wraps than Mo was—a middle-class skill. No one seemed as emotional and animated as he. Especially not Bob, a second-generation Princeton man with a sports car and dressy clothes, who'd rumble off with his girlfriend while Mo studied. "Yes, it made me uncomfortable," Mo says. "But at some point I became aware of the word *meritocracy*. I was part of a meritocracy, having gotten there on my hard work. And Bob and the others were part of the aristocracy—very WASPy breeding stock, handsome, debonair, and polished. My feeling was, I was tougher and better qualified, and I got there in spite of my parents' poor educations. In my own snobbish way, I felt superior. I was the tough kid at medical school. I challenged the professors and spoke out. If a class wasted my time, I'd walk out."

It was hard staying focused, though. For example, Mo had never been hungry before, really hungry. He'd won a full scholarship for tuition and books, but food and rent were on him. He slept in the living room of a place with two other men to save cash. He'd eat macaroni and cheese and cereal. One day, it just got to be too much. Bob was going out to dinner all the time. Others had no problems filling their bellies. Mo craved protein. He walked into Wegman's grocery store and put a few steaks under his jacket. He got caught, but the store manager took pity on the starving medical student and let him go. "I feared not being fed. I was a 300-horsepower engine operating on two cylinders. I didn't want to be poor, and everyone around me was rich. So I had to reach down somewhere inside and come up with whatever it took. That was the pain and the beauty of that struggle. A struggle the others didn't have."

Prep School Confidential

Most Straddlers did not attend college preparatory schools. Blue-collar parents don't have that kind of budget. The few who did got their culture shocks early. And prep-peer animosity was not unusual among Straddlers fortunate enough to go. Pennsylvania attorney and horse breeder Peter Giangiulio attended Malvern Prep in the well-to-do Main Line suburbs outside Philadelphia. His father, a contractor, was a working-class guy, despite the good money he made. "This was a hotshot school, man," says Peter, a dark-haired, mustached man who would strike most people as a regular guy. He lives on a fabulous spread of horses, pasture, and field-stone barns in gracious, hilly country where people still ride to the hounds. There's a law office in one of the farm buildings, but you'll rarely find Peter in it. He much prefers making thoroughbred babies and turning them into racers. It's an addiction. His joke is that junkies might have track marks on their arms, but he has hoofprints on his. I watched him foal out a mare once, little Badger sliding slick and leggy out of

Teedlewinks on a cool spring night. Eleven months of pregnancy, then no more than 20 minutes of labor. So much can go wrong during the intense moments of a horse's birth. Peter stood in the stall and made sure nothing did. That's where he'd rather be—not in court, dealing with the grown-up versions of the preppies he suffered with through high school.

"I hated the rich kids and they hated me," Peter says. Notice he calls his former classmates "rich kids," although he admits that his father, though uneducated, had as much money as many Malvern dads. "The difference was, they were judgmental. I was made to work on the farm every day and my father wore a cowboy hat. He made me develop a work ethic. My classmates couldn't understand why I didn't get days off to hang around with them. And they called my father the 'Marlboro Man.' It was a case of DNOCD—'Definitely Not Our Class, Dear.' Malvern was four years of hell. I never, ever, ever go back to class reunions. If you didn't become someone that you weren't—someone like them, I mean—they wouldn't deal with you."

Two disparate, divergent worlds separated by hours in a given day—this was Jeffrey Orridge's life. In the morning, he woke up in a gang neighborhood in East Elmhurst, Queens, then trekked to Manhattan, where he took his place behind the red doors among the privileged boys of Collegiate School, one of the top 10 private schools in the United States. Founded in 1628, Collegiate is prized among New York parents able to give their children the very best. Jeffrey's graduating class included John F. Kennedy Jr. and the actor David Duchovny, as well as the son of the president of U.S. Steel and a scion of the Newhouse publishing dynasty. Jeffrey's father was a subway conductor, his mother a nurse. An intellectually gifted kid with athletic ability, Jeffrey won a scholarship to Collegiate and was one of two minorities in his class of 30. Now 42, he is an executive at Mattel.

Initially, when he walked to the train station in the morning in his school uniform, he got the business from the neighborhood crowd: "Professor," "squid" (nerd), "punk." Luckily, Jeffrey knew how to handle himself on a basketball court, and the epithets faded as his jump shot improved. He'd play ball with car thieves, pickpockets, and drug dealers. Seventeen-year-old June Bug was the most intimidating of them. Six-two, 200 pounds, and dark-skinned, with a huge Afro, he was the first one around with Walt Frazier Pumas on his feet. Talking was a sign of weakness in the neighborhood. Real men glared and muttered, revealing little of themselves that could be exploited by an enemy. But June Bug would talk to Jeffrey because he seemed to know stuff. "If you break your leg, how do you set it?" June Bug would ask. Or "If you eat something bad, how can you make yourself feel better?" June Bug was a teacher, too, and would tell Jeffrey how to survive the streets: Never look a man in the eye because he'll see it as a challenge; stand up straight and throw your head back if you think you're going to be pulled into a fight.

From this, Jeffrey would launch himself into the world of Collegiate, where eighth-graders sported Rolex watches and deck shoes. They'd invite him to their apartments, where the nannies and maids would wait on them. Parents were often away during the afternoons and weekends, and the children had inordinate freedom. In this environment of extraordinarily wealthy children, the working-class Jeffrey was one of the most popular kids in school. "I got treated with a lot of respect from the Collegiate guys," he says. "I was a very good athlete. And also, there was a presumption that I was hip and cool by virtue of being black. So it was cool to know me. They never made me feel like I wasn't welcome and accepted."

Culture shock absorbed. The dichotomy of ricocheting between June Bug and JFK Jr. somehow worked for him. He got used to it, and he balanced the imbalance. Jeffrey's major adjustment? He had to remember how to curse, depending on where he was. "I had to adjust not only my language, but my vocal inflections. I'd have to flip back and forth between African-American dialect and Collegiate-speak. The Collegiate boys cursed, too, you know. And they had more drugs."

Like Mo Wortman and others from the working class who spent time with the upper crust, Jeffrey developed a sense of superiority over his Collegiate classmates. "I knew I had the perfect combination in my life: street smarts and book smarts. They had half. And I remember feeling these kids would never survive if they didn't have all these trappings around them." Beyond that, Jeffrey felt blessed that both his parents were around, while so many of the kids at Collegiate came from broken homes.

"I was an old head. I was a young, old guy. I felt superior because my father instilled that work ethic in me."

Culture Shock outside School

Some Straddlers tell me that they encountered the upper classes in memorable ways outside of school. For millionaire Don McNeeley, 48, president of Chicago Tube and Iron, who holds a Ph.D. in economics, the day came when he was a teenager in an Irish immigrant neighborhood on Chicago's west side. The family was living tight—12 people in a two-bedroom flat. Don's father was a laborer in a stone quarry; his mother was a switchboard operator. To make some money, Don would caddie at the private Riverside Country Club. One hot summer day, he rode his bicycle to the club and had the great bad luck of having to caddie for a classmate. He was the son of one of the more connected members, a junior member of the club. Things just got nasty. After finding the kid's lost ball from an errant shot, Don returned it. Then, in front of his father, the kid tossed the ball back.

"Wanna clean my balls, caddie?" Don remembers him saying, just like that, snooty and arrogant. Don needed the five bucks he was making for this round, so he said okay, his hands clenching and unclenching. But he got even later on.

"I settled it in a pickup football game we had at school. Elbows can get a little higher in the heat of the game. I beat the tar out of him, and I knew he knew why." Not long before, Don had beaten up a doctor's kid who'd made fun of his brother's hand-me-down clothes. Who did these money kids think they were?

Not every lesson learned about the middle class was so hard-won. Philadelphia journalist Eils Lotozo, daughter of a Polish-Lithuanian watchmaker who died young, was captivated by some wild-spirited golden boys with parental cash flow, disposable income, and outrageous attitude. Living with her waitress mother in Port Richmond, gritty with its soap factories and ironworks, Eils began alienating her neighborhood friends when she went to art school in the 1970s. They didn't get it, and saw her as a three-headed monster. But she was also social poison on the campus of the University of the Arts, to which she commuted each day, lugging art supplies on the subway. Nobody commuted but her, it seemed. She got a part-time job working for a downtown lawyer whose wife bought a house and restaurant in the upscale resort town of Cape May, New Jersey. Eils got invited on weekends and immediately made an impression on the lawyers' sons and their friends. Blond, green-eyed, and beautiful in a Rebecca DeMornay kind of way, Eils was the sort of young woman who got attention. "Those boys were the first upper-class boys I'd met," she says. "And they were so in love with me, maybe because I was so odd and couldn't fit in anywhere."

The boys would drive too fast and take too many drugs. She realized that they could do anything they wanted because someone would always come along and clean up their messes. "Nobody would clean up mine. No one had the money for bail." But the boys had this confidence, this sense of security. "Palms would be greased, wheels would roll their way. Meanwhile, I had this abiding anxiety that if I looked the wrong way, I'd be arrested." Eils was attracted to the boys' confidence, their ease. "It was alluring, their masters-of-the-universe attitudes. They all were big and healthy and strapping, with nice teeth that someone spent money on fixing." And there was this spirit that burned within them—the rocket fuel of their potential, setting off sparks as they moved. None of the boys from the neighborhood were like that. They were all hoping to get jobs in the post office. Eils yearned for these Cape May lives. Envy and self-pity mixed inside her.

Eils remembers one night with one of the boys driving on the Garden State Parkway. They were headed to Stone Harbor for a party. Eils was wearing a peasant dress. The guy had that disheveled preppie-sliding-toward hippie look. As they traveled, the boy got louder and giddier. Then he punched the gas and the old Rambler climbed to 140 mph. Eils was exhilarated and terrified. She couldn't hear the radio anymore. As Jersey blurred green and formless around her, Eils realized something: This guy was a way she could never be. "I had the instant understanding that he had this sense of invincibility. But for me, as I gripped the dashboard, all I thought was that you could get arrested and thrown in jail for this. And he didn't have that fear at all." Working-class girls accustomed to closed doors and meager chances couldn't fake this sense of entitlement, this heady, high-speed deservingness. Eils, now 45, stopped hanging around them not long after. "And," she says, remembering those summers long ago, "what was amazing to me was their lives didn't turn out all that well. With a tremendous head start, these boys ended up nowhere."

Border Crossing

Encountering class differences can obviously be daunting, and Straddlers don't forget the moments they were first reminded of their caste. One woman I met lived much of her life aware of her inferior class position each day. She was born in a blue-collar pocket of one of the richest places in the United States—Westchester County, north of New York City. Her town also bordered one of the wealthiest communities on the planet, Greenwich, Connecticut. Today, Suzanne Bilello, 46, lives in Buenos Aires with an adopted Guatemalan daughter. She works as a freelance consultant to philanthropic foundations. The day I speak with her she is in a New York City hotel with her baby and her au pair, getting ready for her twenty-fifth reunion at Barnard College. Thin and fit in an executive's gray suit, Suzanne has light brown hair, long arms, and a penchant for silver, which adorns her neck, ears, and fingers. Her face tapers to a narrow, distinctive chin. Born to parents who grew up in Dickensian poverty in New York, Suzanne lived in Cheever country among the people who served the rich. A few skilled masons among her kind were responsible for the $100,000 stone walls that adorn the homes of the affluent in the surrounding areas. It was an upstairs/downstairs dichotomy. Despite her background, Suzanne exudes a patrician aura of money and breeding. And that is the crux of her story. It's an image she built out of the raw material of a hard beginning in a border town called Port Chester.

Suzanne's town was where rich kids came to misbehave. The drinking age was 18 in the state of New York, but 21 in Connecticut. Monied brats would scuttle across the border from Greenwich, raise hell among the gas station attendants and motor vehicle workers they'd rub up against in the bars at night, then go home, leaving only broken beer bottles and alley puddles of urine behind. Port Chester had a reputation as the kind of place you could go to and get away with such things.

Suzanne wound up in a public school that actually had a few upper-middle-class Rye-area kids in it. The school bus crossed from the tonier precincts into Suzanne's neighborhood. One day, with the affluent kids sitting in a knot on the bus, they rolled onto Suzanne's block.

"Oh, slum district," one of the kids said.

Suzanne challenged him with a hard stare, and the insensitive child shut down. Mostly, that sort of thing didn't happen with Suzanne because she was in the same advanced-placement classes as the well-off students, and she got points for that. "It's like those racist remarks when people say you're not like the others—'You're not what we expected.' " Interestingly, when some poor African-American girls surrounded her at her locker one day and wanted to steal her purse, one of the girls recognized Suzanne and stopped the mugging.

"She was in my class in first grade," the girl said. "She's okay. She's not one of them." Suzanne says she enjoyed being in this in-between area. "I understood both worlds."

To make money, Suzanne had to venture into the belly of the beast: the Westchester country clubs. Lawns had the best grasses and reflected many of the members: thick and pampered. Kitchens stocked the finest cuts of cow. Chandeliers sparkled on late summer evenings and were reflected in the eyes of tuxedoed men of means and unhealthily thin women, all of whom, it seemed, were cut from the same bolt of taffeta.

The clubs sorted themselves according to background: the nouveau riche divided into Jewish clubs, Italian clubs, and Irish clubs. Old money had its own enclaves, of course, far from the just-made-it millionaires whose jewelry rattled a bit too loudly. Every summer when she was in college, Suzanne waitressed in the country clubs. "I really hated the nouveau-riche ones," she says. "They treated the staff badly. They yelled at you all the time and were never comfortable or satisfied, all style and no substance." Apparently not yet at ease with their wealth, they took it out on the help, needing someone to oppress. Suzanne remembers one big dinner in which the misbehaving nouveaus had eaten only the tails of the lobster and had thrown the rest of the meat away. "That was shocking to me," Suzanne says. "And given how they were acting in general, I didn't want to be around people like that."

Old money, it turned out, was easier to deal with. "The rich treat you well, I learned, if they are secure in themselves." And they liked that Suzanne was an Ivy League kid trying to get somewhere. (The rich, by the way, have a few things in common with the working class, when it comes to that pesky fork question. Truly wealthy folks don't have to know which is the proper utensil to use; they can wield iced-tea spoons to eat their Welsh rarebit, and people will call them colorful. Working-class people don't know; the seriously loaded don't care. Only the middle class and middle-class wannabes seem to fret.)

Suzanne was an ambitious class traveler. She viewed each meal as a seminar, learning about food and wine. And she figured out that Straddler bugaboo, the place setting, by sitting at the tables before the diners did and studying the forks. After six-course dinners at which a different wine was poured with every dish, Suzanne would sip what was left in the bottles, she and a friend holding impromptu tastings. So this is chardonnay, this is rosé. "I was checking out all the accouterments of the middle class without being in it, but with the assumption that I would be there someday." Her newfound knowledge was distancing her from her friends, of course. After her country club wine sampling, she couldn't bear the Boone's Farm swill that her pals passed around at parties. She'd noticed differences between herself and the other waitresses. "Everyone I worked with was in it for life, and they were much more subservient than I was. They were saying to themselves, 'Oh, wow, these are rich people.' But I had no qualms about talking to them, telling them I was going to Barnard. I wasn't intimidated by them at all."

With a kind of startling calculation that's rare among working-class kids, Suzanne plotted out her life. She would have been devastated if she hadn't been accepted by an Ivy League or Seven Sisters school. "I had to make a greater leap than simply going from the working class to college. It had to be a good college to justify my parents' sacrifices for me. What most families took two to three generations to do, I had to do in one. Barnard is the Good Housekeeping Seal of Approval. It means you've made it. And people like me didn't have any other card to play but getting the right credentials. My father didn't donate a million dollars for a new gymnasium."

Before transferring to Barnard, Suzanne was at Vassar. And while she knew she could compete intellectually with students there, every once in a while something would happen to remind her of her place, like back on the school bus in Port Chester. Once, some middle-class classmates from Nebraska asked if they could stay with Suzanne and her family for Thanksgiving. It was a disaster. The kids weren't used to a house that was, by their standards, small and poor. The guests would get up early in the morning, go to the train station, and venture into New York City, not returning until late at night. They refused to join Suzanne when she wanted them to meet some of her neighborhood friends. "That was a function of my denial of who I was, and my naivete. It had never occurred to me that upper-middle-class people like that had never been in a neighborhood like mine. I didn't think they'd be so uncomfortable. But they were, and they never came back."

Freshman Seminar

I wanted to know how young people deal with class differences today, and whether a twenty-first-century college freshman would feel the way baby boomers did when they first entered the academy. To find out, I put together a small group of 18-year-old freshmen from the University of Pennsylvania—three working-class kids in their nascent moments as Ivy Leaguers. I catch up with them midway through their first semester among the middle class and the privileged—the students who were the second, and even the third and fourth, generations in their families to go to college. We meet at a West Philadelphia coffeehouse on a block of middle-class boutiques and restaurants.

Angela Kulp is a blue-eyed, blond-haired Mennonite from small-town Pennsylvania. Mark Natale is an earnest, sweet-faced kid from a working-class Philadelphia suburb, whose father and grandfather have worked at Penn as a maintenance man and a gardener, respectively. Stephen Musick is an erudite, theatrical boy from the woods outside Honaker, Virginia. Both Angela and Stephen will be taking out more than $40,000 in loans to attend college. Their parents can't really help out, and that points out a big difference between themselves and the bulk of Penn students: They're all business when it comes to studying. "I'm paying my own way, and that makes me take more seriously my time here," Stephen says. "I could have gone to the University of Virginia for free. If not for the better education I'd get here, there'd be no point in coming." Like Stephen, Angela can't afford to waste time. But it seems that so many of her classmates can. She had conflicts with a roommate who was more into socializing than studying. "It's clear money isn't a problem for her family, and it doesn't mean as much to her to be here." Angela spoke to the roommate about it, and the woman took just two hours to pack and go.

All three say they feel class differences everywhere, every day. Angela heard a girl talking to her parents, complaining that she was tired of going to Middle Eastern spots for vacation. "I've never even been to Europe," Angela says. "It's amazing someone my age would be tired of traveling." Mark, too, says he feels less traveled, less worldly. "The lifestyles of the people here are so different. I'm just a local kid from 20 minutes away." Up close, the middle class can seem a little spoiled, a little immature. Stephen listened as an incoming freshman berated his mother for forgetting his computer cord. Stephen doesn't even own a computer. "And this kid's talking as if he's always been taken care of, and he can't take care of himself. Meantime, me, I'm on work-study, I'm more independent and serious, and the opportunities I have mean more to me."

Like Straddlers who've straddled before them, the Penn trio have had to endure difficulties separating from working-class roots after learning just how different they were from their peers and families. Odd as it sounds, Stephen's teachers used to complain that he read too much. Too many books would make him antisocial, they warned his parents. Stephen's parents—a pastor who didn't attend a seminary and a stay-at-home mom—cut trees out of a local forest and planed them into logs they used to build the family house. In such an environment, it seemed uppity to be good in school, like he was trying to outdo everyone else. Stephen always hated tests because he'd do so well and classmates made envious big deals about his scores. "My good grades annoyed people, and became more of an embarrassment than a positive thing," he says. His teachers told him the Ivy League was stuck-up, and if he attended, he'd be a C student at best. Mark, too, caught static when the Penn letter came to the house. His friends became hostile. "How'd you get in? You don't belong there," they told him. Meanwhile, Angela shocked everyone by not going to a religious college, as most college-bound kids from her parts did. "I needed to get outside the religious community I was in, but people thought I was trying to get above where I was from, and didn't like it," she says. Already, Angela finds herself in a kind of culture-shock conflict between Penn and home. Her religion teaches creationism over evolution. It's strict and straightforward about the origin of life. Yet Angela, who wants to do genetics research, is working with embryonic stem cells in a college lab. "It's a conflict for me," she says. "You can't see them, of course. Sometimes, I don't think about what they are. But every once in a while it hits you."

After Angela and Stephen leave the coffeehouse to study for midterms, Mark explains that he himself had worked as a laborer at Penn during the summers for the last four years, just like his father and grandfather. Since he was 14, he had thought about attending. One summer, he cleaned out trash cans. From before that, Mark's father dreamed his kid would walk the halls he kept warm in the winter as a campus steamfitter. Mark's mother, denied a chance to go to college, was over the moon about his acceptance at Penn. "She's living vicariously through me," Mark says. "She's so emotional and when I ask why, she says, 'I've always wanted this and now it's come to fruition through you.' "

That is a lot for one 18-year-old to deal with.

"They made so many sacrifices for me to be here, and have so many hopes. It puts a pressure on me that's hard to bear." Sociologists have found that kids in Mark's situation can grow resentful of their parents for heaping on expectations and loading their shoulders with the weight of generations of dreams. Mark loves his parents, but he knows they have a lot riding on him. "My dad worked here 25 years with the hope a kid would come here. It puts so much pressure on me every time I have to take a test.

"At times I think, 'Do I really belong here?' Being the first in the family to go to college, I'm responsible for breaking away. If I don't make it, I'll have to go into a trade. I have a responsibility for carrying my name into something bigger than what the family was. This is so many years in the making for them. I have to succeed."

Learning to navigate such culture conflicts is one of the most challenging, ever-present aspects of Limbo.

5

GOING HOME: AN IDENTITY CHANGED FOREVER

In 1980, after college and graduate school, I was offered my first job on a now-dead daily paper in Columbus, Ohio. I broke the news in the kitchen, where all the family business is discussed. My mother wept as though it were Vietnam. My father had a few questions: "Ohio? Where the hell is Ohio?" I said it's somewhere west of New York City—that it was like Jersey, only more so. I told him I wanted to write, and these were the only people who'd take me.

Why can't you get a good job that pays something, like in advertising in the city, and write on the side?"

"Advertising is lying," I said, smug and sanctimonious, ever the unctuous undergraduate. "I want to tell the truth."

"The truth?" my father exploded, his face reddening as it did when he was up 20 stories in high wind. "What's the truth?"

"Real life. Real people. Writing about that makes me happy."

"No, you're happy with your family," he said, uttering a key blue-collar rule. "That's what makes you happy. After that, it all comes down to dollars and cents. What gives you comfort besides your family? Money, only money."

During the two weeks before I moved, my dad reminded me that newspaper journalism is a dying field, and that I could do better. Then he pressed advertising again, though neither of us knew anything about it, except that you could do it in Manhattan five days a week and still come home for Sunday dinner.

I couldn't explain myself, so I packed, unpopular and confused. No longer was I the good son who studied hard and fumbled endearingly with tools. I was ticking people off. One night, though, my father brought home some heavy tape and that clear, plastic bubble stuff you pack your mother's second-string dishes in. "You probably couldn't do this right," my father said to me before he sealed the boxes and helped me take them to UPS. "This is what he wants," my father told my mother the day I left for Columbus in my grandfather's Cadillac. "What are you gonna do?" After I said my good-byes, my father took me aside and pressed five $100 bills into my hands. "It's okay," he said over my weak protests. "You don't have to tell your mother."

And I was gone.

Over the years, for holidays or just because I wanted to, I went back home for visits. "Isn't it great to be in your old bed?" my father would ask. I smiled at his sweet question, but actually, the bed I had in Ohio was much more comfortable. Columbus friends would marvel at the frequency of my trips home. "I don't see my family as much as you do yours," said a pal whose relatives lived within 20 miles. It's a blue-collar thing, I tried to explain. Middle-class kids are groomed to fly away, and they do. The working class likes to keep its young close to home. Those who drive 600 miles west are the odd ones.

On my visits back, I overlooked working-class Brooklyn's deep flaws—the know-nothingism, the pride in limitation—and reveled in its verve. The quiet, yuppie preserves of Columbus (an Ohio cabdriver described the place as mashed potatoes without salt or gravy) couldn't compare to the tumult of my old town. The genuineness of the people charmed me. And the pizza and bagels were real, too. Once in Columbus, I'd asked a diner waitress for an untoasted bagel. She brought a plate with a frozen Lender's round-bread-thing on it.

Thomas Wolfe wrote a short story called "Only the Dead Know Brooklyn," in which he described its vastness as so great, one would need more than a lifetime to ascertain its totality. That Wolfe also warned about returning to hometowns was always instructive to me.

Practically any journey home for a Straddler is going to inspire pain and nostalgia, guilt and ambivalence. Being class-mobile means you're rejecting at least some part of your past, of your kith and kin. Otherwise, you would have stayed. For Straddlers, it's odd knowing that life in the old place is going on without them. The town or neighborhood you rejected and quit is still there, as are many of the people—perhaps your parents included—whom you told at one time or another, "There must be something more than this." Out in the wide world, the place you left still invades your dreams, still is a part of you. To totally deny its importance is to lose vital parts of yourself. Every once in a while, Straddlers have to go back and touch the place that launched them, the place that repelled them. They need to go back to the world they left, to see what's still there.

When I eventually left Ohio and returned to New York to live and work, nostalgia ended, and my Brooklyn rose up again to disappoint and amaze me. I was working for the *Daily News*, whose editors noted my pedigree and sent me back to my old stomping grounds in Bensonhurst to cover the mess down there after Yusuf Hawkins was murdered. He was a young black man who'd ventured into the predominantly Italian-American neighborhood to buy a used car on a hot August day. He never got out. A mob chased him; some punk shot him. In the ensuing days, Al Sharpton and a procession of black preachers and activists would show up in buses and march up the middle of 20th Avenue, telling the world that a person should be able to walk in any neighborhood unafraid. (A year earlier, at another demonstration I'd covered—this one in a black neighborhood—some people working with Sharpton hadn't exactly followed that credo. As Sharpton looked on impassively, I was punched, kicked, spat upon, and hit with rocks by people who did not want me there. I wasn't badly hurt, but my family first heard about the attack on news radio. It frightened my mother. I wasn't pleased with Al that day.)

In Bensonhurst, the locals saw Sharpton's trips as red-flag provocation. Sharpton knew that's exactly how it would all play out. Dropping work, school, and family obligations to be a part of things, residents formed a counterdemonstration, with all the enthusiasm of a civic group pitching in on a vital community project: "Go home, niggers, go home!" they screamed.

Sharpton and hundreds of other African Americans walked down the middle of the avenue, block after block. All traffic had been diverted. A blue line of cops stood in close ranks near the curbs, keeping the neighborhood people on the sidewalks. It looked like a parade. Except the crowd was purple with rage, their red eyes wild. They yelled the most vile things and spat whenever a black person got close enough. Their hatred inextinguishable, residents kept this up for the five days of demonstrations, crowded together and united. When I was younger, these same people rallied against court-ordered busing. But this was much more vehement. And loud. It was wretchedly, horribly loud.

As a reporter assigned to cover this, I struggled to stay dispassionate. But inside, I was withered and embarrassed by all the noise and bile. It was like watching an uncle get drunk and abusive in a crowded restaurant. Young men were mostly the ones perpetuating the anger, hanging the family's dirty laundry on the clothesline, flapping banners of raw ignorance. A couple of guys nudged me conspiratorially, figuring me for an ally, whispering, "You know what we mean. You understand." I'd heard the croaks of racists there before, but nothing like this, nothing like this 1960ish Mississippi-ization of my city. Streets I'd known since childhood seemed suddenly twisted into a grotesque geography, choked with the menace of neighbors. At that moment, I wasn't sure where I was at all. A few blocks from the house I grew up in, I was utterly lost.

On normal visits back to Bensonhurst, I could walk through the place and recognize pieces of myself in the people, as though basic genetic material is shared. I could hear cultural echoes and feel familiar, comfortable resonances. That's the beauty of a blue-collar neighborhood. But there's a downside to the tug of turf. Some of those screaming guys never ventured outside community boundaries. In Bensonhurst, writes neighborhood memoirist Marianna De Marco Torgovnick, there is a cohesiveness and provinciality in which "difference is unacceptable."[1] And in that insular, isolated bubble in which residents lived and hid, xenophobia cooked like a poisoned soup. Fear, not anger, is what motivated aggression in Bensonhurst among the Italian Americans. People there are flat afraid of blacks. That's why some of the community elders looked the other way when the hair-trigger homeboys "defended" the neighborhood against trespass. (Incredibly, one of the kids who had chased Hawkins was an African American who lived in the neighborhood. That's how strong the pull of territory is.) Affirmative action and

110

special programs to help blacks drive these people crazy. "What about us? What about our struggle?" they ask. The price of staying white, though, is that rough guys run the streets and control the public relations. Heated by TV lights and scorched by headlines, Bensonhurst became raw real estate. The unprejudiced there asked me to be sure I didn't portray the place as a monolith, a homogeneous settlement of like-minded bigots. "Say in the newspaper we feel for Yusuf's mother," a middle-aged woman, literally wringing her hands, pleaded with me. "Say that not all Italians are animals."

On the last day of demonstrations, Sharpton and his companions returned to their buses, which were parked in a school yard ringed by cops and 15-foot fences. As the people boarded the buses, neighborhood residents stood outside, continuing their harangue. A few kids climbed the fences to hurl epithets from a greater height. Then, when I was almost able to breathe again, thinking that it was all over and glad that violence had been avoided, my fellow Brooklynites had one more surprise for me. After the final demonstrator filed onto the final bus, my old neighbors—people who would smile at you when you passed; who'd help your young kid cross the street safely; who'd look in on the elderly woman in the apartment downstairs; who'd wait on you at the pastry shop, winking as they threw an extra cannoli into the box, no problem—these same neighbors passed around fat, whole watermelons and began singing "We Are the World." Incredible. Not only were they racists, they were cavalierly clever enough to make a final, ironic, in-your-face comment about their racism.

After I wrote a story mentioning the watermelon detail in the paper, I was mailed a death threat written in black crayon: "Asshole traitor to the Italians—you're dead when you walk out your office door." Traitor. Disloyal for feeling different from the people I grew up with when I was there, disloyal for leaving, disloyal for coming back to criticize. Uncle Tomaso. The greatest sinners in Dante's *Inferno* were traitors—Brutus, Cassius, and, of course, Judas.

So, yes, going home again can get a bit complicated, especially when the blue-collar populace wants to string you up for your middle-class notions. Not every trip back is so dramatic, of course.

To understand what it's like for others, I followed two limbo people back to the hometowns they had left years before. One man was, still is, and will always remain uncomfortable in the precincts of his youth. The other, haunted by tragic events, has been rethinking his white-collar world and is longing for reconnection with the people he loved but had to leave.

Carolina Odyssey

Roads down here in the South Carolina Piedmont wind through endless stands of pine trees drawing nurture from the red dirt. Every few miles, the thick green is interrupted by a clearing in which huge, Quonset-hut-like churches sit, their metal roofs and walls suitable for baking whole congregations in the hot sun. Along with God, America's other obsession—guns—is available in abundance down here. Fireworks, too, can be bought with ease from obliging purveyors along the side of the road in "towns" that have names that can be found on a map, but don't seem to possess true dimension in any physical sense. You're never more than a short drive from barbecue, or cigarettes, or alcohol. Grasses grow thick and unkempt near rivers that meander like old men lost in the woods. The women's departments of clothing stores are filled with signs declaring that the garments on sale are WASHABLE. On Saturdays, the pulsing night choruses of crickets and cicadas are overwhelmed for hours by the roar of cars racing around NASCAR ovals on tracks cut into the countryside. Confederate flags flap in decades-old defiance.

Once out of the country and into the town of Rock Hill, the landscape alters to a too-familiar American tableau: an aging, mill-town core surrounded by the fresh rot of sprawl. It is here that I meet Doug Russell. A program manager for a high-tech firm in the Austin, Texas, area, Doug is 44 and six feet tall, with brown, intense eyes and a middle-aged physique that is softening from blue-collar muscle to middle-class thickness. He packs his wife and kids in the minivan and comes home every year to see his parents and a few friends. When he was growing up in Rock Hill, about 25,000 people lived here. Now, the population is closer to 100,000, many of them yuppies fleeing Charlotte, North Carolina, 23 miles to the north. They crave closet space, larger backyards, and a "country life."

Doug never felt comfortable here. And you can see that now, today, in the humid, 95-degree heat. He is jumpy, almost agitated. Memories flood and fill him, a saturation that sets him adrift. Restless, he flits around his parents' living room, a cool, dark place from which the sun is banned like an unwanted intruder. It's modest, clean, and comfortable. On a wall is a painting of Doug's father's homestead. Homer, 76, did it from memory—a small, neat depiction of a North Carolina peanut farm. Doug's mother, Zelma, grew up on a farm, too. Her family raised peaches and cotton, among other crops. The Russells bought this small house, surrounded by mulberry, cherry, pecan, and mountain chestnut trees, when the area was practically rural. Homer worked for years at a factory that made filters for cigarettes. Chemicals in there burned his eyes. After that, he started his own construction company, while Zelma, now 71, stayed home to raise Doug and his sister.

Doug always felt different from the other blue-collar kids. "I can't even articulate it. We'd be playing softball in the backyard and I'd be keeping score in my head and they'd make fun of that. They thought it was the weirdest thing." Doug was studious and bright, an anomaly among the working class of Rock Hill. "I knew early it was me against the world." Kids teased him until they grew bored with the torture. Too often, he'd be seen reading a book. "That was the stupidest thing in the world to two-thirds of the kids in the class."

Doug would even notice a difference between his parents and the other adults in town. Homer and Zelma seemed more intelligent; they were energetic, always thinking. Their number one goal in life was to educate their children. Setting precedent for their part of town, the Russells spent a bunch of Homer's take-home pay on encyclopedias for the kids—*Britannicas*, at that. They cost $15 a month for Lord knows how many payments. Homer had wished he'd gotten the chance to go to college, so he made sure his children understood what was at stake.

Still, father and son had problems. Homer couldn't understand why Doug didn't like to get dirty and play in the heat and humidity, like all the other boys. "My dad always had an issue that I was a momma's boy."

"Well," says Homer, a wiry man with a creased face and shining eyes, "he was different. Sometimes, he made you mad as hell. Stubborn. He was fine, though. He'd read the type off a newspaper, or a cereal box. He was just . . . different from us. He could do something in 15 minutes that would take me two hours."

"That's not true," Doug says gently. "You were good at a lot of stuff, too."

Zelma shakes her head a little and smiles. "See, the doctor said Doug needed to get out and get dirty, you know? But I watched over him a lot. I guess I was a little overprotective."

Later, out of earshot of his parents, Doug says simply, "I just wasn't my father's idea of a boy, you know what I mean?"

Friends—even family—tell a story about how Doug would read a book while he was playing the outfield. Doug doesn't know how that tale got going. It's just not true. Homer had been a coach of Doug's neighborhood softball team and would have liked to see more effort, more interest from the boy. But in those days, Doug would rather read than play ball. Still, he never took a book out in the dugout or on the field. Years later, Doug turned into a decent player, he wants you to know. But his father wasn't coaching then, and he didn't see the improvement.

Meantime, Doug was garnering way too much attention as an oddball with his books and that faraway look. "It's a problem when you're interested in stuff other than being a redneck," he says. People notice. "I wasn't very neanderthal-ish, I never had rough edges. I had soft edges." One day in school, a hard-edged kid knocked Doug down, pulled a Hardy Boys book from his book bag—*The House on the Cliff*—and kicked it around the school yard, scuffing it up. That was Doug's own copy, not a library book. The half-life on his childhood anger is still potent enough today to shoot the Geiger counter needle into the red zone. Kids would see Doug and ask, "Hey, what're you reading?" He wouldn't answer because no one wanted to know, really. It was a taunt. And making fun of the kid who'd rather read than sweat became a constant refrain.

Like a lot of Straddlers, Doug found refuge in the library as a child. Zelma would drive him the 10 miles from home, and Doug would load up on as many books as they'd allow him to carry. "It was the most wonderful place in the world," he says. Doug read fairy tales from around the world, because he just wanted to know what people in India were like. He devoured science fiction, and he read about religion. The Christianity that flourishes strong and fervent in these parts did not completely germinate in Doug. He took what he needed from Scripture and discarded the rest. "I hate that holy roller stuff," he says. For some reason, Doug was drawn to New York Jewish writers as well. Why would a Christian South Carolina kid fixate on Philip Roth and others? "I think I understood Jewish neurosis," he says. "I told my wife I think I have a Jewish soul. I'm more intellectual than physical. I see the irony, the comedy in life."

That's not the kind of man Homer is. So it was hard to talk about the Jewish thing with his daddy. Besides, Homer is a man's-man type, physically very strong. Doug couldn't approach his father with an emotional problem because that sort of thing showed weakness. To keep his family going, Homer had worked some awful jobs. He was a tank tester in a shipyard, checking to see whether the seals on fuel tanks were sound. It was so noisy down there in the reverberating ship holds that the men wrote with soapstone on the walls to communicate. Homer's grandmother was pioneer stock and lived on a Civil War soldier's pension. Resourceful in a way no one is today, the woman could dig a better garden with a potato fork than Homer ever could with a tractor. It's not as if Homer wanted his son to be some strapping physical specimen built for the animal work he'd done. In fact, Homer would give his son odious chores to do at home so he wouldn't eschew college like so many of the kids in the neighborhood.

As he tells me this, Homer points to his brain to show he was using it to put his son on the right path. These days, he says, he can hardly move because of the work he's done. Arthritis grips him now. During his last checkup, Homer had told his doctor that he'd worked hard all his life. Yup, the doctor said to him, it shows.

The rough days of labor by blue-collar men are written in the MRIs, CAT scans, and X rays they're forced to sit still for in pain-filled retirement—like models posing for the medical arts. Their wrecked insides tell the stories of bricks and blocks lifted, holes dug, and punishment absorbed. If your rough hands and stooped walk don't give you away, your ruined bones and tissue surely will.

Zelma provided solace for the boy who was growing up different. And she, like Homer, knew education was the key. "Look," she says standing in her immaculate kitchen, "we wanted him to have college because we knew there was no way without it. Me, I grew up grading peaches on a farm to see if they were good enough to sell. I just cried like a baby when we couldn't go to high school because we had to work the farm. You didn't have TV and lived in the country and didn't see friends.

So it was a pleasure to go to school, to get answers to all those questions you had in your head that mommas and daddies didn't know."

After she married and had children of her own, Zelma became concerned about her son. Doug was a difficult problem for farm folk without education. He was . . . well, he was beyond them. And they didn't know how to handle it.

"It was frightening when Doug was 14," Zelma says, now seated at the dining room table, with Doug outside the house, playing with his children in the yard. She is being as honest as she can be. "How were we supposed to handle that—his intelligence, I mean? He read all the books there were to read. We knew he was special. I worried that I couldn't give him what it would take for him to become what he should become. I thought a few times, 'Lord, why can't I have a normal child?' "

"She said that?" Doug asks me when I tell him later. His face grows gray and he winces. Finally, he says, "See, I didn't know any of that. They never told me that. I just felt weird all the time. Nobody ever told me, 'You're fine, son, we like you just the way you are.' You should do that, as a parent. You should do that with your kids, and not make them feel like there's something wrong with them when the other kids pick on them."

Though Rock Hill was mostly blue collar, Winthrop College was there. That meant there were middle-class people around, and they tempered the town, making parts of it seem more genteel. Doug was drawn to the campus, with its brick buildings and cool elegance. It was a break in the landscape, a kind of garden that didn't seem to belong there.

Doug remembers that he loved to sit and talk to his family doctor and his eye doctor when he was a child. "I had no idea why. They just seemed different, more interesting. It was the beginning of feeling class differences for me." He flirted with girls he liked from his advanced-placement classes, but he wouldn't ask them out because they were doctors' daughters. Doug was as smart as they were, but felt socially inferior to these young women who always seemed so well-dressed and clean. "There was that gulf there. I would have felt very inadequate."

One summer, Doug worked in a local country club. He noticed the members' kids his age were more verbally adroit, more confident. "They also were sneakier, not as straightforward as I was." And they acted superior. Doug figures it's all because they were around their parents in social settings, and he and his kind weren't. "Upper-crust kids were just more comfortable talking."

As Doug grew, Rock Hill seemed to shrink—another American no-place with nothing to do at night. Kids would drive up and down the main street, showing off cars and trying to pick up girls. Doug couldn't see himself cruising the same strip year after year. "There's nothing wrong with the people. They're good, honest, try to do the right stuff. But they're not what you'd call generally curious. They don't read; they don't seek knowledge. They're just pragmatic. It comes from that Scotch-Irish stock. I would have preferred to have been comfortable here. But I wasn't."

Scanning the AM radio dial one bored night, Doug heard a distant station play Bruce Springsteen's "Born to Run." He'd had no idea who the guy was, but when he heard the lyrics about blowing the hometown while you're still young, it riveted him. "That really did help focus me. Here was a guy expressing my innermost feelings, feelings in some cases I wasn't even aware of, except in a general anger or resentment."

Doug's dream was to get into Duke University, but that was too expensive. Homer, himself mechanically inclined, pushed his son toward engineering, figuring engineers run the world. Somewhere, Doug remembers, he'd read a book that said white-collar kids study medicine in school, while blue-collar kids go for something more practical, like engineering—if they ever get to college. He attended Clemson, up near Greenville, and Homer and Zelma paid the tuition. At school, Doug didn't fit in with the white-collar crowd; they seemed as foreign and distant as doctors' daughters. When he'd go home for weekends, Homer loved to hear about his engineering classes. But Doug quickly learned to zip his mouth around friends, who didn't want to know about campus life. Rock Hill hadn't improved in his absence. "Visiting the mall when I was home from college, the people just looked more in-bred to me, not diverse. The eyes were duller looking. It's like I was a different species, honestly. And it wasn't arrogance. I still wished I'd fit in."

Doug knew he was trailblazing. He had no mentors, no one to ask whether he should be studying electrical or chemical engineering. Like a lot of blue-collar kids in the white-collar world, he found no one to bounce ideas off of and answer his questions. So he stumbled ahead on his own. Needing a break from engineering, Doug took an entire semester of liberal arts courses and won writing awards for his short stories. "It irritated the English majors," he says with a smirk. "I wanted to study the hardest thing there was for a blue-collar guy like me to study. I wanted to show everybody I could do it. It was a pride thing."

Upon graduation, Doug was accepted at Duke, where he earned his MBA. One bad day, Doug tripped over his working-class roots there. Michael Eisner, the head of Disney, had come to campus for a visit, and he invited some students to lunch, Doug included. Doug had the sense that Eisner was judging how articulate the men were, measuring them for possible employment down the road. Two upper-class classmates kept Eisner engrossed and entertained, weaving charming stories that starred themselves. Doug hardly said anything. "Those upper-crust kids," he says, "really knew how to ingratiate themselves." Eisner never called Doug.

For reasons he either can't or won't articulate, Doug decided to work for the National Security Agency. He's not particularly patriotic. He says he just got a wild idea to go to Maryland and perform security-sensitive duties for his country. Part of the reason he went was to meet a smarter type of woman. "It's true, it's true," he says. "I wanted someone pleasant, kind, smart, and well-read to talk to. I thought I could find her there." Spy for America; meet fabulous women. Doug was an engineer for secure electronics. When I ask him what that means, he tells me he can't explain further. Even former NSA people are prohibited from talking about their work. Sure enough, he met Anne, an NSA analyst from the middle class, who, he says, is smarter than he is. They left the NSA, and Doug and his family moved to Texas.

At the house, Doug decides to take a drive. I tag along and he does some reminiscing as we roll through town. This is where he shot off those model rockets. This is where all the kids would hang out. We find a childhood friend of Doug's whom he wants me to meet. "He's a real Southern figure," Doug says. He's also, I quickly discover, who Doug would have been if he hadn't left Rock Hill. Sandy Hunter is an auto dealer in his mid-40s. Growing portly, he has startling blue eyes and a round face. Highly mannered, he reminds me that Southern people are big on the "ma'ams" and "sirs." "Doug wasn't a nerd or nothin' like that," Sandy starts out. "He could hit and field as good as I could in softball. But he was the brains. Doug was always keeping score of our games, and he never missed a beat." Sandy exudes a gentle sadness, and he looks at Doug with admiration and envy. Doug got out. But Sandy . . .

"You're eatin' lunch one day and then your daddy passes away. Hurts. So I had to take over the auto dealership and took care of my mother till the day she died. That's the way you did it. Did it keep me from doing things in life? Well, you don't know. See, I never married. But it's okay."

Sandy freely tells you Doug was smarter. South Carolina, he informs you, is ranked low in terms of quality of education. "We're not good at it at all. I didn't get the best one-on-one help I needed. You know how there's 35 kids in a classroom and you either get it or you don't? Well, I didn't get it all. But Doug got it. He had a good memory and he read a lot. Reading's good for kids, I guess. I didn't read like Doug." Sandy attended Winthrop but never finished. The school, once all female, went coed when he was there. Ten girls for every guy, including actress Andie MacDowell during Sandy's time. "That's one of the main reasons I didn't pass in college," he jokes. Responsibility kept Sandy anchored in Rock Hill. "I wanted to get away, like Doug. But now that I got his e-mail, we can keep in touch. That's one of the greatest inventions, e-mail."

Doug and Sandy make plans to meet later. We drive on. Each house we pass, each mile we log in the Carolina odyssey, triggers a reaction inside Doug. Traversing the rough terrain of his past, Doug makes slow, painful progress, like a hiker in the woods getting smacked with low-lying branches at every turn. By the time we return to his parents' house, Doug is wide-eyed and overstimulated.

Thinking about his planned meetings with friends over the next few days he's home, Doug is worried. "It's always the same," he says. "We get back together in someone's backyard, and inevitably someone says how I used to keep score in my head. And then they start cackling, 'Hey, what's the score, Doug?' Or, 'What are you reading now, Doug?' And they even get on my wife and me for not eating salad dressing. We just don't. But they wonder about that. It's not hurtful, but it always seems I'm the different one. I remember a friend's wife saying, 'We're not rich like you. We have to work.' And I said, 'You know, we're not rich, either. But I had to study pretty damn hard while you guys were out playing.' "

When you talk like that to people, do they even hear you? Because you read books when you were six and no one else in town did, does that mean you're different forever? It doesn't seem that Straddlers like Doug can change hearts and minds. It's as if someone took a Polaroid of you 100 years ago, and that's the person they know—period. You remain in limbo forever—too restlessly refined for the working class, but not a totally accepted or accepting member of the middle class.

It's the same with Homer as it is with Doug's friends. "My dad still thinks I'm a momma's boy," Doug says, sounding defeated, "because I didn't get under the hood of a car, and because I preferred books. Now, there's this gulf you have to cross. You can't be different from them and still be strong. You're either like them—interested in muscle—or you're weak. You can't be strong and bookish. That's the biggest problem I see with the whole thing. Everybody has to be in some pigeonhole, or people aren't comfortable with you."

Doug's eyes shine. Before I leave his parents' place, he beckons me into a small room. Squatting in front of a low bookcase, he runs his hands over the stored volumes until he finds the one he wants. It's the Hardy Boys, *The House on the Cliff*. He pulls it out and shows me, a little boy still smarting from a 35-year hurt. "That's the book they dragged through the school yard," Doug says. "The marks never go away. You can still see the marks."

Yes, I tell Doug. You still can.

Melrose Places

Melrose Park, Illinois, is near enough to O'Hare Airport that a person can read the logos of planes roaring not far overhead. It can get to you after a while, knowing that all those people above you are going places, and you're stuck in this.

The landscape on the main thoroughfares is eye-unfriendly, with barely a tree to offer a break from the character-free, suburban/industrial tangles: a Ford plant, a Sherwin-Williams plant, a Denny's, a strip mall—it's as though someone forgot to write a zoning code, allowing fast-food restaurants, factories, and big-box retailers to nest one next to the other in disjointed disarray. Acres of stained, gray parking lots thwart rain from penetrating soil, and rivers of oil-ruined water flow toward Lake Michigan in toxic torrents. Surviving on jet exhaust and industrial stink, Armageddon-ready weeds grow unchallenged and unmowed in the cracks of buckled concrete islands that separate endless flows of truck traffic. Pedestrians are scarce. Nothing is of human scale; it's a place for machines and buildings, hard and impenetrable. How tough it must be to live a life here.

Fred Gardaphé did, and it almost killed him. His godfather, his grandfather, and his father were slain here in Melrose, the place some people call "Mafia-town." They were connected in ways to the Outfit, which is how they refer to the Mob in Chicago. It was a gypsy who saved him: "The third Fred in the family will die," she foretold, if he didn't get out. Actually, it was a gypsy, a Dominican priest, and the University of Wisconsin that saved Fred. But that's getting ahead of the story.

These days, Fred is a professor of American studies at the State University of New York at Stony Brook, Long Island. That shouldn't have happened. Guys like him finish high school, maybe, then scratch out a working-class life never more than a few miles from the hospitals in which they were born. But Fred had things chasing him; fear is a great rocket fuel. "It was like being in Plato's cave," Fred says, "then walking out."

He returns every summer to see his mom and his friends, buddies who didn't go to college but remain close. Lately, the reunions have become even more important. Fred's actually been contemplating moving back to the area. "It's to be near what is known, and it's also being known," he says. "To not have to introduce myself to new people all the time."

Can a white-collar person do that—return to his blue-collar beginnings and live a new kind of life? For some Straddlers, the middle class gets to be a burden, its rituals and requirements forever foreign. There's an ease to slipping back to old ways. Another reason Fred comes is to find out more about his father's unsolved murder more than 30 years ago. People must know what happened, Fred believes. But no one ever says. Maybe he'll write a book about all the dead people in his life, he thinks. It's an important exercise in finding order, an action plan to expurgate ghosts. "I need for things to make sense. Because they don't." He's come this time with his daughter, to help her see who he was once.

One thing is for sure: Professor or not, he still looks like a neighborhood guy. Stocky and thick, Fred has a Fu Manchu and receding gray hair he keeps close-cropped. He wears black shorts and a blue, sleeveless T-shirt to show off arms he used to throw around in boyhood fights. He sort of reminds you of Billy Joel in a distant way. Tonight, he'll meet his boys for drinks at a sports bar, then maybe go to dinner. They'll bust his chops about his ride, a 1993 Mercury Sable. They've become plumbers and restaurant suppliers, and they all make more money than Fred, without education. Fred's son once asked him why, with his Ph.D, he has the crummiest car among friends who never went beyond high school.

Right now, he drives the gas-slurper through Melrose Park, once all Italian, now largely, if not mostly, Mexican. "When I come back, I expect things not to have changed. At least there are the same [jerk] drivers. But you see the changes and have to ask yourself, 'Who [messed] this up?' I expect people to still care about the things I've stopped caring about." As we drive, sweet songs like "You Didn't Have to Be So Nice" pour out of the oldies station Fred programmed onto the car radio after his daughter left to hang out with friends. The audio syrup is the wrong flavor for what Fred's telling me. "I come from a long line of violent things. My godfather was killed robbing a golf course." The statement hits you sideways, with its odd juxtaposition of disparate words that rarely work the same sentence. It's awful and absurd. Do things like that happen? Somebody shot the man as he ran off with duffer money, then his buddies scooped him off the lovely grass, drove him to the hospital, and threw him out on the lawn, where he died before ER doctors could stop the bleeding.

Life was that awful. Fred could easily have become a gangster—so many of the adults in his life were. This was, Fred says, "mythic Mafia land," with nefarious traditions tracing back to Al Capone, whose turf this once was. "There are people who still consider Melrose Park the place where the Mafia in America comes from." The Gardaphé family was into laundering stolen money and fencing stolen goods, he said. Their pawnshop was the perfect front. "They were distributors of the stuff that fell off the backs of trucks, essentially."

Fred passes Dora's Pizza and has to stop. He used to deliver for Chucky, the owner, and now the two catch up, as Fred eats a sausage sandwich and drinks an RC standing at the counter. Today the news is not good: Turns out everybody Fred used to know is either dead or on dialysis. "Whaddya gonna do?" Chucky asks, and the two men contemplate the question, so very blue collar in its dual implications that everything is out of your control, but you've got to learn to live with it. "Whaddya gonna do?" practically qualifies as a working-class philosophy of life.

There's a break in the conversation, then Chucky looks at Fred and says, "God, Fred, I remember the day Shadow didn't come in for lunch." That shuts Fred down, and a pall hangs over the men. Shadow was Fred's father. They say their good-byes and in the car, Fred tells me that Chucky has his facts wrong. Shadow wasn't supposed to go to Dora's for lunch. Fred was supposed to bring his father some food at the pawnshop that Monday afternoon. But he didn't want to because he knew Shadow would make him work. So Fred sent his younger brother with the lunch; Shadow took the food and sent the boy home.

"I always felt guilty about that. Maybe the killer would have seen me working there and not gone in." Somebody stabbed Shadow to death. Fred believes it would have to have been someone his father knew; nobody else could have gotten close enough for a knife assault. And it wasn't a robbery because nothing was taken. "It's one reason I keep coming back home, to keep replaying it in my mind. It was the most primal scene in my life and the reason I left this place. When I come back, I look at the people and wonder if they remember. It's not for new leads, really. But to see if his murder had an impact on others' lives as well."

After the slaying, people started telling their kids not to hang around with Fred. He became adept at spotting the FBI surveillance cars on the block, and once put a potato in a fed's tailpipe. Bad times seemed to follow him. When he was 15, Fred was on the phone with his grandfather, who was at the pawnshop. By then, Fred was working there more regularly, but he had stayed home that day. Suddenly, he heard gunshots pop over the phone. He and his mother jumped in their car and sped to the shop, only to see his grandfather lying on the floor, bleeding to death. Fred grabbed his grandfather's gun, saw a guy limping away, and raised it to fire. But before he did, a cop came up from behind and yelled, "Drop it." The shooter was caught and sentenced to 25 years for the murder. It was robbery, pure and simple. But Fred's grandfather wouldn't have died if he hadn't resisted. The only reason he had, Fred claims, is that he was a racist and couldn't bear the idea of being robbed by a black man.

"He used to say, 'When the niggers cross the railroad track, I'll pick 'em off one by one.' I knew my grandfather was a racist. I grew up a racist, too. See, he told me if somebody pulls a gun, give them whatever they want. And he said, 'Never pull out your .25 [caliber pistol] if the other guy has a .38.' Well, this guy had a .38 and all my grandfather had was a .25. Why did he pull it? Because the guy was black, I think." To this day he believes his grandpa messed up.

Mired in hatred and ignorance, steeped in death, Fred was growing up hard. Desperate for Fred to have a man around, his mother asked a neighbor to take an interest. As it happened, he was related to the Genovese crime family in New York. He, in turn, was murdered. Things were not going well for the males in Fred's life.

One day, Fred's grandmother saw a fortune-teller, who foretold his demise unless he sold the pawnshop, which had fallen to him. The family believed, and Fred liquidated the place when he was 16, selling, he said, to the Jewish Mafia in town. By then, he was attending an expensive Dominican prep school, for which his grandfather had paid. On the streets, he was brawling, getting into fights with black kids, and proving he was a man. In the classroom, he was studying philosophy and Latin, being shown another way to grow up. Fred would do his homework on the sly, sneaking books to the park or rec centers. "Around that time, I started realizing that I was trapped in Melrose. But you didn't want people to know that you were escaping." The process was going slowly. Fred got into drugs—speed and acid, mostly. "It was my way of getting out of where I was mentally, because I couldn't do it physically."

Still, the Dominicans were having their effect. He was reading Cicero and Plato. In an irony not uncommon in quality Catholic educations, Fred was being taught to question authority—how, in essence, not to be a good Catholic boy who hangs around and does only the family's bidding without question. "That was the bomb that blew everything up," he says. "They taught me I had to get out of this place. It was getting hard to remain in the world in which I was born while being nurtured out of it by school. The question became, when do you leave?"

Motivated to go but without direction, Fred went to a junior college to escape the draft. When the government did finally send a notice, it was a 4-F deferment, in essence a judgment that Fred had failed his physical exam and could not become a soldier. Good news, right? Well, like a lot of things in Fred's life, there was a mystery to that as well. Fred had never taken an Army physical. To this day, Fred believes his family had any potential draft notice quashed through their long-standing connections to organized crime. But no one at home owns up to it. Whaddya gonna do?

Still connected to the neighborhood physically and mentally, Fred almost lost everything one night. He was driving a car with some guys he knew when they ordered him to pull over in front of the First Baptist Church. A recently slain member of the Black Panthers was having his funeral there, and the boys wanted to disrupt it. Fred stopped the car and stayed in it while the others climbed out. Within moments, they ran back, screaming for Fred to floor it and get going. "We just threw a Molotov cocktail at the nigger church," one of the guys said. Fred doubts it. Nothing exploded and no one ever reported it on the news. The racism was getting old; always having to hate was becoming a burden. One of his college teachers, a white guy, called all the neighborhood guys in the class "racists." He explained how he'd fallen in love with a black woman. He had his students read Richard Wright and other black authors. He showed his ignorant white charges how they'd been getting it wrong their whole lives. "The bad thing about realizing you're a racist is that it means everyone who ever taught you anything or told you anything you believed was a racist, too. It's such an unraveling of all the things that you protected yourself with."

Enlightened and now totally out of step with the neighborhood, Fred transferred to the University of Wisconsin—"where all the good radicals go." Language was the big difference. Suddenly, he was in rooms with people whose English was superior to his. Making things tougher, women were befuddling, too. "I went up to girls and said, 'What are you chicks doing tonight?' and they'd say, 'Why do you cocks wanna know?' My working-class notions about women were they were to be protected. I opened a car door for a girl in Madison and she was insulted. I kind of got dragged into feminism kicking and screaming. You don't know how deeply working-class you are until you're in these situations."

Scholarship lit a fire in his head and Fred straightened out. Now he's a full professor, but he still worries about the clock at work. Is he keeping enough office hours? he wonders. He has a sense the boss is looking over his shoulder somehow. "But," he keeps having to remind himself, "I have tenure. I can't be fired."

Saturday night and time to meet the fellas. Fred drives to a sports bar in nearby Elmhurst, where he hooks up with the old crowd—Anthony, Patsy, and George. They hug like working-class guys do—a quick embrace, hard backslaps, then release. Gotta do it fast, before anyone thinks you're gay. Insults soon follow—jabs about weight, baldness, and creeping old age. That done, the boys are ready to settle in for chicken wings and beers. Balding and in great shape, blue-eyed Anthony works construction. Patsy, who's a little overweight and struggling with the Atkins diet, is national sales manager for a restaurant-equipment company. George the Greek, unique among the group because he still has his hair, is an insurance investigator. All three are 50 years old. Fred is the only one of the four to have graduated from college.

They start with the old stories. Like a vocal group from the 1950s, the guys know all the words. Apparently one day back in high school, Anthony's parents went out of town, the guys came over, and they did something that broke his parents' bed—though no one says what it was. Fred says "fuck" a lot; the others, not as much. "Our seventh-grade teacher called it alley English, the way we talked," Anthony says.

"My wife tells me, 'As soon as you get with those guys from Melrose Park, your personality changes,' Patsy says. 'You say, Fuck this and that.' "

"You learn a different language for the world," says Fred.

Back in the day, there were girls, furtive tries at oral sex, and fights. These guys were in lots of fights.

"The blacks pulled Fred out of the car one night, then they beat the [crap] out of all of us," Anthony says.

"I had no business being there in that neighborhood," says Fred, the reformed racist.

"We had state troopers called out," George says. "There were race riots. I tell my kids it made me a person."

"We all looked out for each other," Anthony explains.

"And we'll do it till we die," George declares.

George has to go, and the others decide to hit an Italian restaurant in a neighboring town. As O'Hare planes roar overhead, Fred reflects. "Back in those days, we would have died for one another. One reason I come back each summer is I want my kids to spend time with my friends. They'll say things about me that give my kids insight into me." The reminiscing reminds him of the crazy years of violent deaths. "Therapy made me realize how strange my life was back here," Fred says. "My life after education, from age 30 on, was boring. Good thing, because it's going to take me the rest of my life to mitigate everything that happened before 30."

The men find a spot they promise has good tomato sauce. On the sound system, Frank Sinatra, with his mellow voice, tells the world he did things his way. The waitress brings three Crown Royals for the guys. Fred, the white-collar one, orders veal, and his two working-class friends protest. That's a switch.

"Fred, they leave 'em in little pens," Anthony says.

"It's bad, Fred," Patsy adds.

"Hey, I like veal."

The men talk about their wives, past and present. "We didn't marry Italians," Fred observes, "because they're too much like our mothers."

"Marrying, we all broke the bloodline," Anthony allows.

"Hey, remember when we kidnapped your daughter from her Indian mother?" Fred asks Anthony. A look shuts down that potential conversation.

I ask Patsy what it was like to hold down the Melrose Park fort while Fred went off to college.

"You know, it's funny, because Fred never talked about going to college," Patsy says. "He felt maybe the rest of us didn't understand his need to go. I really don't remember any conversation about it. Me, I wanted to go to college, but my father said he needed me in the [restaurant-supply] business. It was depressing. I not only wanted to go to college, I wanted to travel, which I can do now. But it took me 30 years."

"You were always a good son to your father," Fred tells Patsy. "If my father had lived, I would have stayed. But there was nothing for me here. Where was I gonna go? But why did I go to Madison? It was totally non-Melrose up there."

"But it gave you an education of how it was in the world," Patsy says.

Anthony chimes in that he actually moved to Madison to be with Fred. For eight months, he painted Wisconsin houses by day, then partied with Fred and his new college friends at night. He never had the desire to actually matriculate, although he once made money by showing up at an ACT test and taking it for a less-smart pal. "I got him a scholarship," Anthony says proudly. "I actually got a better grade for him than I did for myself, when I took the test."

Maybe it's the Crown Royals, but the boys turn sentimental.

"Fred, even with your education, you remained Fred," Patsy says.

"I never felt you thought you were above and beyond us. You always remained yourself."

"And you got rid of that stupid earring," Anthony adds.

"I meet Harvard and Yale people who couldn't hold a candle to you guys," Fred gushes.

"Really, there's been no change in you," Patsy says.

"And you don't insist we call you 'doctor,' " Anthony adds.

"That's the thing I'd never call you," Patsy concludes.

The evening ends that way. In the parking lot, the guys share more hugs and spine-splintering backslaps. Fred is pleased with this trip home. He's happy that he didn't learn anything new about his friends. That means he still understands them, still knows who they are.

He hasn't doped out much about his father's murder, though. Probably, his family knows who did it, he thinks. "They've always known. They just won't tell me the truth." Really, though, what difference would it make now? You come home to sit down with the people who are alive; never mind the ghosts. Fred may finally be figuring that one out. "You know, I live in two worlds. I have to come back from the one at the university to make sure this one's still here. I'm so glad to know that it is."

6

OFFICE POLITICS: THE BLUE-COLLAR WAY

When I told my folks how much my first paper in Ohio was paying me, my father helpfully suggested I get a part-time job to augment the income. "Maybe you could drive a cab." Soon afterward, the city editor chewed me out for something trivial, and I made the mistake of telling my father during a visit home. "They pay you nothing and they push you around in that business," he told me, the rage building. "Next time, you grab the guy by the throat, push him against the wall, and tell him he's a big jerk."

Dad, I can't talk to the boss like that. And I can't touch him."

"Do it! You get results that way. Never take any garbage."

A few years before, a guy hadn't liked the retaining wall my father and a partner had built. They tore it down and did it again, but still the guy complained. My father's partner then shoved the guy into the freshly laid bricks. "Pay me off," my father said, and he and his partner took the money and walked. Blue-collar guys have no patience for office politics and corporate bile-swallowing. Just pay me off and I'm gone.

American corporate culture is based on WASP values, whether or not WASPs are actually running the company. Everything is outwardly calm and quiet. Workers have to be reserved and unemotional, and must never show anger. It's uptight, maybe even unhealthy, and all that pent-up aggression comes out in long-knife ambushes at the 2 P.M. meeting.

Regardless, if you come from the working class, you haven't got a clue how to conduct yourself when you first land in an office. You're lost if you can't navigate the landscape—if you follow blue-collar mores and speak your mind, directly challenging authority. Without tact and subtlety, without the ability to practice politics amongst the cubicles, an executive with a blue-collar background will not rise. And it's a drag watching others get promoted over you.

Language, too, is a sticking point—both what you say and how you say it. If the work environment is particularly sterile, cold, distant, and austere, then anything more than a mild giggle at a tasteful joke will raise eyebrows. And it's no secret that on-the-rise types solicit help from speech experts to bury Southern accents, Brooklyn accents, and any other perceived verbal barbarisms that would offend the ears of a genteel corporate listener. Along with sound, the right picture is imperative. Clothes, then, become vital for the proper office portrait. Straddlers swathed in polyester from birth, or simply unacquainted with the standard-issue Brooks Brothers uniform, report being taken aside by higher-ups and literally told how to dress.

Of course, if people completely give themselves over to this new culture—"improve" to the point of no longer being able to see, hear, or recognize themselves—then they risk kicking off those 3 A.M., "Who am I?," down-spiraling identity crises.

What's a Straddler to do? In the quaintly symbolic vocabulary of psychologists, blue-collar folk have to think of themselves as angular shapes trying to fit into spherical holes. Just shave off the edges, keep your core, and you'll do fine. Maybe.

Here's the dilemma: You come from a culture in which the boss is the common enemy and you're expected to be loyal only to your fellow workers. People are not trying to work their way up to own the plumbing supply outfit in which they sweat. It's noble enough to hang in there and knock out those rent payments. Meanwhile, you go to college, then find yourself embarking on a white-collar career, where you are required to pledge allegiance to the firm, not to your coworkers. And success is measured not by the secure stasis and comfortable consistency your parents struggled for, but by constant movement upward, spurred by a class-taught, sleep-robbing dissatisfaction with your current spot on the corporate organizational chart. Stop climbing and you die. Which reminds me, because middle-class life can include frequent relocation ("We need you in Omaha yesterday, Don"), that creates still more problems for workers from blue-collar backgrounds, who traditionally live closer to extended family and feel a cultural obligation to remain nearer the clan. Oh, and by the way, to facilitate this grand journey, you might well have to shmooze a boss and kiss a fanny or two, anathema to your working-class forebears.

Okay, now try resolving all that.

Not everyone can. Myself, I've gotten into trouble by opening my mouth when I shouldn't have and speaking out when silence was the smart, middle-class alternative. Especially in the early days of my career, there was no such thing as an unexpressed thought. I believed it was more honest that way, more manly. If the boss is wrong, you tell him. You think the assignment is stupid or the editing bizarre? Just say it. That's what my father would have done. Growing up, blue-collar types have no reason not to speak their minds; there's nothing to lose when you're on the bottom. We tell you what we feel rather than what you want to hear.

As Signe Kastberg, the Ithaca counselor and Straddler says, blue-collar people value the direct and honest approach. "I am," she tells me, "unable to be tactful. I cannot waste time figuring out 95 ways to say something that can be expressed in three blunt words. And I know that in some environments, that's not appreciated."

The blue-collar-born are committing faux pas left and right in the middle-class workplace, a panoply of mortal and venial sins of comportment, notes Laurene Finley, the psychologist who makes a specialty of treating people with working-class backgrounds. Meantime, people born in middle-class homes, who attended middle-class colleges, are making the relatively easy transition into the middle-class workplace.

"But when you don't know the politics of a place, you can get slam-dunked," Finley says. Rife with enough difficulties, the office can be that much harder for a person who finds him- or herself tripping over the language and the furniture. Many may actually be ashamed of their backgrounds and try to hide the facts. Frustrated, working-class types sometimes make the mistake of hurling four-letter epithets at colleagues or even getting physical, as they resort to survival tactics from the old neighborhood when they feel threatened. "I've treated people who got directly into colleagues' faces, challenging them. They didn't fit into the culture at all. But nobody ever helped them belong." Needless to say, such folk are soon branded irritant, problem employees, and it isn't too long before bosses are "keeping paper on them"—compiling documentation in support of dismissal. Lots of people get lost, and corporate structure is not accommodating to those who are different. "I know many folks with talent who'll never make it in those circumstances," Finley concludes.

A sad friend of mine used to point out all her bosses' mistakes and found it hard to smile and give them what they wanted. "It may sound like I was being true to myself, but really, it was very self-defeating," she concludes. White-collar colleagues, she says, understand that the key to success is getting along with people. But she was raised on stories of the rotten foreman whom her father stood up to and threatened. She says her dad was a hero to his guys because he didn't take bull. But in the world she lives in now, you have to learn to get around the bull somehow. You can't keep calling the boss a jerk.

Over the years, I've tried to improve my own manner, with marginal success. Now I say things like, "With all due respect . . . ," before I tell a boss I think he's wrong. I try not to be hostile. But I've got a glass head and I can't always hide my feelings, which stage three-act plays for everyone to see. I once told an editor, "With all due respect, I think that's a really bad idea." The man glared and was barely civil to me until he left the paper a year later. Not long after, my blue-collar persona shoved my white-collar self into a corner in a meeting with a top editor. I had challenged the guy, risking months of my work being thrown out and the real possibility of a permanent blackballing. Before doing the story, an examination of bad medical practices, I had elicited a promise from the editor that my wife's name would go on the bottom as a contributor. I wasn't trying to blow kisses to my honey. It's standard practice to include the name of a reporter who's helped substantively, and no financial compensation is involved. Linda, a freelance medical writer for MSNBC.com, Reuters.com, and the *New York Times*, didn't work for the newspaper but had given me numerous sources, in some cases calming skittish doctors who would never have talked to me if she hadn't intervened. Her involvement cut 30 days off the reporting process. Months before the meeting, before any reporting had been done on the story, I explained all this to the boss, a white-collar son of a white-collar dad, and asked his permission. He'd said it would be okay to publish Linda's name in the small print at the end of the story, giving her proper credit.

Suddenly, on the eve of publication, he was reneging. No explanation, really. He was just The Man and that was that. The five other editors in the room stayed mum and studied carpet patterns. But I had to show loyalty to my wife and coworker, in true working-class fashion, didn't I? Most white-collar guys in this situation would have finessed it, maybe met the editor afterward for a private chat. They certainly would not have challenged the big cheese in front of his own cabinet. "We had a deal," I told him candidly. "It was a promise you made. I wouldn't have done the story if you hadn't agreed to her tag line." As I spoke, I could feel my non–poker face register intensifying phases of red: fire truck, white guy yelling at a cop, lobster boiling. There was a loud noise in my head drowning out his equivocations, his smoothings. Brooklyn rose hot in my belly and I felt a righteous blue-collar fury erupting. Just then, my father's suggestion about grabbing my old boss seemed appropriate, almost justified. I didn't move, though. And the white-collar guy inside suddenly lunged for the controls, struggling to keep me employed and manfully preventing personal attacks and curses. "I guess we're at an impasse," I said. I'd decided I would remove my name from the story—a bald challenge to the boss, and tantamount to killing the work. No paper would print such a sensitive story without a byline, and the entire project would have been denigrated as a waste of time and money. As the room began to freeze over with tension, another editor piped up that maybe it wouldn't be so bad to have my wife's name at the bottom of the story. The big man saw a face-saving way out and relented. He also didn't talk to me for a long time. Needless to say, I never got any merit raises from the guy.

Let loose in shirt-and-tie America, the white-collar offspring of blue-collar parents report lots of self-inflicted career wounds. Maybe they try hard to fit in; maybe they don't try at all. Regardless, often enough, their true natures burble forth, and the authenticity isn't always appreciated.

My father-in-law tells me that's the way it's been for him. A tough-guy Irish brawler from Boston, who could throw punches with the best of them, Bob Carroll is a working-class intellectual and sculptor who uses wood to create enigmatic figures and faces. (The first time we met, he told me about how his pals used to beat up Italians in their own neighborhoods. I wasn't sure how to take that.) When my wife was born, he was a blue-collar man with a love of books and a passion for liberal politics, working 70-hour weeks on a Massachusetts assembly line. By the time Linda got to Smith College, Bob himself had graduated from Harvard, after nine years of night classes packed into soul-sapping workdays. Sometimes my mother-in-law, Dixie, would sit in on classes at the school with him, and she'd often type his papers. To participate, though, she had to overcome her childhood antipathy toward Harvard folk. Bored undergraduates used to heat pennies in their dorm rooms, then throw them out the windows. The misbehaving plutocrat progeny would cackle as working-class Cambridge townies like Dixie burned their fingers picking up the needed money. For Bob to progress, she figured, it was worth letting go of the anger. Even Bob's father could boast a Harvard connection; he liked telling people he'd been in all the campus buildings. Then he'd pause and explain he'd painted the interiors of many of them. The degree moved Bob up in his career. Within a few years, he headed west with Dixie and Linda's much younger brothers. He became an executive at a major corporation. While Linda grew up in blue-collar Boston, her brothers came of age in a white-collar household in conservative Arizona. The boys weren't working class like Linda, and their politics suggested more Goldwater than Kennedy.

Still, Bob, now 67, retained that street bravado in his company's hushed hallways. "In the corporate world, I was obnoxious and independent and it hurt my career," he says. "Some people were afraid of me. I don't know why." Well, I could guess. He's got a gruff voice, thick shoulders, and Popeye arms, one of which has "Dixie" tattooed on it. The man used to swim miles-long laps in the icy Atlantic. He became accustomed to fighting against the tide. He also learned that impinging just a bit into a colleague's personal space—a blue-collar trick—could give him the intimidating edge he might need in a one-on-one interaction. Once, when

Linda took a summer job in one of Bob's firms, a middle-class slob pinched her behind. She told her father, and he, in turn, went true blue. To this day, Bob won't reveal what he said to the man. But the pincher wouldn't come within 100 feet of Linda afterward and would hit the stairs whenever he found himself on the same floor as her. I can only imagine the murmured threat—"If you ever touch her again . . ."—delivered, breathy and close, in that impossible Boston accent, rendered all the more ominous by Bob's low growl. It's how a blue-collar man handles his business. I love this guy.

"I could never bring myself to be nice," Bob tells me. "I used to scream back at any boss who yelled. A bourgeois puts his tail between his legs when someone takes him to task. But I confronted. All through my working career, I had this problem with obedience and authority. To make it in the business world, you have to sell your soul, take on a persona that's not you in order to advance. Sell too much of yourself after a while, and there's nothing left. I don't like most white-collar workers. They have no personality left. They give it up to fit in, and they stay bourgeois right down the line."

To Straddlers, many white-collar colleagues seem, well, pale, pasty, and tame. It's their environment that makes them so. Ultimately, a Straddler confides in me, the middle-class workplace pumps cowardice into your veins. As a matter of fact, corporate culture does seem indirect and wimpish, says Dana Gioia, Bush's NEA man and a former vice president of General Foods. Lying, backtracking, and beating around the bush—all the normal stuff of white-collar work life—become unbearable to the blue-collar-born in the office. When corporate shrinks looked inside Dana's head as part of an executive-development program, they reported that he fits the typical CEO profile in every way but one—his attitude toward his career. He'd always say he had a job, not a career. "My profile was exactly like that of a blue-collar worker."

Dana was amazed that being the best at something isn't necessarily how you're judged in the business world. What's more important is how you fit in and get along. A scholarship boy, Dana understood that school was a meritocracy where top people were recognized. It was like sports—everyone knows who can throw the hardest or run the fastest.

Those kinds of distinctions, however, evaporate in carpeted corporate corridors, where no one hears who's sneaking up on them. "To rise in the world, I thought you had to be an alpha type—competitive, self-disciplined. It surprises a lot of us blue-collar men to see how you have to hide strengths like that in the corporation. In the white-collar realm, so much of your success is how you're perceived as a team player. And you can see corporations that suffered severely by lack of alphas' combative energies: Xerox, Procter & Gamble, for example. They were created almost like universities. Everything done the P&G way had lower growth rates. They had to acquire growth because they couldn't generate it." A clear case of a dearth of alphas, according to Dana.

What bothered him most about the corporate America he saw was the waste. That can bug a blue-collar guy—seeing a company spend millions on a project everyone knew was truly doomed, but was kept alive because it had a political champion in the company. It offended his blue-collar sensibility to watch money be spent because of folly and lack of gumption. The make-your-own-soda fiasco was a great example.

General Foods was exploring an in-home carbonation system—a powder mixed with water that could theoretically allow the consumer to create pop in the kitchen. The only problem was that, no matter how hard the chemists tried, it always came out tasting like Alka Seltzer. They could never defeat the salty taste. But somebody near the top loved the idea, and it kept getting presented and re-presented as the method that would reconfigure the soft-drink market within five years. Anybody in the company who understood that market knew the in-home carbonation deal had no real chance to succeed. They had, after all, tasted the stuff. Yet management loved the idea, and the white-collar way is to please the bosses, no matter what. It was funded because someone at the top liked it, but he was never presented with the truth that it would never work. "More than once I got in trouble because I said the obvious truth in a situation that was deemed politically inappropriate. I said it just looked good as something to be done. But it could never actually be done," says Dana.

Other projects worked that way. Teams would meet with the company honchos and present an idea that cost $250,000 just to start, even though all of the executives but the boss knew that the concept would fail for an indisputable reason. And every last college-educated one of them would be mum about it. "Look," Dana says, "I was happy to give deference to authority. But I hated the idea of wasting more money than my father ever made in his lifetime on a project we knew wouldn't work."

Straddlers tell me they play a game: Walk into the white-collar workplace and wonder how their parents might handle the atmosphere on any given day. I've done that. I laughed when I thought about a bricklayer like my father just dealing with the talk, talk, talk—the endless chatter about abstract things. What are we gonna do? How are we gonna do it? What's the budget? What's the target date? Meetings upon meetings would be called for things that working-class guys would simply pick up and do. And are meetings really work, anyway? I've sat in a few thinking my father would be astonished to see a man making money on his butt like this, with doughnuts in proximity. Many Straddlers held full-time, blue-collar jobs before, during, and after college. That, they remember, was true labor. How can meetings ever be considered work?

"Can you imagine Grandpa in a corporate team-building class?" my brother asked me one day. There'd be someone talking about how critical it is to lay brick. Someone else would weigh the pros and cons of using a big trowel versus a small one. Then we'd hear more talk about the need for a good bricklaying team and the importance of a strong relationship between bricklayers and the laborers who mix their mortar. Meanwhile, no walls would go up. Charles Sackrey talks about a class-related study at Cornell as long ago as the 1950s in which a group of students with a working-class background and a group of professors' children who were also students were assigned the same task. The working-class kids picked a leader, then dove in and did the job. The white-collar kids ended up arguing about principles and aims, and accomplished nothing.

One Straddler tells me he can't believe the stuff that comes out of his mouth during interminable meetings among the creased-pants set—especially meetings in which there's a slight conflict in approaches, and he's trying to maintain control: "That's an important point you make. . . . We can't lose sight of how this will affect the stakeholders. . . . I think we can incorporate your thinking into the final report, but I would like to focus us on what I believe is a key issue. . . . If I may, perhaps I can redirect our meeting just a bit to cover some of these key points. . . ." Actually, the Straddler says, what he'd really like to say is, "Get off my back, you moron. I'd like to slap your head with a two-by-four but it would be an insult to the wood."

Straddlers report a communication gap between themselves and colleagues born to the middle class. "The man I first worked for," says Chicago businesswoman Mary Lou Finn, "I couldn't relate to him. Why can't I understand him? I wondered." Then she read her uncle Patrick Finn's book (*Literacy with an Attitude*), with the business about how the middle class and working class speak in different tongues. "I can't understand any person who isn't direct, and that boss wasn't." Mary Lou always wanted to come to a definitive conclusion in conversations, whereas her boss didn't see things in such stark, black-and-white terms. Beyond the language barrier, there was that confidence thing, the middle-class assuredness demonstrated by even junior staff, whose parents were second- or third-generation white collar. "They always assumed they were going to do a good job. I couldn't."

Peter Giangiulio, the Pennsylvania attorney cum horse breeder, prefers his one-man law practice—based in a barn office on his property—because he knows he can trust all of the personnel. That wasn't necessarily the case in prior working situations. He was never comfortable that he was being told the whole story in a white-collar environment. You have to take the little bit someone says and try to glean meaning out of it. It would help if you could be a mind reader, he says. "There's just a huge cultural difference, and it magnifies my insecurity. That's why I like a one-man shop."

The blue-collar world is built on tangibles, not symbols, as the middle-class world is. In blue-collar work, you can study a wall you have put up, two pipes you've connected, or even a box you've moved, and there is no question about whether the task is done. But in the white-collar world, you can expend a huge amount of effort to create something that you believe is right, something that should speak for itself, but ultimately has no meaning if others say it should have no meaning. Trees don't fall in middle-class woods unless some white-collar manager points out the downed lumber. In the inexactness of white-collar work life, a person has to deal with imprecise instructions, shifting paradigms, byzantine politics, and hidden agendas. And when the job is done, the work isn't. A blue-collar woman rearranges the stock in a warehouse and, boom, it's finished. A white-collar woman has to present a report, then justify it, sell it, and resell it to bosses who must decide whether the work is complete. The work doesn't always speak for itself. You need to speak for the work and explain its existence—brag about it—even if it's what some boss told you to do in the first place and then forgot. Lots of blue-collar people are taught as kids that boasting and self-promotion and credit hogging are wrong and unseemly; but that's precisely what's needed to succeed in the office, as long as it's deftly and subtly done. Got that? Good. I never have.

Not the Priest

Learning the white-collar way takes time. And obviously, lots of Straddlers figure out how to do it. That's a matter of survival. Oh, but the mistakes we make along the road to enlightenment! "It would have been better for business if I were more business-like," confesses Veronica De Vivar, the Sacramento pharmaceutical saleswoman who started out working in a tortilla factory with her Mexican immigrant father. "I shouldn't wear my feelings on my sleeve. I actually told people what I really thought when they asked for my opinion. My boss once told me, 'Veronica, if I ask you a question, think twice before you answer, because I'm not your priest.' I'm very honest and people can't believe I've said the things I have in front of others."

Mo Wortman, the Rochester gynecologic surgeon, demonstrated a similar blue-collar lack of restraint that nearly got him kicked out of his profession. He was once asked to resign from an ob-gyn department because he'd been arrogantly honest to all the department chiefs. "I was an academic bully," he explains. "I believed I was the smartest, and I learned from growing up that the solution to the problem belonged only to the smartest." Mo didn't develop the white-collar know-how of consensus building. "I was always going to win alone. Meanwhile, I would have been the first to be voted off the island, every time. I was young."

Brash youth combined with working-class pugnacity almost lost Nick Artim his job when he inadvertently took on one of the most powerful men in the United States. And he would never have become the fire safety engineer for the U.S. Capitol, a job he held for several years until he set up shop as a fire safety consultant based in Vermont. Beyond that, Nick would have missed out on what he calls his "moment of class," a great yarn to tell the grandkids someday.

The son of a Chrysler autoworker and a homemaker from Syracuse,

Nick, 46, grew up wanting to be a firefighter in his hometown. It was the excitement—doing the work of heroes and saving burning chunks of the world—that drew him. Killing time while waiting to be hired, he earned an engineering degree at the University of Maryland. At the same time, he worked as a firefighter in the suburbs near his college. Called to blaze after blaze, Nick knew firsthand the sick-stomach feel of a job gone wrong. One night, the alarm summoned him and his crew into action, the call radio crackling out a calamity and its address. Nick reminded himself to breathe evenly as the wailing truck rolled toward who knows what. (Ask a firefighter what he thinks about on his way to possible death, as I often have, and he will unfailingly tell you about the safety checklist of things his training compels him to consider. That's all. Writers sent to fires would contemplate fate, destiny, and what a man owes himself versus his society. He will consider his all-too-burnable flesh and feel his hot cheek and contemplate what his lungs might look like 20 minutes into the smoke. That is why they don't send writers to fires.)

Nick raced into the blazing building, looking in the thick haze for people to save. As he climbed to the second floor, the disintegrating stairway collapsed beneath him. First there was something solid, then only scorched air and that awful dream sensation of falling. Except this was no dream. In a flash, the rescuer needed rescue, as Nick fell in a pile of splintering, burning wood. He thought he'd die that night. But Nick escaped that and a few other scrapes without serious injury and finally decided there might be other work for a college-educated person in this life.

The blue-collar man wriggled out of his working-class uniform and took a job in Washington as an engineer charged with protecting the Capitol and congressional offices, the Library of Congress, and the U.S. Supreme Court. For the first time, Nick was working with white-collar types. But not just your average middle-class climbers. These were, he remembers, hyper-repellent lawyers/staffers who served senators and representatives. Already entitled by dint of their birth into the middle and upper classes, he thought, many of these guys were even more inflated from the hot air of the politicians who paid them. They were hard to deal with, and Nick much preferred the company of the Capitol Hill electricians, carpenters, and plumbers, whose Christmas kegger parties in the plumbers' shop always attracted the really pretty secretaries from Congress.

140

Nick's job back then was to get smoke alarms and sprinklers into their offices. "We don't want sprinklers," staff people would whine. They didn't like the interruption, they didn't want to be bothered, they were too busy running the nation, blah, blah, blah. Used to rough-boy camaraderie and smart-mouth retorts from living with firefighters on 24-hour shifts, Nick had not yet developed the middle-class tact muscle. Men in blue-collar bunches play the dozens, bust chops, and hurl curse-wrapped insults—essentially, they verbally whack each other in sometimes funny, but rarely subtle, swipes that rip at all the sensitive spots: manhood, mothers, and sexuality. This was not the background one should draw on to suddenly negotiate with the bratty elite. But it's all Nick knew, and he slapped down the golden boys who were too busy to burn in a fire with corner-boy vigor, and he let them know what's what.

"Who the hell do you think you are?" Nick, just 24, started out the conversation. "You're only here temporarily. My job is to protect these buildings. They've got to be here long after you're gone."

No American icon would incinerate on Nick Artim's watch. And no pampered suburban kid with a fancy diploma—which, Nick knew, burns at Farenheit 451, same as everything else—was going to push around the autoworker's son. The sprinklers and smoke alarms went in.

So this was the job; this was the attitude. Then came the day in 1980 that Nick; his boss, the engineering director; and a few others were installing a fire-detection system in the Supreme Court building. Some architects were there, along with a few mechanical engineers and a handful of building managers. The room was crowded. At some point, one of the men started asking questions about smoke detectors. Then, echoing one of those dim-bulb young staffers, the guy said, "I'm not going to let you put a smoke detector in my office."

Red light. Curt, naive, blue-collar Nick stared the man down and, weary of the same rebuff day after day, raised his voice and said, "You know, what this place needs is a good, old-fashioned barn burner. Then you'll see why you need detectors."

Nick's boss shot him a wild-eyed, panicked look that said *you just ended your career and maybe mine, too.* The room went as silent as the law library stacks Nick now believed he'd no longer have the opportunity to protect.

"Okay," Nick remembers the guy—Chief Justice Warren Burger—

saying. "I think you made your point." Then he started to chuckle, and he invited Nick into his office to install the detector himself.

"That was an 'Oh, shit,' moment," Nick says today. "But Burger was surprised. He was so used to having his backside kissed and, in some respect, I know he appreciated the honesty of the statement. It was certainly a defining moment in tact." Nick didn't get fired and would go on to run the office that oversaw fire safety at the Capitol. "I learned how to be more cautious among the powerful after that," says Nick. "And I never forgot my moment of class."

A Little Help

We blue collars grew up understanding at an early age that it's who you know. That was no big secret, really. That was the working-class lament, after all, and after a particularly difficult day of chances squandered or opportunities lost, we'd recite the mantra of the powerless to one another: "Whaddya gonna do? It's who you know." And we didn't know anybody. Oh, once in a while, somebody said they knew a guy who knew a guy who might be able to help. But that fragile connection always frayed; that can't-miss person never came through. I called it the "head-whack rule." As soon as you picked your head up a little bit and stood up to take a shot, something unbidden and unforeseen would slam you with a skull rattling that forced you to sit down and wait for the ringing to end. God doesn't close one door without slamming your fingers in another. Where was the rabbi, the angel, the helper? I did not understand the cultural-capital concept, the notion that aid and influence come with the middle-class territory.

Once, as a young reporter, Rita Giordano had the opportunity to send her clips to Frank Deford, the sportswriter and novelist. A friend worked with Deford's mother-in-law, who had passed on the information that he often read the work of young writers and offered help. Rita sent her stuff, and Deford wrote back that he liked it. Rather than use that acknowledgment as the basis for a beneficial relationship, however, Rita didn't take advantage of her position. "A white-collar kid would have had the confidence and direction from her parents to pursue this," Rita says. "But I was intimidated and didn't maintain the relationship."

Believing that you make your own luck in this life, I decided to take an extremely active approach in my own career launch. After journalism school, I started a campaign to work at the New York *Daily News.* The Caroline Kennedy thing was just a bad memory then, and I was willing to give the place another shot. It just seemed like the right fit for me at the time. Besides, the culture is rife with stories about the plucky nobody who pursues the powerful man to get the job of his dreams. Annoying at first, the job seeker eventually wears down the big shot and impresses him with his persistence. And wasn't persistence a valued trait in a reporter? Naive, unschooled, uncultured, and ignorant, I sent the editor samples of my work; I got the form rejection letter in return. Undaunted, I began writing unsolicited critiques of the paper, offering praise and criticism. Missive after missive went unanswered. I was ready for the third wave: I would simply show up unannounced and chat the guy up. Surely this is how it's done, I told myself, steeling my nerve and talking myself past the security guard and into the managing editor's outer office. This is how you meet the person who turns out to be "who you know." The editor's secretary, a blue-collar woman, was sympathetic to my efforts. She'd read all my clips, letters, and critiques and was rooting for me. "Wait here, I'll see if he'll talk to you," she told me with a smile. Within seconds, I heard the man screaming. It went beyond anger. It was almost a sort of . . . anguish. "Tell him to get out!" I heard him say with a discernible whine in his voice. "No more letters, no more visits. Just get him out of here!" No longer a job seeker, I was now a stalker, an intruder into a man's life. Clumsy and uncouth, I'd gone about it all wrong, and wound up alienating the one person in life I had wanted to impress. "Oh, yeah," I told myself in rueful irony on the F train ride home, "he knows who you are now."

My ignorance continued well into my career. Class-hobbled and unable to understand office politics at all, I didn't realize that doing a job well is no guarantee of advancement and opportunity. There are ways to get ahead that have nothing to do with hard work. But blue-collar people are taught that that's a person's only currency—you sell your labor and give the boss an honest eight hours. I knew an enterprising upper-middle-class guy at a Midwestern newspaper who used his food-writing gig to ameliorate his lucky life. When a new editor came to the paper, he threw the man a dinner party in his own home. Then he charged the cost of the food to the paper. When a hot and influential new columnist was hired, the food man showed up at the writer's house with expensive dope and rolled a few fat joints. When the editor he'd feted at dinner ultimately was deposed, the ingratiating climber took the replacement editor out golfing. I watched in wonder as this approach actually bore fruit, with food boy receiving favors, raises, better assignments, and goodies galore. Sucking up works!

Paul Groncki, who worked for big-time Wall Street institutions like JP Morgan and others, says he often felt that colleagues who were not as smart or as diligent at the job seemed to find it easier to progress. "You can't figure it out. Why is that person getting promoted when we all know he can't even do the job he's doing now? Then you look at their behavior and you see there's something going on that you really don't want to mimic: their total obeisance to everybody above them, right or wrong. I was never afraid to disagree with people, because as a blue-collar guy, I didn't want to be the yes-person. Unfortunately, that's how corporate culture is built—on yes-men."

Along with blatant kissing up, networking and socializing with bosses and colleagues also are dirty words to some Straddlers. It all smacks of phoniness and is antithetical to their blue-collar backgrounds, which emphasize honesty in human relations—"real" relationships. Class-aware Barbara Jensen, the Minnesota psychologist, says she believes that some blue-collar people do network each other. But it's fairly low-key stuff, like one drywall guy asking another if he's heard of any jobs. It's colleagues asking colleagues; nobody crosses any peer lines to hunt down opportunities. Among the working class, there is a belief—a naive one, some say—that you should make it in this world on merit alone. "In my world, you have to prove yourself," says Samme Chittum. "I believe you have to earn everything and am therefore not good at playing games that allow you to get ahead. I don't shmooze well and I really resist it. But that's how the world runs."

Blue-collar thinking goes like this: Networking is making friends with people because they can offer you something valuable. It's therefore not a real relationship, since you're using people. "Networking is a dirty word in the blue-collar world," Signe Kastberg insists. "It says I'm taking advantage of others." Networking attempts can seem forced and unnatural to some Straddlers, one of whom tells me she had an awful physical reaction the one time she broke down and attended a company seminar on how to chat someone up for future work. She literally became nauseous. Others say that while networking doesn't sicken them, it simply doesn't feel right.

"In the last 40 years," says retired academic Patrick Finn, "I've had a business lunch maybe 10 times. I just don't do that. My [white-collar-born] wife, meanwhile, never lets a day pass without eating with people she's networking. I retired as an associate professor. I didn't have the heart to go after a full professorship. And that's because I didn't want to have lunch with people. That's a very working-class attitude. I'm not comfortable with people with power. I've always been intimidated by people like deans. I let them push me until I come back too strong and ruin the relationship. Now, the middle class doesn't see it that way. It's just networking, what's wrong with that? But the working class sees it as highly hypocritical." Charles Sackrey says he's proud that he's managed to pretty much stay clear of the elitist faculty eating club on the Bucknell campus. Did he ever network or curry favor? He was lucky he had tenure for all his working-class posturing. "Personally speaking, people below me in social class, I treat with respect. Everyone above me, it's a freaking war. Provosts were offended when I called them 'boss.' I just presume they're the enemy."

Along with networking, golfing with the boss and other colleagues is a basic way to get ahead in some firms. Cliched, but true. Long-term relationships are built in the short-cut grass; it's big-boy, big-girl bonding, and futures rise and fall during chats on the unnaturally green landscapes. But tee times impinge on hours with family and real friends, limbo folk say. John Garcia, a mid-40s executive with NBC News in New York City, realizes he's not like everyone else who's moved up the food chain. Partly that's because he's Latino; partly it's because he's from blue-collar stock. It can be hard to handle sometimes. "Look, you gotta be smart to manage yourself in the 'hood, where I came from," says John, a product of the projects of Manhattan's Lower East Side. "But as smart as I am, I'm not smart enough to navigate through the corporate culture sometimes. The pressing the flesh, the hanging out— well, I don't play golf. And getting on the golf course and laughing at the boss's jokes, it's just not real. It's a fallacy." John says such occasions are not social situations, they're business meetings. And a working-class guy puts on his play clothes to spend time outside the office with his friends, not his boss. "I'm always on guard in these situations and that makes me uncomfortable." Then there's his working-class tendency to speak matter-of-factly. "And in corporate America, you can't speak honestly like [in] blue-collar culture. It gets you in too much trouble." To protect himself, John says he opts out of golf outings altogether. "And I pay a price for it. I'm fully aware I don't advance as quickly as other people."

Forced socializing with bosses and colleagues is such an intrusion into Straddlers' lives. They react in horror when they hear that a couple must invite so-and-so to their wedding because he does big-volume business with the bride's father. Myself, I generally avoid the company picnics and wingdings, allergic to the false gaiety. I realize that middle-class people may not like these situations, either. But through lessons and examples they gleaned from their parents, they understand that such gatherings can help a career and are more willing to go along with it all. Some Straddlers decide that the career benefits they could reap by drinking and playing games with colleagues and higher-ups aren't worth what I call the "Nathaniel West feeling": It's from West's *Miss Lonelyhearts*, in which a man having sex with the wrong person says it makes him feel like a vessel being slowly filled with warm, dirty water. Who wants that inside? As Amy Reed, a 45-year-old Cleveland marketing manager says, "I just feel extremely uncomfortable at these work-related social activities. So, what, after a long day of work, we're all going to bowl together? It seems so odd." One Straddler's Seattle law firm asked him to make more of an effort to meet lawyers from other firms socially, and to join clubs and societies in which he would run into these folks and perhaps collect referrals. "I'd rather hike with my kid," he tells them. It does not endear him to the partners.

In corporate America, an employee's private house becomes an extension of the office, something that rarely happens in the blue-collar world. Spouses are dragooned into service as ancillary workers. Now, it's a middle-class, home-team effort to help Biff or Marie capture that credenza-ed office at Amalgamated Whatever. Barriers between career and social life blur. I first was exposed to this on television (where else?), watching *Bewitched* as a kid. Darren would always bring boss Larry Tate home, along with a client whom wife Samantha was expected to impress with her cooking and her polished domesticity. It was an experience completely out of my range of understanding. Cook a roast, seal a deal? It's certainly not the way our moms and dads did it.

Lots of blue-collar people I know tell me that after Dad and/or Mom dragged themselves back from the factory, plant, or construction site, the drawbridge went up, the doors were locked, and the outside world remained that way. The working class has so little in life; whatever they've got, they keep separate, sacred, and secret. It would be colossally unimaginable for a UPS delivery driver to call the missus from the hub office and tell her to put another plate out for the guy in charge of Midwest shipping, whom he was bringing home. Nor would the boss host the driver. Precisely because of their backgrounds, Straddlers say they find it distasteful in the extreme to invite people they don't like or trust into their dining rooms and kitchens for a bit of work-related conviviality. In working-class culture, anyone who eats at the table is part of the tribe. Strangers—superiors from work especially—have no place there. None. "I only want people over I like," says working-class studies academic Michelle Tokarczyk, "and I don't use my home to promote my career."

Only relatives came to our house, and, in turn, we visited theirs. Mostly we didn't have dinner with members of the extended family, except on holidays and the occasional Sunday at Grandma's. Even a garden-variety, Friday-night dinner party was just too dear for working-class budgets. My parents would visit after supper, bringing a box of bakery cake—babkas or Danish. The relative whose house it was would make coffee. And that was it.

Unfriendly Territory

Some limbo folk in elite jobs complain that they can never get used to the altitude. Or the company they must now keep up in rarefied air. Even with familiarity, class chasms somehow widen rather than contract, and different-collared people in adjoining offices can barely work together, let alone get on civilly. Everything that's different about them—upbringing, quality of education, family wealth or the lack, personal style—intensifies in close quarters. Ostracized or at least ignored, a few Straddlers can recall some truly uncomfortable workdays. "White-collar people use you," a particularly embittered suburban

Chicago Straddler laments, "until you have nothing left to give. Then you're gone from the company. Good guys get burned."

Philadelphia-born Anthony Lukas says his town is particularly class conscious, dating back to the days of the blue bloods of Main Line society. While that world is much diluted now, Anthony still believes Philadelphia is a more class-conscious city than New York, which he says is more about performance than parents. "I worked my way up and out of working-class Philly, but will I ever be accepted by the blue bloods and invited to join the Union League? Highly doubtful." Apropos of that, Straddler Sal Paolantonio, an on-air ESPN correspondent, tells me that when he worked at my newspaper, the *Philadelphia Inquirer*, in the 1980s, it was still unusual to see blue-collar-born Italian guys on staff. "S.A. Paolantonio," a man who no longer works at the paper said to him when they first met. "That's a name that belongs on the side of a cement truck, not in a newspaper."

During college summers, my colleague Rita Giordano worked as a secretary in a New York publishing house. Other college kids worked there as well, but they were middle-class men and women on paid internships secured by their educated, connected parents. Oblivious and unable to truly see Rita, the boys and girls barely spoke with her. "I had much more in common with these kids than I did with the other secretaries. Those women used to always talk about engagement rings and shopping, and I just wasn't into that stuff." Lunch was the most difficult time. The interns in their crisp cottons and soft linens would float by Rita's desk on their way to salads nicoise. Each day she waited for one of them to look her way, to turn an expensively coiffed head toward the secretary with the high GPA and a writing talent any one of them would have burned for, and say, "Hey, want to join us?" But weeks would go by—summers would go by—without an invitation being proffered. "They never asked me once," says Rita, surprised herself that she's still nursing a class-inflicted wound. "That's how people are in an office. They treat the secretaries, the mail-room guys, the cleaning people, and the security people differently than the executives." It's a cold, distant politeness. Nobody is being rude, but nobody is connecting, either. "I spent my lunches going to the park," she says. "It was like the movie *Gosford Park*, with the servants and the masters in separate wings of the estate. In that office, no matter where I sat, I was always on the other side of the house. And I was very happy when the summers were over."

148

For the most part, the class gap between Straddlers and the entrenched middle class in any workplace is not overt. Few Straddlers tell me they are openly shunned by the congenitally white collar. Many people don't even know their colleagues' backgrounds, and they could not care less. Often enough, middle-class colleagues assume that you're just like them, that you view life the same way, and that you've enjoyed a similar background. But because Straddlers have journeyed from the working class, they are in a distinct position to notice what the middle class may not recognize: its class-bestowed privileges.

In a sense, limbo folk in white-collar America feel like a basketball team that's perpetually on the road, never playing before the home crowd and always dribbling on someone else's court. What's more, they have to adhere to unfamiliar rules and generally play the game in a way no one explained before. With time, quite a few can handle it, difficult as it is. Some, however, never find the rhythm. Stressed and uncomfortable, they trek endlessly through unfriendly territory, always uneasy and unsettled.

That's how it's been for "Donna," who grew up in a trailer park and now works for a national magazine. She asked me to change her name; in exchange, she offers some unvarnished talk about her workplace. Understanding that she won't ever relax on the job, Donna vows not to be defeated. "It's very difficult to work in a WASP-dominated culture," she says. "I don't know the rules and I survive by sheer will. And I will not let them stomp me." Her bosses are from a genteel set, and they assume the rest of the staff is like them. Many of them belong to fancy clubs and live patrician lives. Even the secretaries are middle class born and are graduates of excellent colleges. They work there because of the prestige. "It's a nice holding spot until they marry lawyers," Donna asserts. So many of her coworkers don't need the magazine salary to survive; they possess deep resources. (In Columbus, I worked with a well-to-do gossip columnist who kept confounding the accounting department by forgetting to cash her paychecks. Once the blue collars learned this, they couldn't let it go. The woman would wear up-turned collars a lot; men wearing ties started aping her fashion, turning their shirt collars up in mock solidarity with the rich woman. She didn't appreciate it.) Personal style and comportment are the issues for Donna. White-collar people, she says, learned young how not to be confrontational and how to maneuver behind the scenes: "That's a gift from their parents." At work, she'll say what she wants, but never get it. She'll declare something is a good story and should be pursued, and they look at her and ask, "Who are you?" To get things done, she tells a sympathetic editor, who knows how the game is played. He maneuvers for her. Meantime, everything is cool surfaces and whispered talk. It does not suit. "I need the ridges and valleys. It's hard for someone like me to work in corporate America, which never wants the confrontation. They want it all nice and smooth."

For years, Donna has noted a singular difference between herself and her coworkers from the middle class: "If a blue-collar person like me gets to the top, she asks, 'How did I get here?' If a white-collar person gets there, he's all puffed up with that sense of entitlement they have. Blue-collar people are more self-effacing. These others are self-centered and have high opinions of themselves. Any success I have, it just never crossed my mind that it's something I deserved. But these people with their superior attitudes all believe they did something special to get there."

Needless to say, Donna does not socialize with her coworkers. She is one of those Straddlers who has a hard time hearing how colleagues are moving into $500,000 homes, thanks to hefty mom-and-dad down payments. She and her husband are among the few people they know who've earned all the money to buy on their block. Ironically, Donna says, she never even read the magazine growing up. "It's always been elitist," she says. As a result, she wasn't intimidated during the job interview. It was a different story, though, the first week on the job. "It was a shocker. I couldn't feel like I could buddy up and be part of the scene. Even now, after all these years, I feel uncomfortable."

Donna never found a mentor. She stood out too much among a staff of team players. Yet, she says, people move up at her place with the magical help of corporate shamans, glass-office wizards who nurture and grow careers of the people who ingratiate themselves. "The bosses have a protectorate of favorites—people they like to bring along." One of them was a friend who was candidly told he would not advance without changing his wardrobe. After dropping $2,000 at the local Brooks Brothers, his prospects opened up wide and clear. "His career turned around instantly," Donna says, still in shock. "He'd been a rebel, but he changed, and decided to play by their rules. And the rewards came."

The kind of class divide Donna sees in her magazine exists at others, especially the women's magazines, "the most white-collar profession there is," according to Straddler Andrea Todd. She and I speak in a blue-collar bar in Sacramento, not long after Andrea, 37, put 3,000 miles between herself and the hard, hard world of living and writing in New York City. Back in her hometown, Andrea is looking for work at newspapers, which she believes are more egalitarian than spots like *Mademoiselle, Ladies Home Journal, Sassy, GQ* (the only non–women's venue on her resume), *Seventeen, Tell,* and the other places in which she struggled for more than 10 years. With high cheekbones, light reddish hair, and a runner's taut, muscular body, Andrea exudes an enviable healthfulness. She didn't always look this fit. When I first met her years ago, she appeared beaten down, bullied, and frustrated by her struggle in the white-collar world.

Like a lot of writers, Andrea ventured to New York because that's where writers go. For people like Andrea, there was a romance to it and an excitement about being with other young people burning with the same fever to make it. What you don't hear about are the awful apartment choices, the crazy roommates, and New York's howling, ceaseless demand for money, especially if you're a working-class woman from California. Rent-food-utilities, rent-food-utilities—the staggering everydayness of sheer life-cost can detract from the writer's dream. Nonromantic, mundane needs outshout the muses. If it's a choice between reworking that difficult paragraph and trying to make extra money to get the heat turned back on, which do you think will occupy your time? And if it's been like this for year upon year, how long could you last? Unless, of course, you're a middle- or upper-class woman with a family of resources behind you. "After a while, I felt like my career was falling apart, and I just had no place in this smooth, lily-white-gloved world of women's magazines," Andrea confesses. "The girls who became editorial assistants, like I was at the start, weren't filthy rich, but the families all had summer houses. Everyone had vacationed all over the world by the time they were 10. Their parents knew Peter Jennings, or someone else in the media. You never heard talk about having to deal with financial aid in school, or paying off school loans. They could move to Manhattan and right away get apartments and pay rent without needing roommates."

Through the years, Andrea met a few women from the working

class at these magazines. But one by one, they all dropped away, unable to maintain their dreams on the notoriously low salaries paid editorial assistants, writers, and lower-level editors. Meanwhile, women from white-collar families were able to hang in there, even when they were making just $30,000 a year at their second and third jobs and living in one of the most expensive places on the planet. Andrea, though, had to sacrifice: She wouldn't have a phone installed, or she'd get work on the side, waitressing, tutoring, or doing legal proofreading. Her apartments were cramped and dingy. Bathtubs were in the kitchens; sofas served as beds. Deranged, tofu-eating roommates sucked her into vortices of lunacy. Meanwhile, these women she worked with stretched out in apartments that an aunt or their father owned. Real-estate brokers would not rent to Andrea sometimes, wary of her listed occupation of freelance writer. Though her credit was good, they'd insist on a cosigner. "Couldn't you ask your father?" they'd say. "Well, my dad was afraid of that language, unfamiliar with the situation. Cosigning for an $1,100 studio in New York City when you're a fireman in Sacramento? He's a blue-collar guy and just didn't have experience with this. I couldn't ask him. The idea of debt is frightening to blue-collar people."

Meantime, Andrea's coworkers enjoyed the kind of support that simply made their lives possible and helped them excel. She just wasn't able to compete. Because these women never had to worry about the things she did, it placed them on a whole different social level Andrea could never equal. And social life is tightly tied into magazine success—or, for that matter, just about any real success in the white-collar realm. Andrea couldn't afford the cocktails, the weekends in the Hamptons at some important writer's house, and the uptown restaurants where the impeccably dressed women celebrated their birthdays.

She soon understood that her style differed tremendously from that of her colleagues; it was a collar thing. These women could know from just looking at a guy what kind of shoes he wore, how expensive his watch was, or whether his suit was cheaply made. Andrea didn't grow up thinking about such things. In fact, Andrea's father never owned a suit. On special occasions, such as her graduations, he would make sure he was on duty those days, then sign out for an hour for the ceremony. That way, he was allowed to wear his formal firefighter's uniform in public. Andrea's mother explained that her father was embarrassed about his own clothes, but knew he'd get respect in the uniform.

The white-collar magazine women talked about their summers in camp. Camp? Andrea worked every summer for as long as she can remember, and when she was a girl, she babysat for her money. The women knew about obscure indie films and evolving bands performing at the Knitting Factory downtown. "How could I know this stuff? I was working all my life. And yet you get to New York from California and suddenly there's all these things going on in life that white-collar people seemed to care about." These women had been roomies in Seven Sisters or Ivy League schools; Andrea had graduated from Berkeley, underscoring her outlyer status. Unable to resist tearing at each other, the women would smile in each others' presence, then slice each other, Zorro-like, in private. They dished handbags, clothes, and boyfriends. And no one would dare show up anywhere without $75 Bumble and bumble haircuts. "This just wasn't the way I was brought up," Andrea says. "You don't spend that kind of money on hair. And you don't talk that way about your friends." Unused to snow, Andrea bought a sturdy pair of boots and wore them throughout a winter. Pretty soon, they were salt-whitened and scuffed. One writer snidely said, "Why don't you just get a new pair?"

"I'm not saying it crushed me," Andrea explains. "But there were always bits and pieces like that that made you feel you don't belong."

White-collar language, too, was something Andrea puzzled over. Used to unvarnished criticism from her folks when things were wrong, Andrea marveled at the circuitous machinations of bosses who need to flatter first before delivering the true message. "It's like they picked it up in some manual," she says. " 'Say something positive first, then criticize.' I have no patience for bosses who talk in circles. Just tell me what you want. I learned from these magazine people that I'm way too direct and can't deal with any bull." After she rose and became an editor, people would employ the same infuriating tactics when they attempted to network with her. They'd start the conversation with, "Oh, Andrea, you're so talented" or "Oh, Andrea, you always have the right answer." Andrea hates it and cuts through the nonsense: "Just tell me, what do you want?" she asks them. She can't believe that people who barely know her—people who aren't sure what city she's living in—will still e-mail and ask for favors. "White-collar phoniness," she says.

Many of her bosses could be as annoying as her coworkers—hypercritical, overly privileged, and less than honest. Andrea was shocked to learn how racist many educated people are. "We don't hire Jewish girls here," one magazine editor confided in her. "They're too smart to put up with our baloney. We want Catholic girls. They're pretty, neat, and compliant." This, spoken to a graduate of one of Sacramento's foremost Catholic high schools. "I don't know if that's racist, but if you substitute the words 'African American' and a few of the synonyms, I think you've got a legal problem." Another person she worked with hated Jews and would go on minutes-long anti-Semitic screeds, then kiss up to her Jewish superiors. Not as insidious—but no less loopy—teen-girl magazines without a minority staffer would write articles about the brave step of taking a black date to the prom. "I'll take blue-collar racism over educated rationalizations any day," says Andrea. "Magazine editors pretend to be horrified by events like Bensonhurst and then refuse to hire minorities. Blue-collar racism is at least honest."

When an editorial assistant first starts out, she is at the mercy of the editors. If an editor was from the middle class, she was used to people doing things for her and not uncomfortable with sending employees on bizarre, non-work-related errands, Andrea remembers. An editor at a top women's magazine would frequently dispatch Andrea to get her McDonald's french fries. Ah, but Andrea couldn't go to the restaurant near the office; she had to get in a cab or subway and motor across town to a particular McDonald's on the west side because they used the right amount of salt in the potato prep. No added salt after the cooking could fix the taste. It was these fries or nothing. This was nuts, Andrea thought.

It was this kind of thing—years of this kind of thing—that just wore her down. The class differences between Andrea and her colleagues started eating away her confidence. Any accomplishment by one of Andrea's coworkers, no matter how small—the successful publication of an article about what your shade of lipstick says about how sexy you are, for example—was cause for her middle-class parents to throw a small dinner party at an Upper East Side Italian restaurant. Andrea's family doesn't quite take such direct interest in her work. It's not of their world. Once, her father suggested she try to write something for the *New York Times*. By then, she'd already written a couple of pieces for them. "See, that's hard. The confidence these white-collar people have, from their parents, they just exude it. And I'm not sure of myself, and I'm thinking, 'My stuff isn't even interesting enough for my own parents to bother to read.' That has me constantly second-guessing myself."

To compensate for feeling like the perpetual outsider and for not advancing as she thought she should, Andrea started to work out. This was something she could control when everything else in her world seemed beyond her influence. She says she became a tomboy at 27, soon able to run marathons and bench-press her own body weight. Never at home in the white-collar world, Andrea went the other way and made herself still more blue-collar, reverting to the physicality of her working-class roots. "I watched my body get leaner than my coworkers' bodies and stronger. I have serious muscle now. And I know when it comes to running I am tough and can kick butt like my blue-collar daddy." At one magazine, Andrea remembers, there was an old, heavy electronic typewriter in the hallway. It blocked access and people always fretted that it was in the way. One day, the newly buff Andrea lifted it and placed it elsewhere. Women were dumbstruck. "You're so strong," they gasped. "Like I was Xena," Andrea laughs.

Ultimately, she quit the New York world and returned home. Manhattan is just a memory now. She sips a mineral water at a table under the TV set where a baseball game blares. "I finally just dropped out of New York. It was too many years of not belonging. I never made a real, true friend, someone to count on. I was from a different class. And they never wanted to know the real me."

Figuring Out the Game

For many of the beleaguered sons or daughters of the working class who are toiling in the gardens of the white collars, wisdom comes, albeit slowly. And one day, if it's important enough to them, they can finally figure things out.

That happened to Doug Russell, the former NSA man from South Carolina. At first, he did not handle the middle-class office all that well. At the NSA, his get-to-the-damn-point style won him few friends. "There was this NSA reliability engineer who was just not getting his work done. Well, one Friday came and I just blew a new hole in his body. He felt verbally abused, but I felt he got what he deserved." With others, it was the same way. Doug got into their faces 20 times if he thought the situation called for it. His too-candid, blue-collar style was beginning to create animosity around the office. As one advances in a federal agency or a private corporation, the higher-ups tolerate fewer aberrations. You're not promoted if you're controversial. After a while, Doug learned to do it the white-collar way. "It's only been the last three or four years, in my Texas company, that I got good at being indirect with people. I'm much more effective than I used to be."

These days—surprise, surprise—Doug has done like the others in the sandbox and begun networking. He's finding that it really doesn't hurt all that much. "I became a lot better at it, and the difference in my career is like night and day. I'm doing so much better. I now spend 50 percent of my time networking, instead of 105 percent of my time working. It's wiser doing social lubrication than simply keeping the nose to the grindstone."

Other Straddlers, too, admit they network, without believing it's a betrayal of their heritage. In fact, says Elizabeth Higgenbotham, a Delaware academic who writes about class issues, "I wouldn't be here if I didn't network." Elizabeth, who is African American, says that being mobile for one's race is different from simply class climbing. "African-American faculty take me under their wings. There is a collective interest in my advancement, because I'm helping to advance a race of people." Renny Christopher, a California academic, says she is "humiliated by my talent for shmoozing." Uncommonly gifted at self-advancement, she adds, "I get connections. I'm pretty disgusting. It feels illegitimate. That's why it's my duty to help as many other people as I can." Nancy Dean, the medical researcher in Massachusetts, says there was a time when she'd stand out as someone who wouldn't play corporate reindeer games. Now it's different. She will shmooze, and she will think before saying what's on her mind. They scratch her back, and she'll scratch their backs—not their eyes, like she used to.

Others say they have learned to conduct themselves with a kind of self-conscious care among the white-collar kind. Boston book editor Joe Terry still has a hard time networking. But like an anthropologist cataloguing behaviors in some distant outpost, he has made a comprehensive study of white-collaring during his 20 years in the field. And Joe—with blue eyes, chiseled features, and a balding, Ed Harris look—has been able to find a perch for himself among the natives, living the expatriot's life in the rarefied world of college-textbook publishing.

Most of the meetings in which he participates (yes, there are plenty of those; the natives are partial to groups) are filled with people from multiple generations of college graduates. Over the years he's noticed there are expectations about how one acts and talks. "And you can only learn what they are by paying close attention and reading the situation, which is harder to do if you don't grow up with cultural capital. The higher you go up the corporate ladder, the more people there are who have cultural capital—an understanding of how to behave in a board-room, or corporate meeting. Maybe it's just a matter of learning what the agenda is." (Like a lot of Straddlers, Joe was unaware of the term *cultural capital* until I told him what Bourdieu called the collective advantages of the middle and upper classes; once the limbo folk hear that phrase, however, it makes instant sense, and they immediately include it in conversation.)

Yes, Joe found, the business folk of the middle class speak in a tongue that is not his primary language. But that difference is not insur-mountable. In his experience, blue collars are blabbers of a sort; they believe they have nothing to gain by withholding their thoughts and feel-ings, and nothing to conceal. That makes them easier to read. Joe says he can always spot a person with a blue-collar upbringing in a corporate setting: They're moving their lips more—talking more demonstratively, more loudly, and just saying more in general. White-collar colleagues, however, hide their heads and hearts in a business meeting, Joe believes. White collars have better poker faces. "They must have learned a lot of this in some kind of manual on how to act that I missed out on reading."

To survive, Joe out-white-collars the middle class at their own game. And stays silent. "Strategic silence," Joe says. "You just listen more than you speak. Twenty years ago, I would not have known how to do this. But silence, I discovered, is so effective. I'm quiet because I'm reading the room. I always get the sense there's stuff going on in a white-collar atmosphere that takes me a little more time to read." When Joe finally does speak, people are more attentive. "My business style is to always be quieter than my white-collar colleagues. And it makes peo-ple spend a lot of their time trying to figure me out."

Folks Like Us

Out of curiosity, I asked a few big-time, big-money Straddlers whether they consider class when they hire. Without a doubt. If the candidates come down to a choice between a kid with a 4.0 index from a good school and a middle-class family that takes him/her to Europe each summer and a blue-collar person with a slightly lower GPA from a slightly less prestigious school who works 25 hours a week and every day of every summer, the big-money men choose the blue-collar kid every time. Every time.

"One hundred times out of 100, I'd hire the blue-collar person," says Don McNeeley, who runs Chicago Tube and Iron. "Now, just because you're privileged, it doesn't mean you're a snot. But I want to find a kid whose dad's a plumber. I can't define it. Those kids get it, though. They get life. They absolutely do."

Ed Haldeman, now head of investments at Putnam Investments, a $260 billion Boston firm that manages mutual funds and institutional accounts, will always "cheat" toward hiring the blue-collar person. He hired a guy (at his previous firm) after he heard that the man was one of 14 kids from a Boston family that had one bathroom in the house. "I figured if a guy grew up in that kind of house he would figure out how to get along with people." And it's true, the man's been a success. Ed's not saying his is a perfect filter. But his natural inclination is to hire the working class, even though he acknowledges it's a bias he has. "I like the drive, the motivation, the will to excel." Ed even thinks college-educated blue-collar people have a certain "niceness," a capacity to be understanding that middle-class folks lack. They also display drive and motivation.

Is this really true? It's hard to say. But because perception counts for so much in matters of class, it becomes a de facto truth. As for Ed, who has an undergraduate degree from Dartmouth College and both a law and a business degree from Harvard—he says he hopes his employees think of him as a regular kind of blue-collar guy, up from difficult circumstances, a hard-working blue-collar type who understands them. "Talk to Jim, the shoeshine guy and ask how I treat him." As he tells me this, he tears up and stops talking for fear he'll sob. It's an amazing emotional moment, born of his genuine worry that people will perceive him as a typical Harvard snob. Quickly, he composes himself. Eyes gleaming, he says, "I just feel so strongly that I not be seen as a person who doesn't treat others with respect. I realize lots of people in my position are arrogant, and don't treat working people with respect. But I want everyone who works here to treat every person well."

Dana Gioia says that one reason he did well in the food business was that he was one of the few executives who had actually used many of the so-called lowbrow products growing up. His family ate Jell-O and used Good Seasons salad dressing. "People from more privileged back-grounds didn't know why and how people used some of the General Foods products we made." Pectin, for example. Pectin is a water-soluble carbohydrate used to make a gel that's the key ingredient in jams and jellies. Dana's company sold SureGel and Certo-2, the leading pectin brands. Now, pectin boxes sit dusty and unmoved on most store shelves for months. But when fruits are harvested, stores can't stock enough of the stuff. That's when people are making their peaches, strawberries, and other produce into jams, filling 20 jars in a sitting. Few middle-class-born guys at the company had moms who'd made their own jams. But Dana's mother did, and he remembers how difficult it could be if something went wrong in the process and his mom wound up wasting precious, expensive fruit. So Dana, the blue-collar guy in a high place, paid attention to product failure—the notion that someone could mis-read directions and use the pectin improperly. How much tolerance does a product have to be prepared badly, yet still come out okay? "I spent a lot of time worrying about making pectin work even if someone made a mistake using it, because I knew it was a huge thing for a working woman to have product failure and waste all those strawberries."

A Word about Affirmative Action

A small number of white Straddlers tell me—quietly and privately—that they believe America is blind to the needs of the white working class. When corporations and government dole out help in the form of affirmative action, it is mainly to racial minorities and not to them. Color is held against minorities, Straddlers understand, and skin preju-dice begets a world of pain and poverty. If African Americans can't make it in this country, well, there's a strong reason: The white man has kept them down, our culture says. To overcome that injustice, you invent affirmative action.

Fine, some Straddlers say. But where is their help? Latino and African-American people have an excuse for their disadvantage; they can lay their problems at the feet of the white man. But when you're white and poor or working class and living in an Oregon trailer, the world says to you that you don't have a reason to explain your lack of wherewithal. How come you don't have a job? Where is your college diploma? No one made you ride in the back of the bus, no one burned crosses on your lawn, no one kept you from voting, and no one enslaved your forebears.

When you are merely poor, generation after generation, America does not hold slots for you in corporations. A woman complains to me that she felt she was passed over for a job given to a black man. That's a common enough tale. But, she says, her blue-collar father worked at the lower ends of the food business, and the African-American guy who took "her" job was the son of a surgeon. Was this fair? she asks. Richard Rodriguez, who opposes affirmative action, would say, no, it is not. "I had this excuse to not make it that institutional America assumed, and I hated it," he tells me. "People automatically assumed I had a racial ethnic identity that overrode everything else about me. I could not be just working class and reveal that drama about myself. America gave me the label of numerical minority, which makes me the beneficiary of those numerically excluded."

Growing up among hard-working blue collars, I'd always heard people complain that they were getting shafted in favor of African Americans. I've tried to tell them, you see a black person you say is unqualified getting ahead, but you never talk about the dead white wood that's been hired and promoted for God knows what reason. Without affirmative action it seems, black people would never get hired because bosses hire people who are like them—their college roommates or the nephew of someone with whom they are currying favor. The only way to get used to people who are unlike you is to compel companies to hire minorities, until a point of familiarity is reached and the discomfort is gone.

It's unfair? Well, so is a less-than-stellar student getting into Yale because his father went to Yale and became U.S. president. So is a man getting chosen to work on the docks, or being given a union card, because his father or his uncle was there first.

Affirmative action is a blunt and awkward tool digging and scraping to do some good, to rectify a lopsided system. "Throughout college," says Andrea Todd, "I thought affirmative action should be class-based, because a richer black girl I knew was getting more aid than me at

Berkeley, and I was ticked. After I started working at magazines, where you hardly see any black people, I changed 180 degrees. Affirmative action is not only necessary, it's the only way."

Ideally, there would be a way to take class into account in hiring and university slotting, as the City University of New York tried in its small way when it extended affirmative action to Italian Americans. But it may not happen soon in any real, practical sense. Race and gender have had, and continue to hold, our attention. In so doing, minorities and women have, in effect, disallowed the white working class to be able to say that it's part of an oppressed group. Of course, there are plenty of people who'd argue that whites enjoy cultural advantages, regardless of income. One can hide one's class background and then rise above it, people say. African Americans and women cannot obscure who they are. With labor in disarray in this country, there is no class equivalent of the NAACP or the National Organization for Women. More fundamentally, there is no unified sense of class kinship that can be harnessed into a public voice for the rights of the working class. As a result, things probably won't change anytime soon.

7

CLASS, LOVE, AND PROGENY: THE ULTIMATE BATTLE

Part I: Dating above Your Station

The woman in charge of financial aid at Northwestern University's Medill School of Journalism cornered me one day between classes and, with an odd sort of enthusiasm, whispered that I was receiving the largest scholarship package of anyone in the graduate school. This is not the sort of news one exults over; after all, the school's money awards were based more on need than brains. Besides, the stipend wasn't nearly enough. I had to take a work-study job. And it would be another 10 years before I could pay back the student loans that were keeping me in linguine and ricotta through the cold Illinois nights.

My working-class class standing wasn't the primary message that Ms. Fin-Aid wanted to deliver, though. There was more. Smiling with self-congratulatory delight, she leaned in closer and confided that the person with the second-largest financial aid package in the class was a lovely young woman with whom she had recently chatted. "Wouldn't it be great if you two got together?" she asked. Now, as long as she was in a matchmaking mood, my guardian yenta could have mentioned Karen Florsheim (yes, that Florsheim), who was also in my class and was a pretty, warm, and gregarious person whom everyone liked. She could have mentioned the daughter of a federal judge, who was an equally delightful and popular member of our class. There were, in fact, many women from the middle and upper classes just hanging around without boyfriends who might have had a Coke with me (Evanston, Illinois, was a dry town) on a Friday night. But no, the scheming campus functionary saw my gutter-low bottom line, did some speedy love-calculus, then linked me with another working-class person of limited means.

I was offended for a second, until I realized that she was referring to the woman I had already started dating. Then I was intrigued. Were we together because we were first-generation college graduates—lovers in limbo? I remember feeling comfortable with her working-class background. I realize now it was part of the compatibility and attraction. We had something very basic in common as we attended classes among the better-to-do. Like Americans living alone in a foreign city, we were drawn to a compelling familiarity in one another, a recognizable touch of home in thought and manner. Together we were, as the title of Sackrey and Ryan's influential book on the working class says, strangers in paradise.

Most of the women with whom I've had serious relationships were Straddlers like me. It was not something I consciously looked for on their resumes. Things simply happened that way, with allure somehow tied to collar color. The times I did date above my station, I felt like I was robbing the castle and believed I didn't belong. A sophisticated, older Barnard woman from a well-off New York family asked me out one freshman Friday and, with a sweet leer, suggested I make sure to "bring something" on our date. Understand, I was so inexperienced and so thrown that an upper-class upperclassman wanted to spend time with a collar inferior like me that, for a moment, I actually thought she meant she wanted me to tote along a box of cake or something, like blue-collar folk do on social occasions. She wants Danish? I wondered for the split second before the dim 40-watter over my head snapped on. Neither of us had a room on campus and there wasn't enough cash in my wallet to pay for a New York hotel; we wound up at a Brooklyn trysting site in my father's car. Now this was during the era of the .44-Caliber Killer, the

Son of Sam. He had been stalking lovers' lanes and, in fact, had shot a girl from my high school class as she made out with a guy very near the spot where I took Ms. Barnard. But none of this mattered to us as we breathlessly went ahead with things. I had expected a transcendent experience, as though being with her would alter me somehow—make me less of a nobody, less like a boy from the neighborhood. Of course, that didn't happen. She was nice, though, and we remained friends for a while. I think she ended up marrying an investment banker from a prominent Manhattan family.

One night in Ohio, I kissed a surgeon's daughter who was leaning against a center island in a kitchen in a rambling house on a quiet cul-de-sac. Having never seen one in person before, I thought the island was as exotic as Tahiti, and I believed that possessing one was proof of making it. Impressing an island woman meant I had arrived, I thought. This was a period of time in my life when I simply felt unworthy of these women's attentions—an uncouth pretender come to grasp their cool, smooth hands in my large, sweaty paw. For their part, a few of them were attracted to a perceived erotic primitivism, I came to understand, born of a stereotype injected into the culture by the swarthy casts of *The Godfather* and *Saturday Night Fever*. The women were blond-haired, blue-eyed Mid-westerners, and I was a dark, East Coast Italian. We were exotic to each other. To my shame, I have to say I slightly exaggerated my Brooklyn accent for maximal effect. It was that rough-edged, bad-boy thing they responded to, and I laid it on by the trowel-full when I was in my mid-20s. "You don't wanna know the things you gotta do to make it alive to age 21 in Brooklyn," I admit I once told a wide-eyed, impressionable woman from the right side of the tracks. "Only the strong survive." Years before the movie *A Fish Called Wanda* came out, with Kevin Kline as a Lothario who lists Italian foods to arouse a lover, I was entertaining requests to speak the language to well-bred Columbus women during private moments. When I ran out of ideas (my Italian classes took me only so far), I slowly and emotionally recited an Italian patriotic song that I had learned in fourth grade that went on and on about equality and liberty. This did not disappoint. "You see, that's what we working-class Italians are for," Dana Gioia tells me, half-seriously. "We're sexual playthings for the wealthy." Those women and I did not quite mesh, and I wound up marrying a Straddler who's tougher than I am. It just feels right.

A New Terrain

Straddlers who have had cross-class relationships acknowledge that class becomes part of the conversation at some point. How could something as fundamental as your background not be important when two people become involved? It may not be as profound as a *Guess Who's Coming to Dinner* interracial scenario, but it has resonance and meaning. Everyone believes that the values and customs they grew up with are the proper ones to live by, regardless of class. And everyone can defend those values and customs, attacking any deviation from them with unending arrogance and unyielding obstinance: His blue-collar family is a howling crowd of unsophisticated World Wrestling Federation disciples who believe there is such a thing as Velveeta with honor; her spoiled, white-collar bunch ties pink sweaters around their necks and falters like a Yugo in the rain when the going gets the least bit rough.

Did your family of origin have supper or dinner? "Supper" is blue-collar eating, implying big-pot cooking—meats and bones and gobs of carbohydrates—all ladled out in hot, brown heaps on dishwasher-safe plates, accompanied by not more than one fork. "Dinner" can be more refined, a middle-class meal in which prettified food presentation is as important as taste itself. I know a Straddler who says he and his middle-class wife battle over the time she takes to prepare an haute dining experience when all he wants to do is fill his belly with something warm, then leave the table.

Did your family take you on mind-expanding, Machu Picchu vacations, or were they plotz-at-the-beach, two-week affairs in summer rentals where your mom fried little-known fish every night (for supper, not dinner)? I know Straddlers who still believe plotzing holidays are superior, and get into tangles with high-minded, white-collar spouses who look to re-create the brain-stimulating good times of their past.

Did your family buy everything with cash, or was a parent's wallet thick with plastic? Money can kick off seismic disturbances in even same-class marriages; collar-based differences on how it should be handled can get awfully unfriendly. A blue-collar-born friend from New York balks at her middle-class husband's Christmas Visa extravagances, fearful, like her father, that debt will sink them. If we can't buy it with cash, she says, it's not worth having.

We like to say in America that the heart doesn't know from class. And indeed, many Straddlers insist, in the end, love is a great leveler, and class becomes just a minor consideration, a small aspect of the relationship that does not play a primary role in how two people get along.

One of our cherished myths is the Cinderella scenario, with love conquering class differences between people with uneven pedigrees. Countless silly books and movies build plots on that very foundation. One notable exception is *The Philadelphia Story*, in which the rich heroine, played by Katharine Hepburn, learns she's much better off with Cary Grant, the blue-blooded guy she grew up with, than with the ambitious, working-class fellow to whom she is briefly engaged. Turning on its head the populist American notion that the rich are useless and evil, Jimmy Stewart instructs us that just because a fellow is born to the purple, it doesn't mean he's a bad guy. And, he adds in a kind of wonderment, a guy who's worked his way up from the bottom can still be quite a heel. It's naive to believe that no one ponders class in love relationships. In his tart cynicism, Paul Fussell writes that if an upper-class person marries downward, it's mainly for beauty.[1] Blue-collar boys like me remember living-room grillings from the middle-class dads of our dates, who inevitably asked, "So, what does your father do?" You may say class is of little consequence, but it seemed to be of vital significance to our interrogators. From our end of the conversation, some of us believed, correctly or not, that middle-class men and women were more desirable and had more to offer than potential mates from the neighborhood. A few guys I knew wanted their blue collars stained with middle-class lipstick because it symbolized success and mobility.

Class is not benign. It is in fact, an invisible, powerful force that influences what people expect out of a relationship and how they communicate with one another. Rarely do people understand that class differences are causing the rift or argument, although it's sometimes quite obvious. Straddler shrink Barbara Jensen recalls that in a couple of her marriage-counseling cases, class was clearly the problem. The middle-class husband wanted to socialize more often with his boss as a way to network and get ahead. The wife, on the other hand, developed a blue collar's enmity toward that kind of get-together, which she saw as uncomfortable and contrived, with a false conviviality that left her cold.

And she wanted the couple to spend more time with her family. But for some people from the middle class, Jensen says, spending time with one's family is seen as very déclassé, and the husband believed such enforced gatherings were a waste of time that could be better spent with his boss or even his friends.

Jensen tells of another couple in which both partners started out blue collar. But the wife began attending college and was soon enraptured by the books, the talk, and the possibilities of campus life. The husband wanted more bowling and TV watching time. He'd make fun of her college chums and things the professors said. One day, after it had become clear that the woman was growing into someone unfamiliar, the husband's fears exploded. He grabbed one of his wife's books and waved it wildly in the air. "This crap is more interesting to you than the kids and me," he yelled. Then he threw the book against a wall, smashing the spine of the outside irritant that threatened his happiness. The woman cried as she told the story—her book like a broken bird in a heap on the floor; her husband breathing hard and beyond reason; a rift in the marriage hastened by an imbalance of education. Working-class studies professors tell me it's a common enough tale among their older students, who confide to their teachers that the very scholarship that nurtures them is tearing apart their marriages.

Jensen says it's unusual for class issues to exhibit themselves as baldly as that. More often it's subtle and hard to see, embedded in the language of lovers in trouble. In counseling sessions between couples from different class backgrounds, Jensen has noted that working-class people are more likely to believe someone who shows emotion when he talks. But in therapy, a partner born to the middle class will explain him or herself rationally in lawyer-like recitations of fact and circumstance: "What I actually wanted from him was . . . ," or "What I was trying to do in that situation was. . . ." Middle-class clients often avoid emotion at these moments. The working-class-born person, however, comes in splashing emotions around, unable to stay rational and explain his or her side calmly: "How could she say that to me when I . . . ?" "Doesn't she understand how hard it is to . . . ?" Says Jensen, "The more calm the middle-class person gets, the crazier it makes the working-class partner. I help the working-class person hold it in more after the middle-class person has trashed them with better skills. I work with the working-class person to pick up more of a middle-class style, and I try to get the middle-class person to open up more. In the end, it's harder to get a middle-class person to open up than it is to get a working-class person to pick up the middle-class way."

Buffalo scholar Patrick Finn says most conflicts between his middle-class wife and his Straddler self are class related, and all of them have to do with language. Working-class man that he is, Finn tends to be more silent than his wife. "With the working class, people tend to rely on shared knowledge. Everything is implicit, and they aren't as used to talking to strangers outside the circle. My wife will say things I already know—she's middle class and tends to be explicit. I always find myself asking, 'Why is she saying that to me? I already know that.' "

For Amy Reed, the Cleveland Straddler, the problem wasn't language as much as it was money. There was a values gap between her and her former husband, a second-generation attorney. Her father had been extremely conservative with investments and paid cash for everything. Amy's ex had what she called a "white-collar casualness" about money that stressed her no end. "He never filed our taxes on time and always got extensions. This horrified the blue-collar person in me. My father was always on time, and even paid off his house early." A Washington attorney says he and his middle-class wife similarly clash over fiscal management, with the monied wife bouncing checks, while he has never incurred credit card debt in his life.

Miles from Monkey Run

For Straddlers, class differences between themselves and the opposite sex pop up early in life. You can achieve a fairly sophisticated grasp of life's pecking order just by cruising the cafeteria at school. Clothes, attitude, and ready loot for that extra pint of chocolate milk: It's fairly obvious who's who and where. A few people tell me that when they chose to step out of line and flirt above their stations, they were slapped off those higher ladder rungs they'd climbed to and were forced to recognize the rigid rank of things. Such humbling lessons in matters as sensitive as love are never forgotten. Forever after, stung people remember to look for class in all situations, constantly measuring themselves against others purportedly above them in the social hierarchy.

Joe Terry, the Massachusetts college-textbook editor, was 16 when he first learned about love and class—and their close relationship with scallops. The son of a carpenter/fisherman living in a working-class area near the outrageously wealthy Hamptons of Long Island, Joe would fish for his spending money. He remembers one particular school night, opening scallops he'd collected in the 20-by-15-foot, wooden, one-car garage that Joe's father had built. Having made a date for the weekend with his girlfriend, who came from a monied family and lived in a nice house, Joe was standing in the cold fish stink under fluorescent lights, trying to figure out how many scallops he'd have to open and take to the Fulton Fish Market in Manhattan to come up with the $6 he'd need to take the girl to the movies. It was freezing and a relentless water wind rattled the windows. Joe was tired and was cutting up his hands with the shucking knife. In nervous need of cash, he was hurrying the process, grabbing shellfish from the bushels stacked in front of him, sliding the knife into the three-inch shell, cutting out the meat, and adding to the pile. Joe's two sisters had taken pity, slicing open their own gray mounds of shells and donating the wet fish to him for popcorn money. He doesn't remember the exact number, but he figured six bucks' worth of scallops required about three hours of work.

As the night wore on, it occurred to Joe that the girl didn't think about any of this. She did not picture his routine in her mind: Joe waking up before the sun, fishing for a while, going off to school, then returning home to stand in his father's garage and extract beige plugs of fish from their unyielding casings. This thought took up more and more space in Joe's head: She has no idea what it takes for me to come up with enough money to take her to a movie. "It was such a telling thing," Joe recalls. "It indicated to me all our differences. My girlfriend's worries were more about what she was going to wear and which movie we'd see. I never heard her worry or talk about money. It was understood I would pick her up and take her to the movies. And I would pay."

After saving scallop and other fish money for a year, Joe accumulated enough cash to actually take the girl to dinner. It was, at 17, the high point of his adolescence—the first time he had ever phoned a restaurant and made reservations, his very first grown-up date. He even wore a jacket. But the night didn't feel right from the start and wasn't going the way Joe had planned. The girl was not wowed by the tablecloths and enchanted by the feeling of being treated like an adult by waiters and water bearers. She had eaten out before and was not impressed by how very far out of the ordinary this evening was for Joe. She hadn't worked for her place at the table by struggling in the predawn hours on pitching boats in dangerous waters. The girl had not yanked up wriggling ocean crop in heavy nets or scrubbed extra long in the shower to expel the odor of fish guts that seemed to invade the skin like tattoo dye. And she could not share his thrill over the heft of the wad of bills in his pocket, which was usually the repository of a crumpled buck or two and a few jangling coins. "I remember being struck by the distinct feeling that it wasn't the event for her that it was for me. And I had intended it to be a big deal for her. It became clear in a moment that she just had no idea of the sacrifices a person like me would have to make to take her out. We graduated and she moved on. I never saw her after that."

Already vulnerable because they were revealing their hearts to boys or girls they liked, a few Straddlers remember that the added pressures of class differences made love life all the harder. It was excruciating for Gregg Andrews, the Texas history professor, when any date of his visited his house in Ilasco, Missouri, and asked to go to the bathroom. Without indoor plumbing even into the 1960s, the place looked shabby, a hick outpost decades out of step with the rest of society. It seemed doubly bad when a middle-class girl from a nice house needed the facilities, Gregg remembers. He would just cringe when she asked, "May I use your . . . ?," and he had to see the look on her face when he chuckled and stammered and pointed toward the outhouse. Then he watched her put on her coat and make her way to the ugly, freezing anachronism hunkered in the trampled grass, shutting herself into its stink and poverty. He'd wait for her to come out, then show her where she could wash her hands. Angry at his circumstance, embarrassed for himself and the girl, Gregg would hand over a towel and hope that she could rise above this, laugh it off, roll with it, and allow him a nugget of dignity.

One of his most vivid memories of the time was a country club dance that could not have gone more wrong. Gregg had been dating the daughter of the city attorney of Ilasco, a cement-manufacturing company town of little charm or significance. (Much of the town, in fact, was destroyed by mutual decision of the company and the state in the 1960s to build State Highway 79, an easier conduit for tourists seeking the environs of area hero Mark Twain. Gregg's house survived the wrecking ball, but nearly everything else was knocked flat and hauled away. So he lived in a house without a toilet or a town.) The girl invited Gregg, who showed up at the genteel soiree in his best paisley shirt and blue jeans. Everyone else at the dance wore suits. "We never went out with each other again," he says. "I felt terrible and embarrassed. I know she wasn't trying to embarrass me. She assumed I would wear a suit appropriate to the occasion." The two never discussed what happened. But they both understood—she in her dress and he in his awful clothes—that they could not progress another day together as a couple. "I knew without her saying a word that I had failed on some very important level. And I knew that this was not my world."

Another middle-class girl delivered yet another mortification. This was the daughter of the high school principal. Gregg was visiting with the girl at her house and needed a ride home. When the girl volunteered, the father stopped her: "I don't think you need to be going down there," he said, making it icily clear that he saw Gregg's neighborhood, known as Monkey Run, as poor, white, outhouse country—no place for middle-class daddy's girls. Obedient and maybe a little frightened of Gregg's neighborhood because of her father's reaction, the girl drove Gregg a little closer to home, but still miles from Monkey Run. He hitchhiked the rest of the way. "Inside, I burned and was humiliated at the same time." But as with the country club girl, Gregg said not a word about the incident to the principal's daughter. Class inequality rendered them mute. Both instantly understood the caste system that her daddy had tactlessly illuminated. But there were no words. It was as though no language existed to describe her obligation to follow the tenets of her kind or his utter exposure as someone not worth knowing.

In graduate school, Samme Chittum fell hard for a guy whose family could trace back its accomplishments for generations. While he liked spending time with her, he made it clear to Samme that she wasn't the family's type of gal at all. "He liked little, pretty, perfect women with social skills," she says. "And I was never the kind of girl who showed up preened, presented, and groomed. I was, and still describe myself as, a mutt. And that was not elite enough to be a wife candidate. I was not pretty enough to be a trophy wife. And being the pugnacious, blue-collar person that I am, I said to the guy, 'Fuck you.'"

Problems with the Clean

I am struck by how often Straddlers use the word *clean* to describe would-be paramours of the middle and upper classes. It's not that their own blue-collar kin were unhygienic. This was a state of unsoiled being they were beholding, a smudge-free refinement. Clothes were wool or cotton, tailored and dry-cleaned, with a fine drape. Hair shined from gentle shampoos and conditioners, and not from Ivory soap. Shoe heels and soles were always thick, keeping the upper classes that much farther from the pavement. Their newer cars hummed unplagued by the demons that settle into machines that have been coaxed beyond their natural expiration dates. Their nails and teeth looked nice. These people, scrubbed and luminous, possessed an ease of manner, a kind of grace you didn't see on your own block, where life was haphazard and uncoordinated. The white collars were quiet, unethnic, and poised. And they smelled good, too. "The clean upper crust," says Doug Russell, the Texas high-techer from the South Carolina working class, "are good-looking people, with confidence. I was so impressed."

So was Mo Wortman, the Rochester ob-gyn. Yet he understood there was something wrong with worshiping the tennis-at-10 A.M. set. He fell in love with his first wife's family, middle-class types with an iconic, all-American glow. "It was an Ozzie-and-Harriet attraction I had for my first in-laws. I don't know, they were Ward and June Cleaver, what the American family is supposed to be." They lived in a house, not a cramped apartment as Mo had. They spoke English and ate out in restaurants, two things Mo's parents weren't able to master. No matter how nice they were to him, though, Mo felt unable to completely fit in. "I was always aware I was from a different social class, and that these were polished people." After a time, Mo began to feel a different kind of uneasiness, a sense that he was being too much seduced by the white-collar clean. The family offered him money to defray medical school costs. Mo refused. "I developed a certain lack of comfort. It was like wanting to be one of them was a betrayal to my background, and it had that element that I was becoming embarrassed about where I came from. There was something nice about being part of the Cleavers. But I still retained a great deal of pride in being blue collar."

Dana Gioia also dove headlong into his rich lover's world of swank and polish, only to smother in the opulence. He met the daughter of the president of a major American bank in the dorms of Stanford. To give you an idea of how wealthy they were, the father had a Chagall above the toilet. In the beginning, it just didn't sink in how different from one another they were. "You know how it is. You like each other. You're both smart, sexy, and normal. We had fun correcting each other's pronunciations of European movie actresses from the 1930s." He was nothing like the preppies she had known and dated. He was Italian and Mexican, with a swagger and physical self-confidence she found attractive, not to mention an IQ that equaled hers. She was clearly upper class—stratospherically upper class, as it turned out—but down-to-earth, fun, and unpretentious.

The first indication of their colossal class mismatch came when she invited Dana home to her Gatsbyesque Long Island estate. "Bring a dinner jacket," she said. "What do you mean?" he asked. Dana didn't know what she was talking about. Turns out, what the working class calls a tuxedo, the upper class labels a dinner jacket. Dana rented one and off they went. Dana and the woman were permitted to sleep together in a guest house on the estate. It shocked him. "My parents would never have allowed their daughter to stay in the same room with a guy overnight at their house," he says. Not that he was complaining. But it underscored that we're-not-in-Kansas-anymore thing that so many Straddlers in love with the clean people talk about. Old-world old-schoolers like Dana's folks clung to a working-class code that made no allowances for young people to express themselves sexually.

The couple's first New York date was a debutante ball for one of the girlfriend's pals. Dana had seen nothing like this; few people ever have. The estate where the party took place was enormous, with the endless driveway lit by torches. Revelers strolled by a private lagoon, deep and cool. A dance orchestra and a rock band alternated sets through the night. Dana had never seen plenty before, never known abundance. For his family, shrimp was a luxury, and here were boatloads. In his house, electricity was a commodity to ration and monitor, and here were rooms and grounds ablaze with endless utility product. "My thought was, 'These people sure must have clipped a lot of coupons.' I'd thought places like this no longer existed." Oddly, many of the people he'd met didn't match the setting. They weren't excellent; they weren't sharp.

Lots of guys his age at the ball seemed like lazy goof-offs who spent their days drinking, the ne'er-do-well sons of privilege who never bothered to map out life plans. There was nothing in Dana's life that could compare to this. The experience existed on its own plane, inexplicable and unreachable.

The trip was cut short after his mother called to say his grandmother had died. Dana flew back to L.A. "I was suddenly back with my family," he says. "All these really strong working-class men in their dark suits. My family was smarter than anyone I had been spending time with. And no one was divorced, like everybody I'd met in New York. Suddenly, with my family, the world made sense again."

But love operates beyond sense, and Dana needed to be with the banker's daughter. He made more trips back east. This time, the woman's father began to show his true feelings about the boy with too many vowels in his name and not enough zeroes in his bank account. "The father disliked me but the stepmother loved me," Dana says. "It was her way of showing off her liberal credentials—being nice to the poor kid." Dad argued politics with the boy and became frustrated by two things: the fact that Dana could hold his own, and the emerging realization that their views did not differ all that much. Dana was a Republican, after all. That just made the father madder. He tried to stir up trouble by ruminating aloud that Dana was probably in the Mafia, as all half-Italians must be. Meantime, Dad would do what he could to make Dana feel uncomfortable, the white-collar way. "He sat me next to a gay Spanish count at a dinner party and gave me a malicious look from across the table.

It went on like that for four years. In the end, Dana says, he bailed. "She wanted to marry me, but I knew I had to make my own way in the world. Besides, hers was such a weird world for me. In the end, she made a dynastic marriage with an investment banking family. She made the right marriage. Class discomfort was part of the reason why we never progressed."

Twenty-five-year-old "Tina" fell out of love with her bad-boy rich guy in such a moment of class discomfort. She admits it was fun to hang out with a guy whose father paid for everything. "That boy," she reminisces fondly, "that boy always had the best herb." But one night at a party at some rich someone's lovely home, the guy announced that he wanted to get going, and Tina said to hold up until she could find a place to set down her beer. Impatient, the boy knocked the can out of Tina's hand and told her, "Someone else will pick it up. That's what they're paid for." It was as if all the love drained out of her in a gushing moment, the full flow of it washing away. She was shocked and could never look at him the same way again. Tina came from the kind of family that was paid to clean up beer spills and other messes of the well-to-do. It was inconceivable to her that someone she'd spent so much time with could actually act and think this way. She had misjudged him. Though he had money, he had seemed like a regular guy. But it was just a pose.

Nancy Dean dated someone like this years ago—a 19-year-old who liked to portray himself as the ultimate blue-collar sufferer, someone who knew what it was like to come from nothing and had to work for everything he had. The problem was, it was all a lie. Nancy finally found out that both his parents had master's degrees and had provided a comfortable home and a smooth ride for the guy. "In the end, I couldn't match up with him. He had the money, the educated family, and the support for continuing his education. He was simply contrary for the sake of being contrary." Straddlers tell me that white-collar lovers who fake blue somehow reveal their true color in the end. Pretenders believe it makes for a more romantic profile to boast of a journey that started from nowhere: "And just look at me now." (Some people find it embarrassing to have to admit they were born with compasses, maps, and means. Sacramento Straddler Andrea Todd's middle-class-born husband told her that she's a threat to insecure white collars who measure the distance she's traveled with practically no help. It makes their own accomplishments appear less special.) Nothing angers a blue collar more than someone with a fake passport and a phony story. Unless we're talking about an Eliza Doolittle situation. Then it's infuriating.

At first, Southern California Straddler Renny Christopher submitted to her (now former) husband's rehab mission. She had, after all, come from an uneducated world in which her family of carpenters openly disdained the middle class as parasitic drones who fed off the working class and offered little to the world. But as she progressed in her education, Renny grew fascinated with a previously unseen life.

Meanwhile, the man, doing some carpentry of his own, went to work on Renny like one of those *This Old House* restoration guys. "He thought he could civilize me," Renny says. He knew she was smart, so there were good bones to work with. Still, the woman was too loud, too forward, and too pushy for him, a middle-class man taught to prize subtlety and understatement. It was the way she took up space in the world that bugged him—her blue-collar lack of refinement. "He wanted to change me. He saw me as clay he could mold." When they met, the man represented the world Renny wanted into. She had recently gotten her master's degree and was applying for a teaching job that, it turns out, the man was just leaving. He was confident, smooth, and erudite. Fabulously well-read, he knew everything and made references to books Renny hadn't heard of. Suddenly, she burned to read them all, in a desperate hurry to fill the gap between her knowledge and his. He provided reading lists and encouragement, the patient mentor (he was 12 years older) with his student, all edgy potential and earnestness. Working hard to expand Renny's world, he introduced her to music, art, and foods. "I was not very experimental in what I was willing to eat. He kept coaxing me to try different things. That actually turned out pretty well. He was right about the food."

It all worked for a while—the little-known texts, the sushi, the life coaching. Eventually, though, the charm of it all started to wane. "After a while, it wasn't so romantic that he knew everything about everything. And I began to realize that he'd pretend to know something even when he really didn't. The more I came to know, the less he seemed to. And he was overbearing, treating me more and more like a father." Renny says his attempts to change her manner ultimately failed; the blue was too deep to wash out. She's still loud and forward, and the guy is, well, an ex. "A great deal of the problem in our marriage was class conflict, in the end," says Renny.

In a twist on old Henry Higgins, Barbara Jensen worked to remake her middle-class husband by trying to get him to be more blue collar. There's a simple reason why, she says: "Working-class men are sexier." Her husband, the son of an architect, is quite handsome. "But he's a little dorky compared to a working-class man. I bought him a black leather jacket and black jeans and he looked at the clothes and said to me, 'You're dressing me working class. That's not me.'" Though he prefers to be called David, she convinced her husband that it made more sense to be a Dave when he was with her family. And Dave/David gave in—not on the clothes, but on his name. Now her family loves him. Barbara told her father he can't fix anything around the house, like a blue-collar guy should. That's okay, her understanding dad said. You wouldn't want a guy like that, anyway. "It was sad but true," Barbara says. "I'd been in the middle class longer than I was in the working class, and in the end, I wanted an intellectual. That was a bittersweet moment when I realized it."

Obviously, cross-class relationships can work. Besides, people with many more dissimilarities than collar hue build strong unions. Some even find their class differences to be mutually beneficial. "My wife and I are perfect for each other," Straddler attorney Dennis George says. That's because Michele, a social worker who grew up in a high-income suburb, smooths out Dennis's rough edges, having spent the early part of their marriage correcting his English, especially his penchant for using the forbidden plural form of the word *you*. Michele, in turn, rejected the guys from her neighborhood who inherited wealth and was drawn to Dennis's born-with-nothing, work-till-9 P.M. manner. "She wanted somebody like me, who was book-intelligent and streetwise, both."

Movies You Don't Talk About

Is it a betrayal to eschew love with your own class kind? There were so many lovely girls from high school whom I ignored. Singer John Gorka has a song called "Italian Girls," in which he rhapsodizes about the beautiful working-class women of his youth for whom he fell. I know how he felt, but I could never love a woman whose greatest ambition was marriage. Relatives scratched their heads at this perceived flaw. "Why do you go for the complicated girls with the steel-trap minds?" one of them asked me. "Just find a nice girl who can make you a nice home." Why didn't I want one of Gorka's Italian girls?

The problem was, all that niceness wasn't enough. I was bucking custom, I knew. Everywhere around me were examples of how you were supposed to do it: Scout the neighborhood, find someone, and make her pregnant. By not following the program, I was a snob, a classist too good for the women around me, who were trained to love me, whoever I was. Don't misunderstand, I would melt, smolder, and pine whenever I met a lovely blue-collar girl in my school or neighborhood. But then— and I don't know how to say this without sounding snooty and high-handed—I would hear them talk about this new lip gloss they bought during a triumphant shopping trip to Kings Plaza Mall, and suddenly their hair wouldn't look as lustrous, and their mouths would no longer beckon. This is not to say I never met bright blue-collar women— proud, independent-minded, wonderful people. But I wanted to be with someone who yearned for college and loved books, who was taking orders from a voice in the brain telling her to move beyond herself and the stasis of neighborhood. I remember wishing this one girl IQ points, just wanting her to be someone I could talk to. I didn't want there to be limitations on what we could share and understand. And high-functioning brainpower is attractive, let's face it.

I did try to fit in. I spent time with Miss Nice; I dated She'll Make You a Good Home. We saw movies we didn't talk about and had thoughts we never shared; we didn't stay up late arguing about Nixon or Vonnegut. Make no mistake, these women were nurturing and kind and wanted to please me. They cooked me elaborate dinners that cost them time and so much money, and they smiled watching me enjoy them: "Of course there's more. Eat." And there I'd be, forking in the food, want-ing the perciatelli or the stew or the latkes to be enough, hoping I could simply ingest what they made and have love fill me like a sacrament. Then, too, I would sit there looking at them, wishing they would dazzle me with some insight that could make me fall at their feet.

A young woman who liked me once begged to read something I'd written. She saw the word *juxtaposition* in the text, thought it was a typo, and said, "You meant to write, 'just a position,' right?" I remem-ber feeling crestfallen, just absolutely saddened, when she said that, as if I'd seen her slap a puppy. "No!" I said to myself. "Please don't be this way." In the movie *Annie Hall*, the Woody Allen character is freshly broken up with Annie and is dating another woman. He makes a joke that the woman doesn't understand—a joke that Annie would certainly have laughed at. His face registers the awkwardness, the wrongness, the bleakness of that awful, awful moment when romance is forced and two people are simply not getting each other. The girl was sweet and sexy and her mother loved me. We had spent a lot of time together, but I could never feel love or make myself want to be with her more. And I'd always wondered what it was. "Just a position" told me.

For Veronica De Vivar, the pharmaceutical sales Straddler from California, the moment of class realization came during a frustrating argument with a guy. They were both 18, and he had been complaining about her inattentiveness. The young man was a blue-collar Mexican kid, very good looking, and he impressed Veronica's girlfriends. Still, something was wrong. "What is the matter with you?" the guy asked Veronica when they were out some night. "You're half here. I am so much like your dad. What's the problem?"

"Oh," Veronica said to herself, finally getting it. "That's why I'm half here. He *is* like my father." Veronica believed blue collar meant macho dominance, and she wouldn't have it. She broke up with the guy, then later started seeing an Anglo, purposely dating the opposite of her parents. He was liberal, vegetarian, and atheist—nothing like the family. This was at a time when Veronica had moved out, shortened the family last name ("bastard daughter," her father called her), and started acting independent. "I was very happy, because this guy was my excuse for being how I wanted to be." Veronica's family saw the changes in her and thought it was the white guy's influence: "He's bewitched you." That was fine with her; it made things easier for them to think that. But she knows that if she had stayed with him, she would have lost her family forever. Eventually, she married a Mexican-American Straddler like herself. "And that makes things easier with my family."

Veronica's sister did what Veronica could not and married a blue-collar guy. It was a revelation. "My brother-in-law is 6-foot-5, muscular, and really nice. I told my sister I would never have gone out with him, but now that I know him, he's a great guy." The sister called Veronica narrow-minded. Veronica does not want to be viewed as arrogant, but she knows that class makes a difference. "Look, I love my brother-in-law, but his idea of an anniversary celebration would be to take you to an action movie, and not to see *Phantom of the Opera*."

When Veronica was looking for a husband, she knew she had to find a man who could tolerate her having business dinners with male doctors at night. "Someone from a working-class Hispanic background without a college degree might have been too possessive for that," she believes.

Veronica's father, now dead, demonstrated his own class awareness whenever he greeted his two sons-in-law. He always offered Veronica's husband a glass of wine and her brother-in-law a glass of beer, regardless of their preference. "My father and my brother-in-law were always closer than my husband and my father. It was a class thing, in the end."

Part II: Making Middle-Class Babies

Bill Cosby once joked that the first rich kids he ever met were his own. Straddler parents with a bunch less money offer similar reports. Some even go a step further, saying they don't like the middle-classness they see in their children and wish they could scrub it out of them. Yet Straddler moms and dads don't want their kids to grow up with the feelings that they had as children—their lack of comfort in the middle-class world, their inability to speak with adults, and their sense of inferiority. They want them able to compete with the truly entitled, because they know firsthand how difficult that is.

My wife and I are unable to have kids and plan to adopt. I wonder what kind of parent I'll be, class-wise. What will I use from my blue-collar past, and what will I take from my middle-class present to create a human I could respect? How do I keep from spoiling a child when I can afford to give them more than my parents could? How do I build in a work ethic when the only example I can offer is that of an office person who types rather than a bricklayer with rough hands? (Doug Russell says his kids are missing something vital that he had: the grit and determination that his father exuded, the unkillable notion that he was going to survive, period. They also think money comes from an endless supply.) Finally, how do I teach a child about her place in the world when I'm living in limbo myself?

"A lot of middle-class people from the working class regret that their children will assume privilege and not know anxiety," Richard Rodriguez tells me. "They will not know that none of what they have is inevitable. We know it's not inevitable because we come from different circumstances. It's not written in stone what we become. But children of the middle class assume it's all given to them." He has a 17-year-old nephew who speaks three languages and figures that, if he wants to go to Spain, his parents will underwrite it. "There's nothing remarkable about air travel, nothing remarkable about Spain to him."

Upstate New York Straddler Gillian Richardson says she and her husband, the son of a dentist, get along quite well, considering their collars. But their class differences manifest themselves in child rearing. In the working class, Gillian believes, a child is supposed to be independent by 18. "By then, you've done your job as a parent," she says. But her husband says that your kids never grow up and you're always working for them. When it came time for her son, Joe, to pick a college, Gillian harkened back to her own upbringing. She had no car; there was no money. The University of Buffalo was down the street. So that's where she went. And that's where her son should go, she told her husband. But he disagreed, saying the boy deserves to go where he wants. "To me, his going away to school was a waste of money," Gillian says. "What is this 'deserves' stuff?" Gillian's husband has a sense of entitlement he's passed on to Joe, Gillian says. And it's evident throughout their neighborhood, an upper-middle-class enclave. "It drives me insane the way people here raise their kids, acting like the world revolves around their little darlings."

While she was careful not to bring up her boy that way, something must have rubbed off. "My son is absolutely middle class. There is no working class in him whatsoever, and I find that very sad. He's got entitlement, I can see that. If he needs $50, he just asks for it. When he gets this entitlement thing going, I really go ballistic." Once, Joe decided he wanted to go to Mexico during spring break. "Mexico, huh?" Gillian said. "So, how are you going to pay for it?" Joe said, "You can give me the money, can't you?" Gillian started laughing. Then Joe sank himself by using the precise wrong word with Mom. "You know, I worked really hard in high school. I'm entitled to this." There was a silence in the room like in the movies, before the bomb explodes. Only this time, Gillian laughed even louder. "He got angry with me, but I found that entitlement stuff hysterically funny. I didn't have that growing up and I really hold to that." Joe, by the way, never got south of the border.

Middle-class living has lots of limbo parents worried. They got kneesocks and underwear for Christmas, but they shower their own children with acres of pricey under-the-tree booty. Then they fear their children are developing warped ideas about what's appropriate and what's expected. Taking art lessons and piano instruction for granted, Straddlers' kids are growing up with completely different value systems than Mom and Dad had. "Gee," Ithaca Straddler Signe Kastberg says, "my friends all wonder, are we even going to like these kids when they're adults? Are they going to have values we can live with? I can't tell you the end of the story."

Some Straddlers confess they couldn't articulate exactly how their middle-class children differ from them. They only know that they do. Detroit Straddler Larry Gabriel says he feels bad that his four-year-old daughter won't be working class. "She'll miss out on being who I was—shaped by a lack of money. I'm not sure what it brings out. It's just who I am and what I identify with being like." Not that being without money is something one aspires to. There were too many nights Larry's parents had to instruct him to stay quiet and pretend no one was home while a bill collector banged on the door. No parent wants a child to know that. But Larry understands that a connection to the past is severed. That leaves him with a nagging worry: "Not growing up among the working class, will she even develop an appreciation for working-class people?"

Counting Entitlements

Outside Joe Terry's house north of Boston, men herd leaves into piles, wielding high- and low-tech implements—their choice depending more on aesthetics than cost. Everyone in this neighborhood can afford a leaf blower. Muscular SUVs, looking like Chevettes that worked out and took nutritional supplements, sit at the ready outside multivehicle garages. Wood smoke curls out of chimneys, creating a smog of burned supermarket logs: sweet bourgeois air freshener. It's comfortable, safe, and predictable—all the things Joe's life in Long Island was not. So here's the problem: How does he teach his three boys (ages 10, 7, and 3) not to be arrogant, entitled brats? They are, after all, white-collar kids. Now, Joe is certain he's a better person for having struggled on a journey from near-poverty to this place. Short of casting his children into the streets, how does he educate his boys about that?

"I'm always on guard to how they react to their lives. My kids don't know what collar they are." Joe's solution is to reveal to his children as much about his childhood as he can. He goes out of his way to make sure they know his parents—really know them. "I want them to have the values I had growing up." There is, Joe says, no foolproof way to avoid a sense of entitlement in children, except to constantly remind them not to take for granted the stuff they have. Joe is always bringing up such things: "What a nice fire we have going tonight." "Isn't this a great room?" Sensitive to working people, Joe makes sure his children view any painters, builders, and garbage collectors they might see as people to be respected. Joe purposely tackles repair jobs himself—though he can afford contractors—to show his young men that no one is above such labor. Still, there's a problem with the plan. "It's arrogant of me to watch out for entitlement in my kids," he says, "because my father raised us with things he didn't have." Although, to be honest, those were luxuries like light and heat.

Lately, Joe's been having these ideas about showing his kids what real work truly means. His middle-class-born wife, Lisa, for whom country clubs and cocktail parties were not foreign entities when she was growing up, has not warmed up to the notion. It does sound a little out there, despite the obvious symmetry: Joe wants his kids to learn how to fish, just like he did. His brother-in-law is a commercial fisherman on Long Island. "And what I'd like to see happen, when my oldest can work, is for him to spend time on a fishing boat." Now, commercial fishing is considered one of the most dangerous jobs on the planet. Remember *The Perfect Storm?* But Joe sees other perils. "I think about the danger of having your kids grow up and not know what it's like to put in a hard day's work. Raking leaves is not the same thing. It's just easier to learn that satisfaction of work through manual labor." Beyond the life lesson, the kids could actually pick up marketable skills—being a bay man, a fisherman. Joe likes this idea for his children because it's already an in-case-of-emergency-break-glass option for him. Blue-collar people think this way: "I know that if my career flames out, I could go make a living on the water somewhere. And that's the kind of insurance worth having: knowing you have another way of putting food on the table."

Another blue-collar parenting notion that Joe is having a hard time selling to Lisa has to do with college. Specifically, his not wanting to pay for it. It's not that Joe's overly parsimonious. He just believes that, like hauling squirming fish out of the cold Atlantic, paying your own way through school is an important part of feeling like a self-made person. "It always disturbed me seeing my upper-class peers in school who thought they were entitled to their educations. Somebody was always writing a check, so it was no big deal." But for Joe, paying his way through St. John's University in Queens was a major accomplishment, a B-12 shot to the old self-esteem. He wants his kids to go through their college years feeling like they're earning the education. Of course, Joe knows what this sounds like. "It makes me look like a terrible person. And I'm going to lose the argument because my wife thinks I'm nuts. I know I'm going to write the checks, and that's the way it'll be. But it's still a position worth taking—that my kids can choose what they want to be, and be masters of their own destinies."

Jerks in the Next Generation?

A number of Straddlers tell me that the experience of struggling for everything they ever got in life was so valuable to them, they consider it bad parenting to simply hand over things to their children—including (especially) education. Leticia Vega and her Straddler husband had a fight about it before they even got married. At the time, the children were hypothetical, but Leticia's feelings were quite real. "My husband-to-be said over dinner once he wanted to send any kids he would have to Harvard or MIT, and he'd pay for it. I told him, 'That's the most stupid thing I ever heard. If you give kids something, they'll never value or appreciate it.' It was a big blowout."

Leticia, 38, has an undergraduate degree from Berkeley and an MBA from Stanford. Her twin sister, Betty, also has a Berkeley degree (the two won full scholarships) and a master's in engineering from Stanford. The daughters of Mexican immigrants, both women now work for Sun Microsystems in Silicon Valley. A diminutive woman with dark hair, brown eyes, and nicely tailored clothes, she suggests we meet in a noisy Palo Alto coffeehouse frequented by other high-tech executives. She is in her element. But it was a long trip to get here. Leticia was raised in Northern California among apple ranches. Her father was a ranch foreman and her mother cleaned hotel rooms. For 18 years, Leticia would watch soap operas like *General Hospital* and *The Young and the Restless*, her primary exposure to people who'd gone to college.

At least, it seemed like the characters had degrees. She entered the business world because she wanted to wear high heels and nylons to work, as the soap actors did. To her it was glamorous and so very different from the kinds of clothes Mexican-immigrant ranch workers wore.

When her father retired, Leticia and her husband bought him a house and 11 acres of orchards near the very land he used to work. Leticia's husband once said that eventually the ranch will go to their children. As she did in the college argument, Leticia laid down the blue-collar law again. "I'm not going to protect assets just to pass them on. You can't instill values in kids if you just give them things. The things I most cherish are things I worked for. And so many times, inheritance leaves kids at each others' throats."

While it may not seem like much of a problem to the middle class, money—specifically, the abundance of it—gets to be troubling for limbo folk who believe working-class values are as important a legacy as wealth. Ed Haldeman, the Boston investment guru with millions, had a very specific concern about what money might do to his son and daughter: "I worried we'd get jerks in the next generation." When the children were growing up, Ed purposely lived well below his means. In his lifetime, he has accrued the kind of fortune that allows a person to own planes. He purposely avoided them. Neither did he travel to Europe with the kids, nor live in a 20,000-square-foot mansion. Don't misunderstand, they wanted for nothing and lived comfortably. But it was a consciously scaled-down lifestyle, fashioned so the children would not know extreme opulence. Ed tried to go further and replicate the privations of his working-class past, telling the children they had very little. But this wasn't possible because the kids knew there was always a safety net stretched tight below them.

"There's a joke among people like me: 'My dream is to come back as my kid someday.' " Unable to pretend he was strapped for cash, Ed did the next-best thing, taking his son and daughter on frequent blue-collar field trips to the poor North Philadelphia neighborhood where his family had worked, telling stories of how hard it was to grow up with so very little, and how important it is to help other people. When Ed started putting money away for his children, a few friends advised against it, saying they'll turn 18 and buy drugs or give it all to the Hare Krishnas. But Ed took the gamble, telling his son, Matthew, essentially, that there was enough money for him never to have to work. Rather than chase debutantes and race cars, he's used the flexibility and freedom to do something reflective of his parents' values: Matthew graduated from college and plans to attend a seminary, then start a ministry in inner-city Washington.

Ed had always worried the money would soften his son, rob him of the blue-collar drive and ambition he'd possessed. The kid wouldn't be tough enough. "But you know what I finally figured out?" Ed asks. "Although toughness is usually a good thing, an awful lot of self-centered aggressiveness comes with it. Matthew doesn't have any of that. He's not selfish. And that's good."

To assure himself that he would avoid what he calls spoiled-brat syndrome in his children, Chicago millionaire Don McNeeley practiced a kind of segregation, keeping his kids away from the offspring of upper-class parents as often as possible. Earlier in his career, part of Don's compensation was a country club membership, but he vowed his kids wouldn't see what that life was like. He swears to me that he once saw an 11-year-old boy at the club sign for a milkshake he had just gotten for a friend, saying, "Come on, Tommy, let me get this one. You got the last one." So he banned his kids from the club. From the time they were very young, Don's children had to stack their empty plates at their table in restaurants, to help the waitress or busboy carry them away. "Somebody like your grandmother is doing the cleaning-up here," Don would tell them. Like Ed, Don made sure to live below his means. His first house cost $30,000, which he sold for $60,000, the price of his second house. That sold for $120,000. His current house cost that much, though he can, frankly, afford any domicile on the market. That would be losing perspective, however, and that's something he won't do in front of his children. "I haven't taken a pledge of poverty, but I don't like gluttony. How much it takes to make you satisfied is a function of where you come from," he says.

Don wanted his kids to start work young. Too many middle-class kids don't have before- or after-school jobs, he believes. (Fred Gardaphé, in fact, says his son is 17 and hasn't worked a day in his life. By the time Fred was 17, Fred says with a smirk, he was ready to retire.) In Chicago, a child can't work until he or she is 16. Don circumvented that by buying a summer house in a resort community 200 miles north, in Wisconsin, where children can work starting at age 14. They began by picking up papers blowing around the parking lots of resorts. Having his children earn their own spending money was vital to Don, although he knows he can't always "protect" them from his wealth. "I was coaching my daughter's hockey team. One day I watched as each kid popped onto the ice, each with $800 of equipment, including her. This is on top of ice time at $300 an hour. And I remember thinking to myself, 'These are the kids I hated as a kid.' And she's my very own child."

Straddler parents insist their children not think of themselves as better or superior people. They straighten out their kids when they make a remark about a child at school with holes in his or her pants. If there's a homeless person on the street, parents tell them not to shun them, not to ever view humans as nuisances. They scrutinize their kids for signs of elitism as scrupulously as they check their eyes for drug use. Helen Tom, a Straddler homemaker living in Washington, says she and her husband eschew the fancy private schools for their children. The daughter of Chinese immigrants, Helen grew up on New York's tough Lower East Side, then went on to Yale, and received an MBA from Columbia. She worked for a time in the upper echelons of New York banking. "After my work experience and exposure to the affluent at school, I don't aspire to being affluent," she says. "Affluence generates elitism in children. And there's always someone wealthier than you. You don't want your child to be the poorest kid in an elitist group. I've felt like an outlyer enough in my life. I don't want my children to have to deal with that."

At the same time they're guarding against creating middle-class monsters, Straddler parents try to teach their children to speak up for themselves to adults—not obnoxiously, but in constructive ways. Remember, as children, these people were taught to stay mum and to fear and respect grown-ups. What they said or thought could not have mattered less. Many Straddlers could barely speak to adults as children, let alone voice their preferences. They felt unworthy of people's time or consideration. The difference between my childhood and that of an entitled middle-class kid's was brought home to me the day I had to interview a well-off guy in his Upper West Side apartment in Manhattan. I knocked on the door, and the man answered with his six-year-old son in tow. The boy purposely stood in front of me, blocking me from going in. "Now, Evan, don't we want to invite Mr. Lubrano in to sit down and talk with Daddy?" the father said.

"No, no, no, no!" the kid screamed. The father continued to try to convince the little prince to let me in, saying the word *please* a lot and essentially asking the child's permission to allow my entrance. Finally, the boy relented and I could do my job. All I could think about was what my father would have said had I been insane enough to block a guest from coming into our place. My guess is it would have been very loud.

Jealous

The unalloyed self-confidence of middle-class children is something Rebecca Beckingham still marvels at, and she's living with two such kids, ages 9 and 11, the sons of her fiancé. Rebecca can't help comparing her put-upon farm childhood to her soon-to-be stepkids' sterling upbringing on Manhattan's Upper East Side, where great swarms of uniformed private-schoolers take over whole sidewalks and intersections—like Canada geese in riotous ground formation—on their daily way from gorgeously appointed apartments to staggeringly well-supplied schools. She finds herself divided sometimes on how she feels about all this. When you have kids, Rebecca tells herself, you want them to be self-possessed enough to say, "I want this." That's a good thing that can only help them later in life. But at the same time, it absolutely blows her away to actually witness entitlement in action. "I see them having no qualms expecting X, Y, and Z. Not even expecting—more like saying to themselves, 'I should get this and this.' Invisible forms of power go into growing up middle class, in things like life chances and quality of education. You have parents who support you and are educated. And from these life chances come the self-confidence and the sense of entitlement. They don't have to worry, 'Do I belong?' They don't even entertain the idea of whether they belong. They're just there. And that's a great gift, when you're starting off life with that."

Dinnertime, especially, is when Rebecca is convinced the children are living golden lives. What happens around the table is precisely what she'd yearned for as a little girl, during those sullen, silent meals where children were, at best, tolerated. The child is accorded godlike status in the middle-class home, or so it seems to Rebecca. Every utterance, every piece of art or writing, is treated with near-reverence. Every event, no matter how small, is seen by a parent as a teachable moment that can impart an important lesson. "At the table, I giggle to myself, it's so fantasy-like," Rebecca says. "It's exactly what I imagined the other students at my graduate school grew up and felt like. I had so many gaps in my knowledge and never felt I could keep filling all the holes in the dike. And I never believed I could ever catch up."

The children and their father (and now Rebecca) have philosophical discussions about Sartre over the potatoes. Rebecca's fiancé, a downtown attorney with educated parents, takes pains to explain everything. A word will come up that stumps the kids and he'll suggest they go to the dictionary. He will suspend dinner to have his children look up a place they never heard of in the atlas. Rebecca cannot imagine a working-class family interrupting mealtime to ascertain the latitude and longitude of the Marshall Islands. "He quizzes them in the shower about foreign countries. It's amazing to me. I find myself jealous of their childhood."

Renny Christopher was, if not jealous, then keenly aware that her stepdaughter has had markedly better opportunities in life than she did. Fortunately, they like each other. The young woman is the daughter of Renny's former husband. Like Rebecca, Renny found herself comparing her own background with the stepdaughter's—not in a petty way, but with a sense of head-shaking wonder. For example, the only reason Renny took the SATs was that, at the last minute, a counselor told her it might be a good idea to sit for the exam. She had never heard of it. Meanwhile, with the help of a father with a master's degree, a mother with a Ph.D., not to mention Professor Renny, the stepdaughter took the PSAT, the SAT (twice), read up on potential colleges, and made visits to the places on her shortlist.

When Renny was young, her parents' greatest ambition for her was that she live to adulthood and not get pregnant as a teenager. No one mentioned college. The stepdaughter, on the other hand, has had endless numbers of family conferences in which concerned people have quizzed her on what she might do with her future and how she could get there. They helped her fill out all of life's important forms and applications—made sure her boxes were checked and her papers were in order. There was continuity between her family life and going to college, and beyond. The young woman actually had a crowd of supporters at her Ph.D. dissertation defense.

"For her," says Renny, "there were people at home who could help, people who valued school and knew its importance. That's the kind of difference cultural capital makes. My stepdaughter—with whom I'm still close—has had a more holistic life. There was supportiveness and connectedness all the way through. And that's something we never had."

8

DUALITY: THE NEVER-ENDING STRUGGLE WITH IDENTITY

How, ultimately, is a Straddler to live?

If you learn the language of the new world, can you still speak with the folks from the old country? Do you cross the border and try to pass for white collar, until you totally assimilate? Do you stay true blue and risk alienation and career stagnation among the middle class? Or do you blend town and gown, creating a hybrid who is, at the end of the day, at home in neither world?

Ideally, a Straddler becomes bicultural: Understand what made you who you are, then learn to navigate the new setting. If you were to leave your family and completely give yourself over to the new mainstream, disavowing your background in the process, you'd risk distancing yourself from yourself. It's a form of self-hatred. As Laurene Finley says, you internalize the stereotypes—believe you're trash without refinement— and wind up disowning yourself. How does that help? The best situation has people maintaining connection with their families, while simultaneously supporting the things they need for themselves in their new middle-class worlds. And they work to cut down on that imposter feeling.

Ah, but duality is tricky living. Most of us Straddlers hold within ourselves worlds that can never be brought together. I often feel inhabited by two people who can't speak to each other. Limbo folk like me, Jake Ryan says, are "torn between competing loyalties." Maybe there's a way to change the outer package, to self-gussy until you look like one of Them—until you drive what they drive, live where they live, and on and on. But how real is that? "If you are born into the working class," Janet Zandy, the upstate New York academic tells me, "and you're willing to change your speech and appearance, and deny the culture of your working-class background, then you could pass as a member of the dominant culture. But you will never belong there." In her writings, she invokes W.E.B. DuBois's sense of "two-ness" regarding race, and suggests it applies to class as well: being in two worlds at once and belonging to neither.[1] I can say I've moved beyond Brooklyn, but it always has a way of finding me, calling me out, and reminding me it's in there somewhere.

The days that you thought you were done with are never done with you.

All the (Expensive) Pretty Horses

I am sitting in the worn and graceful stands at Devon, historic horse stomping grounds on the Main Line outside Philadelphia. Throughout much of the twentieth century, the Main Line suburbs were synonymous with über-culture and breeding in America—the height of WASP high society. Hope Montgomery Scott, the woman on whom the Katharine Hepburn character in *The Philadelphia Story* is based, helped make the Devon Horse Show into a prestigious annual event. The Main Line is a lot less WASPy and more diverse these days, inhabited as it is by educated-class "meritocrats," according to author David Brooks in *Bobos in Paradise: The New Upper Class and How They Got There.*[2] Essentially, bourgeois bohemians (bobos)—an educated affluent class—have supplanted WASPs as the ultimate cultural power, Brooks says. But let me just say that there are enough plaid-worshiping, bourbon-and-marbled-beef-indulging, Bitsy-and-TiTi-nicknamed, Roman-numeral-appendaged, Dr.-and-Mrs.-So-and-So, Friends-of-the-Harrimans-Vanderbilts-and-Bushes, old-money types at Devon to make you at least question the notion that the WASPs are no longer running this country. Here, horses' bloodlines are studied by folks with impressive breeding of their own. Cast your eyes around the robin's-egg-blue grandstands, with the cupolas and flapping pennants; see the fussily maintained flower boxes around Dixon Oval, where pampered, strutting mounts compete—some of them worth hundreds of thousands of dollars; marvel at folks who can pay $29 for a couple of sandwiches and some soup, not to mention $450 for paddock boots meant only for trudging through manure, and you may be reminded of Jimmy Stewart's line from *The Philadelphia Story* about the pretty sight of the privileged class enjoying its privileges.

So why am I here for Dressage at Devon, a kind of horse-ballet exhibition? How does a working-class, sweat-sock-wearing ant get to crawl into the picnic among the D.Q.s (spoiled and demanding teenage dressage queens), the horse-hobbyist second wives, the write-off-ready burghers in rainproof L.L. Bean hats? Appalling as this sounds, the white-collar me stole the car keys while my blue-collar self was asleep, and today two horses that I own with my wife are on display. How did this happen?

This is embarrassing, and requires some explanation. I met my wife at the Loma Prieta earthquake outside Santa Cruz, California, in October 1989. The *Daily News* sent me to cover the event; Linda at the time was a geophysicist working for the federal government and living in the Bay Area. I interviewed her about the shaking. She was, at the time, indulging in a lifelong passion: equines. Linda was unable to afford horses as a child, but made up for it in a hurry with a nifty bit of blue-collar business savvy. In exchange for caring for a rich California entrepreneur's stallion, Linda negotiated free breeding rights from the guy—all the horse semen she could use. She then sought out mare owners and offered them a deal: Loan her their horses' wombs for a year, let her flood them with little squigglies and keep the subsequent babies, and she would return the mares to the owners several months pregnant. Thus, she parlayed the free breedings into free babies, and started building a herd. She had her first horse when she was 24. Shortly after we started dating, she took me out to a barn that she rented. "See these?" she said, smiling in that way she has. "They're non-negotiable." She offered me an out, though, saying that I could still run away before I became too deeply involved. You have to understand that, as she told me this, she was stroking the neck of a nickering little foal at sunset, while puffs of dandelion and milkweed blew through Woodside's autumn air and snowed into her dark, shining hair. Way too smitten to think straight, I said no problem, bring them on. Today, we own 11 backyard-bred horses on a farm in South Jersey. I measure my love in horse manure, mucking stalls for my baby when I can. It keeps us close, though I don't even ride.

To me, horses have always been symbols of the rich. Now, I must reconcile the irreconcilable and deal with being a guy from the working class who owns slick and lovely hay-burners. I hate the idea that some people in our area think I'm well-to-do. In their eyes, I am the kind of guy I grew up blindly disliking and mistrusting. Near-strangers come to the farm to borrow money, and I give it to them—maybe because of four-legged guilt.

What can I say? I love a woman who loves horses. So here am I at Devon, the son of a construction worker among the upper classers. Part of me worries that at any moment they will demand to see my bank account and cast me out. Part of me burns to tell all these high rollers to kiss my horse's butt. It's confusing. I hold our chestnut yearling Beau Soleil as a friend French-braids his blond mane in preparation for his Devon debut. I keep thinking about that Talking Heads song in which David Byrne wonders how he got to where he is. I whisper to the horse that I shouldn't be at a horse show, that this is not my beautiful life. He has no sympathy. We did geld him, after all. "Don't let the duality bite you," I think I hear him say.

Ambivalent Schizophrenia

Straddlers tell me it's crazy to be middle-aged or approaching it and still be struggling with identity. "This is about your very basic being—who you are," says Gillian Richardson, the Buffalo writing teacher. "But you're in a limbo, just not fitting in. You can't be the total person you are with family, and you don't fit in among the brownnosers at work." One never truly crosses over, Barbara Jensen asserts. Because it's hard to live in a kind of no-man's-land, she likes to tell people who aren't sure where they belong that they are creating something, inventing their lives as they go.

Of course, it's important to remember that Straddlers consider themselves lucky to have escaped the need to debilitate their bodies and deaden their minds in working-class jobs. Carlos Figueroa, a 33-year-old research assistant in American politics at New School University in New York City, forces himself to remember all of the faces he saw on the assembly line in Central Jersey, where he worked during teenage summers, making computer fans. Sunken eyes, premature wrinkles, and unhealthy skin from too much smoking—these were people who wore out young, with decades of work ahead. Carlos's father worked in the factory year-round, but made sure his son would not permanently fall into it and develop an assembly-line face. "Every time I achieve, I see the images," Carlos says. "I think to myself, 'Move forward, but don't forget.'"

Still, some say that the submersion of their old selves in order to better fit into the middle class is debilitating. They experience what Barbara Jensen calls a "survivor's guilt" of becoming educated and moving away, while family and friends remain blue collar. Also, Straddlers often become irritated at people around them who never had to be self-conscious about class. It's a tough way to get through the day.

What's more, Straddlers retain the blue-collar suspicion of anyone in authority, only to quickly realize that some of *them* are now actually the ones in charge. Many eschew the boss's job, because it comes with too many negative connotations from past family life. Needless to say, ambivalence is a unifying theme among the middle-class children of working-class parents, says scholar Jack Metzgar, as class-mobile people see a downside to pushing off from the working class and a not-so-upside to reaching the beckoning shores of the middle class. Their schizophrenic lives of mobility don't allow for the comforts of tradition and memory—what Richard Rodriguez calls the "consolations of regularity." That's because everything has to change.

Always, it seems, people living the limbo life have a relationship with the world that is complex, contradictory, and difficult.

Paul Groncki, the New York businessman, is putting a deal together with partners willing to contribute $500,000. Heavyweights with impressive backgrounds, one guy has a place on Nantucket, the other on Cape Cod; both are middle-class-born. Though he's an economist with a Ph.D. and years of banking experience, Paul still feels as though he's out of his league, outmanned and outclassed, because he was born to blue-collar parents. "It's incredible how this stuff stays with you."

The start of every semester is the tough time for Loretta Stec, because she still doesn't buy the notion of herself as a professor, even though she's been teaching at the college level since 1986. To help herself believe she's capable of running a classroom, Loretta literally has to put on a jacket. Dressing up looks professorial to her and lends her a sense of authority. So she will rely on her clothes for aid and buoyancy—a life jacket to float her through the rough waters of September and January. In her spiffy formal clothes before those opening sessions, Loretta will regard the fit and the lapels in the mirror and tell herself, "You are the professor. You know a lot. Go and be the professor now." She always has struggled with an absurdly inflated view of what a professor is supposed to be. They had transformed her life, after all, changed her collar and her outlook, and therefore possessed powers she surely lacked. "It is so hard to reconfigure myself after every semester break to move myself back into the place of authority, because I come from working-class Jersey, come from a house where I was the daughter who didn't do the things a working-class girl is supposed to do, like marry and have kids." So why would anyone listen to her? she thinks.

Renny Christopher didn't follow the route her parents had prescribed for her, either. As a consequence, she's lived through some heavy-duality days. At the same time she was attending San Jose State University, Renny was working with her carpenter father, doing a commercial remodeling job on yuppie-palace health clubs. She'd literally rush from the job site to class in the middle of the workday, paint and putty on her pants, a sweaty bandana on her head. She remembers putting in a beautiful hardwood floor for a basketball court in one of the clubs. That felt like an accomplishment, a tangible piece of work that meant something. The stuff she was learning in school was so abstract. Today, she contemplates that dichotomy still and asks herself who is more useful to society, the carpenter or the professor? "Those two halves of me can't talk very well with each other and can't occupy the same space at the same time," she says. "Half the time, I regret the path I've taken. And the other half, I feel there was no other path." Renny's brother has lived a blue-collar life more like their parents', working as a 911 dispatcher and living near the folks, a geographical metaphor for remaining in the world of his upbringing, integrated and close. Renny still remembers with some guilt the sign her father had made for the joint carpentry business that never was: "Christopher & Daughter." She wishes it would have been enough, to be able to work with her dad and become a less divided person. But the blue-collar work got to be boring. While she'd been laying that lovely basketball floor that shined and sat plumb level, she'd been thinking about the books she was reading. Her father, she knew, was thinking about the wood. And that was enough for him. Renny has strong loyalties to the world of her origin, which she thinks was better in many ways than her current place. Yet she did opt to leave that world. The truth is, there is no answer for her. "I am a person with a divided consciousness. I live in a permanent sense of dissatisfaction."

At the same time they wear their working-class backgrounds as a badge, Straddlers still look for acceptance in the middle-class world they don't believe they're good enough to join. "Even though I went to an Ivy League school," says Marianne Costantinou, now living in the Bay Area, "it never absorbed into my skin, never became who I was." Though she's a college-educated writer, Marianne will describe herself first as Greek, then as a child of immigrants. In kindergarten, Marianne couldn't speak English and didn't know how to ask the teacher for permission to go to the bathroom. She wet herself, and the teacher made Marianne sit in a corner of the room with a curtain drawn around her. Children would peek in and laugh as Marianne waited for her mother to come and pick her up. "All my life I have felt like the little girl in the corner with wet pants," she says. "It's got to be the reason why I work so hard. I mean, I work constantly. I'm forever seeking validation from the middle class, because I don't feel good enough in their world. I'll never change the way I speak, dress, and act. I definitely have a working-class . . . attitude. But I still crave validation to prove I made it with them, in the middle class, in some regard."

Enduring what can only be described as a kind of lifelong shame, some people will hide their dual citizenship and not let the white collars know that they're different. It's like that for Cleveland Straddler Amy Reed. She's long had a sense that she doesn't belong in the executive setting in which she works. When people ask her where she grew up, she'll lie and say the tonier eastern suburbs, where well-appointed streets wind upward through the hills like flute solos, rather than in working-class Maple Heights to the south. "I'm embarrassed by the blue-color origin of that. I don't want to feel inferior. I'm dealing with coworkers and bosses who grew up on the East Coast. Some of them make millions, put their kids in exclusive schools. I don't want them to know what my origins were. We're not classless in this society. My mother said education would raise us up, but I'm still blue collar. It doesn't go away."

Who wants anyone to think your parents were too stupid, lazy, and unmotivated to make it out of the working class? Signe Kastberg asks. Newly minted middle-class Americans don't admit to their blue-collar heritage because it's not safe, she believes. They run too much of a risk of being looked down upon and rejected. Charles Sackrey understands this: "There is great contempt from the upper classes. There's an assumption that you're dumb." Signe calls herself fortunate for having grown up with a Scandinavian background; she thinks it has hidden her collar like an expensive silk scarf. "Scandinavians are aloof and reserved. I grew up that way and behave in that way and it stood me in good stead. Blue-collar people are demonstrative, show anger. The upper class doesn't show anger. So I've been able to blend in. In my family, no one ever yelled."

Maybe people shouldn't have to resort to subterfuge, but they need something to feel comfortable in their skins. Some go the other way, of course, using that blue-collar swagger they learned back in the neighborhood to advantage. "I never hide my background," Philly ad man Anthony Lukas asserts. "I use it to surprise people, to have them ask where I'm from, then shock them, wave it like a flag. I like making them feel uncomfortable, standing right in their space. My business partners and I look at the middle-class ad guys and say, 'If this is the competition, bring it on.' " In quiet moments, though, Anthony will admit that he's not relaxed in middle-class places, and will always believe he doesn't belong. "I'm stuck between two worlds. I tell my wife I'm the Great Pretender. I fake it a lot. Maybe people like me should find each other and form some type of club."

Rebecca Beckingham once actually did just that. When she was studying at New School University, she "came out" as working class; Rebecca purposely borrows from the language of self-revelation used in gay discourse. She "disclosed" to all her professors that she was a farm girl from uneducated parents. Then she put up posters around campus with questions: "Are you from a working-class background?" "Do you feel uncomfortable talking about it?" For a while, Rebecca had tried to hide her past. Then she decided the more healthy course was to publicly embrace it. There was no significant talk of class—shunned as the "C-word"—on a campus that prided itself on being steeped in the politics of self-identification: race, gender, and class. She organized meetings, and between 6 and 20 students came for around six sessions. Shy and unsure at first, like first-time 12-steppers with something big to reveal, the kids started opening up and talking about feeling outnumbered and misunderstood at an elite school. They went up to Rebecca after each meeting, brimming and aglow: "Thank you. This is so great. I've never seen anything like this before." One day, a woman in her late 50s showed up at a meeting. All eyes locked on her, and everyone instantly recognized her as one of the deans of the school. She took a seat and listened. Afterward, the dean told Rebecca that she was from the working class, and had always been uncomfortable at the school. She had felt overlooked because of her background and believed that she had to overcompensate by asserting herself in more and more strident ways, which felt false and awful. The woman thanked Rebecca and left.

Not surprisingly, you'll find among the limbo set people who are totally at ease, despite the duality. When I meet such a man, I linger in his presence, hoping to glean a secret or two. Milton Sommerfeld and his wife Carolin live on a lush golf course in a gated community in Chandler, Arizona. Their large, comfortable house has soaring white ceilings, white carpet, a Jacuzzi, and a pool. Milton teaches at Arizona State University; Carolin used to teach elementary school. Both of them came up from hard-working, blue-collar backgrounds in Texas. Carolin's father was in the dredging business on the Gulf Coast; Milton's family had a Central Texas farm. As a young man, he used to spend eternal, hot days on a roaring tractor, rolling up and down the rows of corn or cotton, one growing cycle after another, a few yards at a time, his entire world as big as the field in front of him. The ocean of crop made Milton feel lonely, a tiny boat adrift on an undulating sea. The nearest neighbor was 5,280 feet away. When you get to the end of one row, all you do is switch direction and go back up the next one, the boring symmetry of the field meager stimulus for a brainy boy with potential. After a while, a low-boiling panic bubbles in a row-riding man who believes he has more to offer the world. A voice in Milton's head eventually grew louder than the rumbling machine he commanded: "What am I about? And what am I going to do? Is this going to fulfill me?" Milton thought it could if his parents had owned 1,000 acres or something, and he could grow the farm into a thriving, diverse agribusiness. But the Sommerfelds didn't have much land. "It would have been very difficult to be the level of farmer I wanted to be if I'd stayed on that farm," he says.

Milton went to college, became a professor, and built a life among southwestern academics. He bought the family farm, which he now rents out. Often, Milton will return to Texas to see old friends and family, and fish the river that runs through his property. To him, it feels like he didn't skip a beat. "I can go back and be a good ol' boy. I don't see a real gap between myself and the people I grew up with who never went to college. We go hunting together. We fall right into place." Talk comes easily and the food tastes the same as when he left. Similarly, Milton has no problems at ASU. "The white-collar world was never a big adjustment to me. Be trustworthy, live your life with integrity, and people will respect you. I feel I belong easily in both places. I can go back; I can stay here. I can be a good ol' boy and interact with the hometown folks. And then I make the transition to ASU. I'm always comfortable."

So is Jeffrey Orridge. We talk in his office at Mattel headquarters in El Segundo, a large, character-free high-rise in an office park of similar, unimaginatively designed buildings sitting along one of the endless clogged arteries in Southern California. Jeffrey's office has a window, unlike most of his colleagues'. The symbolism is clear enough: Those with vision get views. He's got that corporate-casual thing down, wearing dark wool slacks and a cream-colored, soft, and roomy shirt buttoned to the neck, without a tie. Behind him on shelves sit boxes of Hot Wheels cars, brightening the drab decor and lightening the corporate vibe. Guys who make and sell toys must have some fun in them, right? Jeffrey used to display his diplomas to afford himself a kind of home-court advantage whenever somebody born to the middle class would walk in. He wanted that person to know that he belonged here as well, even though his parents were blue collar. After a while, though, Jeffrey realized the sheepskins were a crutch, and that he himself was proof enough of his worthiness.

Born into hard-time Queens, then schooled with capitalist-cream kids at Collegiate—arguably, the mother of all preps—before graduating from Amherst and Harvard Law School, Jeffrey has the singular ability to balance street and boardroom in one high-functioning head. He can't really tell you how he does it. That's just how it works.

His best duality story is set in his blue-chip, corporate law days back in New York. At the same time he was helping the rich stay that way at his firm, he was promoting nightclubs around Manhattan, and in fact was a co-owner of one spot. It was some balancing act. "I lived in both worlds, carrying myself very differently in each," he explains. "The people you deal with on the party circuit are a lot different than the ones in corporate law." Why he needed this is hard to say. Jeffrey now says that he was simply expressing the two major parts of himself: the urban party guy and the brainy overachiever. He had fun being both of his personae—just as long as he remembered to change clothes. The wrong costume in the wrong place would be a disaster. The law firm uniform of a blue or gray suit with 1¼-inch cuffs and muted tie would not play in the club. And Jeffrey would have been sent home by the partners had he shown up for a day of lawyering in his black silk mock-neck shirt, leather pants, and sport coat. He always kept spare clothes in the car.

On one duality day, Jeffrey was closing a deal with a huge revolving-credit facility at the opposing counsel's firm on Wall Street, another top-tier blue-chipper. Negotiations had been complex, stretching from 8 A.M. to 8 P.M. Jeffrey then left work and headed to a club in which he was hosting an event. He changed clothes and when the doors opened at 10 P.M., one of the first guys in turned out to be carrying a gun. The bouncers stopped him, saying no firearms were allowed in the club. The guy then started yelling about how he knows Jeffrey and that they go back a long time, and if I wanna carry a piece, I will, and who are you to stop me? Jeffrey was summoned and, sure enough, the gun guy was someone he had grown up with—one of the crew with June Bug, the young criminal who had taken a liking to the bookish, athletic Jeffrey and allowed him to live back during the days when not so many boys in the neighborhood were managing to do that. "It was just yet another negotiation," Jeffrey says. He let the guy know delicately that firearms were not permitted. The Queens man felt he had needed it for protection, out of his territory in Manhattan, but Jeffrey assured him it was not the kind of place where he had to worry about watching his back. The guy trusted Jeffrey and gave up his gun to a bouncer.

"Two very different kinds of negotiations in a 24-hour period," Jeffrey says, smiling. "It was just that easy for me. I had been immersed in both environments for so long. You just learn to speak to people in the idioms of the particular cultural environment. When you're throwing parties at nightclubs, your demeanor, the way you speak, the way you carry yourself—it's just more blue-collar-aggressive and loud. It's very urban and very real. You're just as self-controlled and poised as in the law firm, but in a different way. Your language is more colloquial, and you use slang. You'd never curse at the law firm. I'm not suggesting the party promotion business was any less important than the firm. You just use different tools to get the job done."

Jeffrey's friends had difficulty watching him ricochet from corporate days to party nights among the working class and were worried that he was literally displaying a form of schizophrenia. He laughed and said he was fine. He was just reconciling his two halves, which seem to always have lived amicably inside him.

Like Jeffrey, Suzanne Bilello lets the dichotomy of her Ivy League/working-class background work for her. Doing foundation work in South America, she can just as easily sit down with the president of Brazil to develop some philanthropic program as she can walk into a slum in Rio de Janeiro to help the impoverished. "Very few people I know can do that," she asserts. Interestingly, Suzanne has moved so far from her working-class roots that her refined manner initially lends people the incorrect impression that she is incapable of dealing with the poor. Only after reciting a resume and pedigree can she convince doubters that she has the flexibility to talk to all kinds of people, and that she's not the aristocrat she appears to be upon first impression. "I've been there" goes a long way toward making that point.

Unfortunately for me, Milton, Jeffrey, and Suzanne cannot offer any single tip, any true guide, for being well-adjusted. Self-possessed and centered, they easily handle the dichotomy of their past and present circumstances. For them, it just happens. For the rest of us, however, duality is hard work.

You Haven't Changed a Bit

For the fish-out-of-water set, flopping on the gleaming floor of the middle class gets exhausting. That's why formal reunions are important for Straddlers—they serve as refreshing dives back into familiar waters. The Straddlers join up with the old crowd and become recharged with the legitimacy of their own backgrounds. Unfortunately, the high only lasts a little while. And people who've traveled sometimes great distances to revisit their roots because of dissatisfaction with the white-collar life learn that these all-blue weekends are not the ultimate answer. After the nostalgia clears like burned-off fog and the remember-whens are all carefully recited like verses of an epic poem, something will be seen or said that will remind the reminiscer of why he or she left in the first place. Then there will be a slow, sad dawning in the brain: "Oh, now I remember. I'm the one who doesn't really belong anywhere."

When Susan Borrego, the Cal Tech associate dean, went back to Detroit for her twentieth high school reunion, she was extremely nervous, worrying about her outsider status. She was, after all, one of just two people from her class who had graduated from college. What's more, she was bringing her daughter, and Susan didn't know whether the girl would have a good time. On top of that, Susan had come out as a lesbian since she last saw her classmates, and she was accompanied by her partner. At first, all anxieties melted away when her classmates saw her. The guys from the football team crowded around her and made a lovely fuss, one of them taking her face in his hands and literally petting her head in a gentle, adoring manner. They didn't have any problems with Susan's partner and marveled at how her daughter looked exactly like Susan did at 18. The class clown told Susan's daughter that Susan was the one who had taught him how to French-kiss. The guy had gotten a job with the railroad and worked with Susan's mother, a brakeman. There was a great deal to talk about, and Susan was enchanted. "It was like I'd never left," she says. "I didn't talk a lot about what I did. And they didn't care. It was a great evening. And I knew it was a very different life than I live now. With some sadness, I knew that."

But the next day, while Susan was still thinking that her white-collar life was devoid of the warmth and camaraderie she had just experienced with the old crowd, things started to change. The gang had reconvened, but now people were starting to tease her about her job, her status, and her effulgent white collar. "I'd become the symbol of the 'haves,' and to me, that's an insulting, almost despicable thing to be." And anyway, in the world of the true haves, Susan believes she is a have-not, especially out in Los Angeles, where ostentatious wealth is on daily display. For the longest time, Susan chose not to buy a house, so vivid was the association of home ownership with the despised upper classes. "For me, the house is the symbol of rich people, and the rich didn't care about people like my family. It's funky, I admit, but it's in my head." In the end, Susan realized that she could never fully explain herself to her friends. Her lesbianism they could deal with; her class differences, however, became too much. "Too few things in our lives are similar," she understands. "And I'm not what I knew myself to be."

Not long ago, Dennis George returned to South Philly for a grade-school reunion that followed an arc similar to Susan's. At first it was fun to be busting chops with the fellas, and he no longer felt like the fancy lawyer, as he joked around in a room full of bakers and city workers. But by the end of the evening, Dennis understood that he couldn't be around these people every night. For a moment, when the reverie was at its height and it looked like beer-soaked men were working up to a group hug, Dennis projected himself into his friends' lives, and what he saw wasn't pleasant: eight-hour blue-collar days at tough jobs. No tennis, which he loves. His kids not going to their nice schools. His wife being someone else, someone he can't talk to about President Bush's last trip to the West Coast. It was the language that sucked him in at first: He was uncorsetting his vocabulary, just letting the F-word rip with the guys, and it felt like fun. "At one point, though, I think I yelled out, 'Fuckin'-A,' and my wife looked at me, just looked at me." Between Dennis's vision of what a blue-collar life with his pals would be like, and that stare from Michele that showed him just how far off base he'd strayed, Dennis realized with absolute certainty he didn't belong in South Philly anymore. The evening was instructive. But it was time to go home.

It's tempting for people to say they want a simpler life, one not so fraught with stress and complication. People from blue-collar backgrounds can look at their friends who stuck with their kind and wonder whether they made the proper life choices. Mary Lou Finn, the Chicago Straddler, used to have days when she contemplated whether she wouldn't have been happier as a cop or something. Then she attended the reunion of a neighborhood football team her first husband had played with. She was shocked that so many of her working-class friends had not insisted that their own children go to college. "How did they not know?" she asked. "What did I get that they didn't? I wish I knew the answer." Mary Lou theorizes it's all about fear: People stay blue collar, she thinks, because they're afraid to move out of the neighborhood, go to college, and build new lives. "They do anything to keep their jobs, and then they pass along that ingrained fear they have to their children. So they wind up never knowing there's something better, never fully realizing what they're capable of." After the reunion, Mary Lou stopped thinking about strapping on a gun and enforcing the Chicago penal code. She was cured, at least for a while, of searching out the simpler life.

On Strike

The discomfort of duality—the internal imbalance of class—rarely materializes outside a Straddler's head. The feelings are real enough; they just don't normally manifest themselves in the everyday world. One exception, however, is the odd and dangerous exercise known as the newspaper strike. The bitter 19-month Detroit newspaper strike that began in July 1995, as well as the less damaging five-month New York *Daily News* strike (in which I participated) that started in October 1990, put class on display. More to the point, the labor actions showed duality in stark relief and had the white-collar kids of blue-collar, union parents minutely examining their lives, creeds, and values.

White-collar unions are oxymorons, but that's what you've got at newspapers, representing reporters, among others. The press workers, the drivers, the mailers, and all the other blue-collar crafts at newspapers have their unions as well. When management at the *Detroit News* and *Free Press* put a merit-pay system in place, the Newspaper Guild protested, saying it was a blow to collective bargaining and workers' rights. The strike was on. Right away, some say, the reporters' union erred by aligning itself with the blue-collar craft unions that had grievances the writers were not part of. But, others say, that's what union brotherhood is all about, especially in a town like Detroit, where so many people have worked so long at auto union jobs. So, middle-class, college-educated reporters were on the picket lines along with working-class folks. A newspaper delivery truck was burned, riot police were called, and replacement workers showed up and put photos of their loved ones on strikers' desks. Some reporters crossed the line, ending years-long friendships that are still being mourned.

For Straddler Larry Gabriel, the whole thing was a mess. The strike was eating time voraciously—days and days without pay. A reporter at the *Free Press*, he had bought a house and moved in one week before the strike had started. But his role was clear from the start: "Solidarity with the union was automatic for me." He wouldn't scab because his father, who'd worked in the paint shop at Ford and was a member of United Auto Workers Local 600, had told him throughout his life, "Always stick with the union." A loyal son, Larry had filled himself up with hot dogs, cake, and ice cream at UAW picnics, along with the rhetoric and lore of the great labor battles of the 1930s. His father had long preached the gospel of unquestioning solidarity of the workers against the bosses. With a deep blue-collar allegiance, Larry supported the other classes of workers—the custodians and mail workers—that he thought management was treating unfairly. "I had a good deal at the paper. For an African-American kid to make it to the *Free Press*, that was a big deal. I was a golden boy, all the editors told me. But I saw the way people they didn't like were being treated, and I said I'll stand up."

Even for Larry that wasn't easy. Six wearying months into the strike, he wavered, and began thinking about crossing as he saw his hard-won, white-collar life crumbling. "But a friend and I talked and it helped set me straight," Larry says. "He and I both write poetry and he said to me that the words 'poet' and 'scab' don't go together in the same sentence, or in the same person. I realized it was just the wrong thing to do. I could not go into that building."

Ultimately the strike ended, and the editors offered Larry his old job back. But there had been too much acrimony for him to return. He had bristled when an editor tried to entice him to cross the line during the job action, telling him that as a professional man, he had nothing in common with the blue collars. Today, he edits the UAW magazine, firmly adhering to his working-class roots. "Class never really made a big difference to me until the strike came. Then I realized my orientation was the same as custodians'—we're workers, together." Not many people see it that way at newspapers, where the reporters and the press workers and drivers never drink together or socialize at each others' homes. Larry doesn't hate the reporters who crossed the picket line, trying to save their jobs and houses. While some autoworkers' kids thought it blasphemy to disrespect a strike, others said, the hell with it, I'm finally out of the working class and I don't want to go back. "What can I say?" Larry explains. "That stuff didn't play with me."

My reaction was more ambivalent. I thought our strike at the *Daily News* had been misguided and ill-timed. The job action was, in fact, spurred by a surprise, unilateral walkout by some members of the drivers' union, as other unions were negotiating with the company. Our union went out in solidarity. The company was right when it charged that some of the blue-collar unions were featherbedding and fighting to remain male and white. But the union assessment that management was looking to bust them apart by bringing in replacement workers, including reporters, was also correct. There was a creepy zealotry to management's methods—which included hiring a brown-uniformed "security" detail— that left a bad taste. Besides, my pop was a union man, and I knew that, as his son, I was biologically precluded from crossing a picket line. I don't even know where that comes from; it's not as if we ever talked about it, as Larry and his father did. But that's how blue-collar workers act, I told myself, and I was born blue. I felt more loyalty to my fellow workers than I did to the company, though I never really understood why we were striking. It's not as if reporters regarded themselves as laboring brothers and sisters toiling for meager pay in awful conditions. Still, to earn my strike pay, I dutifully walked my picket on 42nd Street in the winter cold, making crisp, sharp turns when I got to the police barricade, like a tight end faithful to his assigned play pattern.

Our strike became popular among New Yorkers and others. Lou Reed, Pete Seeger, and Jesse Jackson showed up to sing and preach. It was cool to be on our side—like when people were anti-lettuce, anti-Coors, or anti-grapes at different times over the years. The *New York Post* sent Danish. New York *Newsday* delivered sandwiches and certificates for Christmas turkeys.

After a while, though, the duality was gnawing at me. White-collar man in a blue-collar fight—that's what it felt like some days, especially after guys from one of the blue-collar unions allegedly torched a delivery truck. What am I doing here, what's my issue? I'd ask myself. Then I'd think about the company trying to unilaterally change work rules, scuttle the unions, and put out the paper with replacements. Back and forth I'd go, never able to join with the idealogues who sang union songs (they actually did this), but soul-certain I would not cross the picket line. One day, I was asked to distribute leaflets in front of stores that advertised in the scab paper that the replacements were putting out.

"Union busting is disgusting," I chanted, and I thought things couldn't get any lower in my life. Then a friend got me a temp job in *Newsweek* magazine's public relations department for a month. I had to write fawning letters nominating *Newsweek* writers and reporters for magazine journalism awards. The magazine people were impressed because they'd never had professional writers doing these letters before. I made it sound like Hemingway, Tolstoy, and Maya Angelou were on staff, churning out graceful paragraphs of clarity and light. To strengthen one letter, I walked into the office of a writer to interview him about how he got the story I was about to exalt and glorify. What I saw stopped me. On the wall behind his desk, the guy had a framed *Daily News* front page that read "Man Feeds Baby to Dog." I had written that story with the help of various reporters some time before the strike. It was a gruesome tale about a Nebraska dog trainer who had come to New York to breed guard dogs. He had been angered when his infant son urinated on him, and the father shook the baby to death. He then cut up the child and fed him to a German shepherd, trying to blame the animal for his crime. (The guys who write the TV show *NYPD Blue* used the story as the reason the main character, Detective Andy Sipowicz, started drinking on the job. A few commentators—notably Pete Hamill in *Esquire*—used the story as a basis to essentially say the world was coming apart.) It was awful, and I purposely wrote the story in a careful, quiet tone. But it got that screaming, black headline on the front page, and the *Newsweek* man—who had been treating me in a high-handed, snootily white-collar manner—saw it as a piece of cultural kitsch. His displaying it was an ironic celebration of the kind of garish, blue-collar journalism he was above. Here I was, in the midst of a New York labor war, fighting to pay the rent and keep the lights on by being compelled to praise some white collar's mediocre output, hoping to return to a job that this imperial clod thought was a joke. Needless to say, I didn't exactly put my heart into his nominating letter. I don't think he ever won that award.

Soon after, the strike ended, and we went back to work—under a new boss who, by the way, made many of the changes for which we struck the old boss in the first place. Then the new man—who had lived on his yacht—drowned at sea, leaving staggering debts. It was a circus. But I never scabbed.

Pick a Place

For some Straddlers, reconciling their hybrid lives with the expectations of family and neighborhood friends started as a problem in college and continues today. They are never fully understood by people who want them to bend in a way they cannot contort themselves. What's amazing—and sometimes sad—is how hard limbo folk still try to please their relatives and connections, even after living so many years in the middle class. Often, nothing they do is good enough: overt gestures, grand accommodations, acquiescence on matters great and small— none of it matters. The person is left lost and frustrated, never seen as having done things the right way.

Talk to Veronica De Vivar long enough and she will tell you this. The vulnerability she guards with her professional's veneer pokes through as she struggles to figure out the doubleness of her life: How can she live the way she chooses, while making her family happy? The ultimate answer is, she can't.

Before her first child was born, Veronica suffered two miscarriages, each in the second trimester. That's unusual, and both occurred while she was traveling from her Sacramento home to her pharmaceutical company headquarters in New Jersey, part of the so-called Pharm Belt of drug companies in the central part of the state. Nature had failed her utterly and mysteriously, and the doctors told Veronica to quit searching for a cause because the events were inexplicable. This didn't stop the fami- lies—hers and her husband's—from telling Veronica precisely why this happened. It's your job; you work too much, the families said. Point- blank, they accused her of valuing her career more than having a family. Her parents, who lived six blocks away, wanted to know when she was going to quit work and be like all the other blue-collar Mexican-American daughters. They thought she was too driven and didn't understand Veronica's need to be challenged and to grow, and her notion that mothers who've been educated and allowed to develop offer more to their kids. These ideas of hers always seemed misguided to her family, her priorities a puzzle.

"My blue-collar family thinks it's terrible that when I think about my children, I think about how many I can afford. They tell me, 'How dare you look at children in those terms? You can always afford children.' But I say I want to send them to good schools and colleges, and that costs money."

They always make Veronica feel different. Just the other night at a Halloween party, everyone started in with the looks. Nobody said anything, but Veronica could tell. All the moms were fussing over the kids as they bobbed for apples or whatever. But Veronica asked her husband to keep an eye on things as she caught up with an old friend she hadn't expected would be there. Out of the corner of her eye, though, she could see the disapproving glares from elders, cousins, and friends. On the drive home, Veronica asked her husband, John, "Did you see how many times I got the head-shaking look? Why don't you just get up and tell everyone, 'I enjoy being a father? I enjoy my wife hanging out talking to a friend from college and I don't mind changing diapers and taking care of the children when she does?' He's very easygoing and he says, 'Just let it go.' But it's hard for me. I always walk a fine line and ask myself, 'What would be acceptable for me, and make them happy?' The question is, why do I need to make them happy?"

Because blue-collar kids are always expected to please their parents first. Stray from that law and risk family censure. It's becoming a problem at work, where Veronica's career is on hold. Upper management believes she's ready to advance, but she's got considerations that many middle-class-born executives don't ever think about. "The bosses show me a map of the United States where I could work for them and they say, 'Pick a place.' But how do you tell these folks that my family in California wants me to stay close by, without them thinking less of you, without them thinking that there's something psychologically wrong with you? I have created problems for myself, in rising up through management. The minute relocating is not an I issue, I could move up.

"Meanwhile, everybody in my family thinks there's something

wrong with me because I left a one-year-old behind with my husband while I left town for a three-day seminar. How do you win?"

When Veronica's second child was born, the pregnancy had been uneventful, and there hadn't been any business trips. "See what happens when there's no stress?" the family said. And when he turned out to be a boy, oh goodness, someone must have been trying to tell Veronica something because that's a bigger reward than a daughter, the family enthused.

Duality is stress, Veronica knows. She feels it at every family gathering, and it bubbles up every day at work, where her blue- and white-collar needs collide. "At first, it really took a toll on me, and I looked at ways to please both the families and myself. Lately, I've been telling myself, 'You are just going to have to accept that the family will never understand.' And you have to move on."

Life, Death, and Money

Like engineers looking to harness a kind of raw, natural power, some employers actively seek white-collar workers with blue-collar backgrounds. As Ed Haldeman, the megarich Straddler, says, they like the combination of book and street smarts and use it to advantage. This is especially true in the world of finance, which has traditionally attracted a great number of first-generation college graduates. Acting on the working-class imperative to make money to support a family (and not worry too very much about finding self-fulfillment), these people discover that working in brokerage houses and other financial shops makes the most sense for them. Not long out of the old neighborhood, these hard-charging money folk use tough-guy shrewdness and gamesmanship to score big for their firms and to fatten their own bank accounts. Ed says street-smart people like him understand the rules of the risk/reward financial game intuitively because they possess a blue-collar-born instinct to work efficiently and make the most of what they have. Also, there is a kind of ruthlessness to the job that attracts the macho broker set. It's simple stuff, really. "On the investment side," Ed says, "if old Bob here produces 12 percent, while the other guy does 8, I say, 'Come here, Bob.' Maybe if I'm hiring lawyers I want to pick one who knows what high tea is and has the best suit. But in finance, I don't care what suit you're in. If you do 12 for me every day, I'll tolerate anything you do. You are my guy, Bob. I love that. It's the only business in the world with a report card at 4 P.M. each day."

Wall Street called out to so many guys from my neighborhood. It was the logical next step for the sons and daughters of Brooklyn shopkeepers and sanitation workers, who did not entitle their youngsters and did not endow them with cultural capital or fill them with kitchen-table talk about the wide world of possibility that was out there. No, you went to a reasonable college and then you got down to business in Lower Manhattan. That's the kind of mobility and the kind of work blue-collar parents embrace and understand.

Straddlers whose duality skewed more blue- than white-collar were notable among those who died at the World Trade Center on September 11, 2001.[3] My high school friend Billy Bernstein was among those lost, a bond guy at Cantor Fitzgerald. His parents ran a silver shop in Brooklyn. A pragmatic son of the working class, Billy tried law school after college, but didn't like it. So he simplified things and hooked up with the neighborhood bunch out to score a buck or two. Making sure to still live in working-class Brooklyn, where he felt comfortable and at home, Billy spent his days across the water at the grand party. I could never do the requisite math to understand finance, but Billy doped out the bond market and started making at least four times what I did. Once in the go-go 1980s, Billy's boss reprimanded him for inadequately lavishing clients with entertainment. He'd spent something like $7,000 in restaurants and bars in one month, and still his overseers whined that it wasn't enough. So there he was, like a lot of neighborhood boys on September 11, up 101 floors in blue sky, looking down on Brooklyn, a big success.

Much has been made of the fact that many of the firefighters and cops who rushed to rescue the brokers and traders and died trying were themselves products of the same neighborhoods. It's true. We all, in fact, had played basketball together on the same broken-down, netless courts; we all tried picking up the same girls at Brighton Beach. Our parents—many of them the children of immigrants—were the people who built the towers that burned and buckled. We were Irish, Italian, Polish, Jewish, and mutt. In summers, we ventured to places like Asbury Park and Wildwood, New Jersey, blue-collar beach towns that attracted the overheated guys from the city that Springsteen sometimes sings about.

Our neighborhood rock band played down in Wildwood, or in schools and bars in Queens and Brooklyn, and Billy—more loyal than musical—would always be with us. Charming, cute, and funny, he'd collect young women's phone numbers as we sang, then help us load up the amplifiers at the end of the night.

The kinds of people we played for—who danced to our music; who started microphone-stand-swinging fights with us when we didn't play the songs they liked; who once swiped the battery out of our sax player's car during a gig—were like us, blue-collar kids with a restless energy and a ragged promise, at best. Nobody expected much of us. Some, like me, left town to pursue dreams, if they had any; but many of the ones unsure of what they wanted out of life stayed close to home. The people who made better grades or who harbored the belief that school might offer them a slight edge attended city or state colleges and changed their collars. As soon as possible, they found jobs where the money was. They knew where to look; they just cast their eyes upward at those towers. A lot of the other guys for whom school was a waste of time went into civil service. The pay was decent, you could afford a home in Staten Island or Rockaway, and you got a certain amount of respect as a firefighter or cop.

The traders and the cops and firefighters could all be tough guys. They were, after all, blue-collar people working in elemental conditions, dealing with the basics: life, death, and money. What did you expect? Billy avidly lifted weights and built up his body, which had been thin and small in high school. He was balding, and people joked that he looked like Mr. Clean. But his bulk gave him a kind of authority in a profession where strength is understood and respected.

On September 11, people who had grown up in the same neighborhoods—some of whom had remained blue collar, some of whom had gone white—were reunited in Manhattan hellfire. I went up to New York soon after to see things for myself and instinctively tried to scout the towers, like an amputee scratching a leg that isn't there. In the days that followed, I recognized the anger that came out of Brooklyn, the kind of heat and bile I'd seen as a kid, pouring out of people born on tough streets. Now middle-aged, the blue-collar guys of my youth cursed Mohammed Atta for unbuckling his seatbelt and standing up on a westbound plane, cursed Osama bin Laden, and screamed at the sky: "Is that all you got?"—a fighter's taunt to an opponent who has hurt him badly. Billy had a brown belt in karate and might have liked that. But I can't really know.

Sitting in the Duck Blind

Straddlers tell me that, although duality can be vexing, it can be worthwhile. Mo Wortman says the patients he feels closest to are the ones who struggled to get somewhere, because he believes the struggle says a lot about a person. It's enriching. He doesn't have a single friend who's second-generation wealthy. Nor does he want one. "Having the money, or the opportunity to make money, handed to people really pushes my buttons." He can't abide the country club set, because the members stand around and complain about the cost of good labor all day. "And I've been the laborer, and that's a big part of me. I identify with that."

Mo says his duality causes confusion in his life—"What class, exactly, do I belong to?"—but he believes that doesn't necessarily require an answer. "Maybe it's enough to recognize the difficulty of putting a neat, clean answer to it. And maybe there's enough of a fraternity of people who understand that."

It's not surprising that limbo folk are drawn to people like themselves. It may not be a conscious tropism. But when they take stock of their friends and the relatives they're closest to, they can't help but notice that those people happen to be straddling. "I just connect with white-collar people with a working-class background," says Dennis George. "I find they're more open and honest." They are the ones who moved beyond the original neighborhood folks intellectually and culturally, and now enjoy classical music, goat cheese, literary novels, and movies in which nothing explodes. But they retain a raft of working-class characteristics, and a kind of pugnacious resistance to a full embrace of white-collar life. They've picked and chosen the characteristics they believed were right for them from both collar groups.

The Plan-B types possess backup skills and an internal strength tempered by hard times. They're confident they could take care of business by signing on for a blue-collar gig, should the middle-class day job crash. "I like people like me," Peter Giangiulio asserts. "Blue-collar types who've achieved. Blue-collar types with an education—that's powerful. We can sit and talk like real people, without putting on airs. You don't ever lose that working-class practicality, and that ability to have a good old time. But you've achieved a little more than the average blue-collar guy has. It's perfect."

There's a nostalgia some have for their blue-collar past, a wistfulness for their younger selves. Richard Rodriguez is like that. He had been a laborer as a youth and was sorry to leave his body behind. He liked being strong as a young man. "Now I go to yuppie gyms to try to recover the sheer bulk of the body I didn't take with me," he says. "Middle-class men on Stairmasters I find much less sexy, much less interesting. A labor-shaped body is different than Nautilus-machined abs. I was always enchanted by the world of physical labor. I never was happier than when I was a laborer, working with my body, doing the kind of job in which you are not defined by your work. But I always knew this was somehow a sin, a violation of this other person I'd become."

Still, duality being what it is, Richard cannot enjoy this other person, either—not fully, anyway. He has never learned how to sit in a limo. While he derives a gaudy delight from the occasional stay in a five-star hotel, the experience is invariably leavened by his worries about the maid. He believes her needs and her schedule take precedence over his, and he feels awkward in her presence. And when the *New York Times* offered him a shot at one of the marquee jobs in American journalism—a column on the op-ed page—he said no thanks. "Am I crazy turning down the *Times?*" he asks me in the San Francisco twilight as he sips coffee in a sidewalk café. This has been a pattern for him. He will get close to things—lovely middle-class things—then back off. Richard has literally walked to the doorbell at dinner parties, then turned and gone home, leaving all those fancy buzzers unpressed. "I'm tantalized about being in the room, but I know I would feel uncomfortable in it. I don't belong at the *New York Times.*" It is the kind of upper-class institution in which a working-class man has no place, Richard believes. They wanted him, he says, because he's Latino. "That's interesting to me, because that was more important to them than my class, my blue-collar background." That, Richard says, is something the paper did not want to hear about.

Richard's duality is a powerful thing. In his travels, he has attended several college graduations and has always marveled at the photo ops, when working-class kids in joyous triumph throw their arms around their parents and smile for the cameras. That was not something Richard could do with his parents when he graduated. "I never had that grace. I wasn't able to put my arms around the two worlds. And I've still not done that." I ask him if he regrets the dichotomy and the difficulty of the crossover from one class to another. Doesn't the duality weigh on him? He looks at me, surprised that I don't get it, surprised that I don't see that the lives people like us lead are enriched.

"This movement in a life is nothing less than remarkable," he says. "Yes, this movement produces anxiety. But the quandary of being in two worlds deepens your humanity rather than restricts it. Why should you want to be less?"

So many Straddlers complain, though, that the movement costs them their families:

"I can't talk to them."

"There's nothing to say when we get together."

"They don't like who I've become."

It's sad when it happens, and the people I talk to about this live in real distress about the permanent disconnect. But the shrinks insist it doesn't have to be this way. Straddling doesn't automatically mean the end of all meaningful communication with the family. If the emotional life between the white-collar kids and their blue-collar parents was healthy from the start, then there is hope. Of course there'll be distance in terms of ideas and lifestyle. But maybe it's up to us to bridge it, some Straddlers tell me. After all, our parents and still-blue-collar siblings didn't cross the class divide with us. We are the bilingual ones, able to speak the language of both classes. Don McNeeley says that, despite his millions, he will never live in a gated community because he wouldn't want his seven brothers and sisters to have to announce themselves at the guard gate. "My siblings aren't going to have to go through a gate to see me. That's rubbing it in their faces."

Similarly, Nick Artim says that he's taken to looking at himself through his parents' eyes. The children of miners, they would see that he's moved from the valley to the house on the hill. That's fine, but Nick is always afraid of appearing ostentatious, of seeming as though he forgot the old values. Sometimes he thinks about buying a Porsche because he appreciates the quality, but he believes he'd have to give up too much

218

of his identity to climb behind that particular steering wheel. "I don't want to be the kind who would embarrass people like my parents and grandparents. I have to keep my humbleness."

When Joe Terry told his father he'd been having trouble sleeping, his dad said, "You must not be working hard enough." Joe laughs while repeating his worker father's simple explanation for the complex anxieties that can cause a sleepless night. But, Joe says, he's learned that his parents' blue-collar bromides that he once dismissed as overly simplistic really do have resonance for him: Work hard, and take care of your family. There's nothing better than a good work ethic and nothing more debilitating than not having one. "I work in the realm of ideas," Joe says. "But at the end of the day there are some absolute truths in terms of how I ought to live that I got from my parents. You need a code. There's a lot of cultural relativism in life, but those truths help me get through the day, and help me maintain a close relationship with my parents." As Joe walks through his house at night, snapping off all the lights, remembering the look on his father's face when the electric company cut the power, he understands something important: "Education divides you from your parents only if you let it." So, despite his dislike of duck hunting, Joe will sit in a duck blind with his dad, because it's what his dad likes. "If that's the only way I'm going to have contact with him, I'll do it."

For years, Susan Borrego kept in touch with her grandmother, who raised her. So it was natural for Susan to want her grandmother to attend a ceremony in which she would be getting an important award related to her doctoral program. Susan's grandmother traveled from Michigan to California to be there and was seated at a table with Susan's peers and supervisors. Susan's brother, who was supposed to keep an eye on Grandma, didn't show. The "barfly, kick-butt, salty broad," as Susan describes the old woman, was in rare form, saying things like, "For Chrissakes, how come we're eating all this fancy food?" It was, Susan remembers, "the most amazing moment of my life. I was sitting there thinking, 'Here's where east meets west, my blue-collar past, my white-collar life.' "

Susan began to feel embarrassed, as her grandmother fussed in front of high-level faculty—polished, accomplished people who had a lot to say about Susan's future. Her discomfort level rose as she tried to explain to her feisty grandmother that the dinner was only chicken and

219

okay to eat. But as she leaned over to scrape away the fancy sauce to reveal the humble bird below, Susan looked into her grandmother's eyes. Susan began to see scenes from her own life, disparate and yet somehow connected, always tied to this tough and rowdy old lady. She remembered how her grandmother had driven from Detroit to Idaho, sleeping in her car overnight, just to see Susan graduate from college. Susan used to play under the card table as her grandmother and her friends played pinochle. Later, Grandma would tell these same women that Susan was college president, though she was a dean. This was the woman who told Susan, "I'm sorry I didn't teach you more. You know I'm proud of you."

In an instant, the growing sense of mortification ebbed, her worries about what her colleagues were thinking drained away. Susan smiled. "Right at that table, I decided, 'F— them, this is who she is.' " When Susan got up to speak, she was overwhelmed with love. "I was able to say thank-you to her, as she sat in the middle of the world I live in. I told everyone that she taught me to read, with Dr. Seuss, when I was four. I said that's what set me on the path. I told everyone that my grand-mother is how I got here."

The Lower 40

My father had some difficulty accepting my being a mere reporter when I could have chosen swankier careers. But he had an experience once that helped him understand a little about what getting educated was like.

Thirty years into his bricklaying life, my dad decided he wanted a civil service bricklayer foreman's job that wouldn't be so physically demanding. There was a written test that included essay questions about construction work. Why they needed bricklayers to write essays I have no idea, but my father sweated it out. Every morning before sun-rise, my brother Chris would be ironing a shirt, bleary-eyed, and my father would sit at the kitchen table and read aloud his practice essays on how to wash down a wall or how to build a tricky corner. Chris would suggest words and approaches.

It was so hard for my dad. He had to take a Stanley Kaplanesque prep course in a junior high school three nights a week after work for six weeks. At class time, the bricklayers—the outside men—would come in: 25 construction workers squeezing themselves into little desks—tough, blue-collar guys armed with No. 2 pencils, leaning over and scratching out their practice essays, cement in their hair, tar on their pants, and their work boots too big and clumsy to fit under the desks.

"Is this what finals felt like?" my father would ask me on the phone when I would pitch in to help. "Were you always this nervous?" I told him yes; I told him that writing is always difficult. He thanked Chris and me for the coaching, for putting him through school this time. And the big guy made us proud: He aced the exam and became a foreman for the city.

For a while after that, my father would persist in asking me how the money was. "You know, you're not as successful as you could be," he said one day, while we were driving around Brooklyn, shopping for some things he needed. "You paid your dues in school. You deserve better restaurants, better clothes." Here we go, I thought, the same old stuff. I'm sure every family has five or six similar big issues that are replayed like well-worn videotapes. I wanted to fast-forward this thing when we stopped at a red light. Just then, my father turned to me, solemn and intense. His knees were aching and his back muscles were throbbing in clockable intervals that registered in his eyes. It was the end of a career of lifting 50-pound blocks. "I envy you," he said quietly. "For a man to do something he likes and get paid for it, that's fantastic." He smiled at me before the light changed, and we drove on.

He retired not too long after that, and he and my mom moved to an empty-nester condo on a golf course in Central Jersey. It ain't Pebble Beach, and the course is crawling with bad swingers whose shots go awry. Often, the balls will clank off the house, infuriating my folks. Neither of my parents plays golf, mind you. After years of staring at brick walls outside their windows in Brooklyn, they just wanted to see something green every day. But ignorance of the game does not stop my mother from critiquing the duffers. Nothing she says is constructive; she just doesn't want them hitting her house. So my mother will walk out of her backdoor to address the wall bangers, speaking with such authority and self-assuredness about straightening their shots that sometimes the golfers think she actually knows what she's talking about and take her criticism for instruction.

221

In his retirement, my father has been spending too many days in doctors' offices, his body all at once collecting on a bill. The tonnage he's lifted brings night pains that interrupt sleep. More and more lately, I consider the differences between our ways of life. I'll catch myself complaining about a silly story assignment, something I believe is beneath me. Then I think about men who really had to work for a living. And the thought diminishes me.

I tell my father he was half right when he predicted I'd need a professional to come over and hammer a nail into a wall for me. Some simple guy-like things I can do, but when it comes to stuff like plumbing and electricity, I'm lost. The times that I have to summon workers bristling with tools to come and fix something that's well beyond my capabilities make me feel rotten and low. These I call my tiny-manhood days. When blue-collar fixer guys are around, I try to stay out of their way and hope they leave quickly. Sometimes, I lean against the sink and stare at them, wondering whether I can beat them up. (In fact, I often enter a room, blue- or white-collar, wondering whether I could beat up the occupants, a true trogolodytic thought marinating in my brain since the old days. I was so happy when Joe Terry told me he sizes up guys, too, and calculates his chances in a potential brawl. I'm not alone in the blue-collar madness.) During the time Linda and I were building a 700-foot fence across our property, I reveled in the backache I got from using a posthole digger, and—after the initial pain and swelling abated—I admired the black, purple, and yellow rainbow thumb I'd won by accidentally whacking it with the hammer my father had given me to nail up fence boards.

Once, I mentioned to my dad that I'd been seeing a physical therapist for the repetitive strain injury I got from years of journalism. "RSI? What's that?" my father asked. "Are you gonna be okay?" I told him, then just laughed. Yeah, good one. Tell a man who once had a wall fall on him, who once fell off a scaffold and impaled his forearm on a nail, that it hurts when you type. Perfect.

Since I've married and done a wider variety of writing, the old man doesn't carp so much anymore about the money. "I do okay," I tell him, and now I think he believes me. My being a homeowner earns me a little respect, too, I guess. If we make him a grandfather, I might score even more points.

He still likes to kid me about cleaning up after horses and living on a farm, though. He and my brother have taken to calling me Dinty Moore, their blue-collar chop-busting skills still honed. "Hey, Dint," my father asks, "how's the lower 40?"

He'll never understand it. But he lets it all slide now. I don't know if it's old age or a blue-collar man's acceptance of his white-collar son's choices. At this point, I don't really need to know. He talks to me like a man, not a child.

And I can live with that.

Conclusion

For Straddlers, life's ultimate goal is reconciliation: finding peace with the past and present, blue collar and white, old family ways and the new middle-class life. That is a challenge. Different values and different views often seem to get in the way. Now-vegetarian Loretta Stec will never be able to talk about the fine points of cooking meat with her family. Manhattan resident Rebecca Beckingham will probably only exchange polite, perfunctory chat with her folks on the farm. Doug Russell has gone far in his company, but he knows that his blue-collar background will forever hold him back. "I want to fit in and grow with the organization," he says. "But I feel people will always talk about me in a different way: 'Will he be running the company in five years? Oh, no, he's a little rough, he's a little loud.' And I think, 'Why wouldn't you want to have people like me?' "

The phrase "people like me" is telling. Limbo folk remain aware of their otherness throughout their lives. Often out of step with their parents, their coworkers, and even their born-to-the-middle-class children, Straddlers can feel like perpetual outsiders.

Still, as tough as limbo can be, it does not have to be debilitating. The more successful Straddlers—and by this I mean people who are comfortable with their lives—embrace their middle-class reality while honoring their blue-collar roots. Though they live in limbo, they choose to concentrate on the upside and what makes them unique.

Another straddler, Jeffrey Orridge, always knew that he was just as good as those prep-school kids he ran with years ago in New York City. His working-class family imbued him with a strong sense of self. Living a profitable corporate life that includes international travel and major responsibility, he exudes confidence without being pretentious. People feel comfortable around Jeffrey because he's bright, accomplished—and grounded.

Joe Terry had his doubts about his worthiness and his suitability in white-collar America. A carpenter's boy and an avid fisherman, he had believed his right hand would always be too rough to shake in the boardroom. Nowadays, he celebrates the successful blending of his past with his day-to-day life. He looks at his working-class background as the strong foundation upon which his life is built. Possessing both calloused hands and corporate smarts, Joe has become a balanced person—more accomplished than his parents, more complex than his colleagues.

Some Straddlers will tell you they are successful *because* of their working-class roots. "I sometimes think that I'll never be what I could have been if I were born middle class," Doug Russell says. "On the other hand, I might not have gotten anywhere if I'd come from the middle class. I had such drive and ambition to get somewhere because of where I came from. I pushed and got somewhere." Straddlers can take pride in a resilience born of relative deprivation. As battle-tested as marines, Straddlers have no doubt they possess the stuff to get themselves through the hard times. That's because they've almost always had hard times. Limbo folk carry within themselves a "strength-from-struggle" ideal that can keep them afloat and move them forward. "I was never afraid of my employers," working-class studies scholar Charles Sackrey says. "I was always willing to say, 'Take this job and shove it,' because I knew I could survive no matter what. And most of my white-collar colleagues seemed not to know that at all." I too have always planned for the potential "crash." I've survived as a temp and a secretary at different times in my life. My years in newsrooms have honed my typing skills. If I had to, I could get by on my own.

I think that Straddlers enjoy the advantage of knowing they are self-created. "My identification is rooted in the family," says Peter Ciotta. "But I made my own identity." I take satisfaction in that notion myself. I don't work in my father's law firm; I'm not a third-generation surgeon. I am the bricklayer's son who made himself into something new.

Straddlers come to the table without the same assumptions or the same take on life that middle-class people have. There's an independence of thought that makes for interesting perspectives. It's a kind of diversity that human-resources types don't normally strive to achieve. A mixed-class workplace is more energized and dynamic than a same-class shop; the dialogue is much richer.

Ultimately, Sackrey says, white-collar people from the working class can consider themselves lucky because they have escaped the drudgery of "real work" in which their parents engaged. That's an advantage we have over people from elite families. We will always believe that we got to some place better because we became educated. We will always know that we avoided the construction site and the coal mine, the bus route and the assembly line. We will always understand that whatever we do for a living is safer, cleaner, usually more profitable, and often more engaging than the truly hard jobs at which our parents were compelled to toil. We won't take ourselves for granted and we won't stop working hard to avoid the alternative lives we could have lived.

My father was a bricklayer. I am a newspaperman. He got his wish—that I graduate from college and not live the life of the outside man, excluded from life's better buildings.

I got my dream—that I leave the neighborhood and get a chance to write about the world.

We Straddlers know there are costs and consequences for all the wishes and dreams. They are inevitable. Limbo folk can consider themselves fortunate if they can be upwardly mobile but still rooted in the blue-collar world. Peaceful reconciliation comes to us when we can finally meld the two people we are.

Endnotes

INTRODUCTION

1. David Brooks, *Bobos in Paradise: The New Upper Class and How They Got There* (New York: Touchstone Books, 2000), 11.
2. Curious to know just how many Straddlers there might be, I called on Tom Smith of the University of Chicago's National Opinion Research Center. His figures, from the General Social Survey, show that out of a workforce of about 141 million Americans, 30 percent, or roughly 42 million people, are professionals/managers. Of the 42 million, 23.6 percent, or approximately one-quarter, are college graduates whose parents did not attend college at all. So, about 13 million people (25 percent of the 42 million) are the college-graduate, professional/managerial kids of blue-collar parents who did not go to college. In other words, there are about 13 million Straddlers.
3. Paul Fussell, *Class: A Guide through the American Status System* (New York: Summit Books, 1983), 27.
4. Jake Ryan and Charles Sackrey, *Strangers in Paradise: Academics from the Working Class* (Lanham: University Press of America Inc., 1996), 107.
5. Patrick J. Finn, *Literacy with an Attitude: Educating Working-Class Children in Their Own Self-Interest* (Albany: State University of New York Press), 108. Finn is himself quoting from James Paul Gee, "What Is Literacy?," in *Rewriting Literacy: Culture and the Discourse of the Other* ed. C. Mitchell and K. Weiler (New York: Bergin & Garvey, 1991), 3.

CHAPTER ONE

1. Fussell, 27.
2. Pierre Bourdieu, *Distinction: A Social Critique of the Judgement of Taste*, trans. Richard Nice, (Cambridge: Harvard University Press, 1984), 12.
3. Bourdieu, 66.
4. Bourdieu, 12.
5. Dennis Gilbert, *The American Class Structure in an Age of Growing Inequality*, 5th ed. (Bont, Calif.: Wadsworth Publishing Co., 1998), 144.

6. Michael Zweig, *Working Class Majority: America's Best Kept Secret* (Ithaca and London: ILR Press, 2000), 44.

7. Lillian Breslow Rubin, *Worlds of Pain: Life in the Working-Class Family* (New York: Basic Books, 1976), 48.

8. Rubin, 163.

9. Rubin, 186.

10. Gilbert, 121.

11. Lareau says middle-class kids were taught to speak up among adults, and were told that their opinions and happiness mattered. This fostered feelings of entitlement. Working-class kids were not solicited for their opinions, judgments, or observations.

12. bell hooks, *Where We Stand: Class Matters* (New York and London: Routledge, 2000), 112.

13. Fussell, 26.

14. Yet another example: Annoyed female Straddlers will tell you that the women's movement has always been more about the middle class than the working class, says Straddler/scholar Rebecca Beckingham.

15. E.B. White, *Here Is New York* (New York: Harper & Brothers, 1949), 17.

16. Richard Sennett and Jonathan Cobb, *The Hidden Injuries of Class* (New York: Alfred A. Knopf, 1972), 128.

CHAPTER THREE

1. Sennett and Cobb, 131.

2. Richard Rodriguez, *Hunger of Memory: The Education of Richard Rodriguez* (New York: Bantam Books, 1983), 46. Rodriguez himself quotes from Richard Hoggart, *The Uses of Literacy* (London: Chatto and Windus, 1957), chap. 10.

3. Rodriguez, 128.

4. hooks, 143.

5. Rodriguez, 49.

6. Louis Alvarez and Andrew Kolker, producers, *People Like Us: Social Class in America* (New York: Center for New American Media, 2001).

CHAPTER FOUR

1. Michelle Tokarczyk and Elizabeth Fay, eds., *Working Class Women in the Academy: Laborers in the Knowledge Factory* (Amherst: University of Massachusetts Press, 1993), 74.

2. hooks, 144.

3. C.L. Barney Dews and Carolyn Law, eds., *This Fine Place So Far from Home: Voices of Academics from the Working Class* (Philadelphia: Temple University Press, 1995), 216.
4. Tokarczyk and Fay, 132.
5. Barbara Ehrenreich, *Nickel and Dimed: On (Not) Getting By in America* (New York: Henry Holt and Company, 2001), 2.

CHAPTER FIVE

1. Marianna De Marco Torgovnick, *Crossing Ocean Parkway* (Chicago: University of Chicago Press, 1994), 7.

CHAPTER SEVEN

1. Fussell, 51.

CHAPTER EIGHT

1. Janet Zandy, ed. *Calling Home: Working-Class Women's Writings* (New Brunswick and London: Rutgers University Press, 1990), 12. Zandy herself is quoting from W.E.B. DuBois, *The Souls of Black Folk* (New York: New American Library, Signet, 1969), 45.
2. Brooks, 54.
3. Janny Scott, "A Nation Challenged: The Human Side; In Neckties or Fire Helmets, Victims Shared a Work Ethic," *New York Times*, 4 November 2001, sec. 1A, p. 1.

Source Notes

Although more than 100 people were interviewed for this book, not all of them are named in it. Some preferred to be anonymous; some had experiences similar to those who are included and were therefore omitted because of repetition. In some cases, there simply wasn't room for everyone. Still, the book includes their echoes and flavors, and is informed by what they told me.

Many of the people I have quoted—both experts and Straddlers—were interviewed more than once, in some cases two and three times, over a period of several months. I wanted to hear what they had to say at different moments, in different moods. After interviews, several people would phone or e-mail me to impart more information and fresh thoughts.

Because so many of us are not used to thinking about our lives in terms of class, it took some Straddlers a little time to connect an event in their lives with the notion that they indeed live in a kind of class limbo. These "aha" moments were especially gratifying for me, first because they validated the premise of the book and helped me realize I was on the right track, but also because I witnessed someone "getting it," putting together puzzle pieces that had eluded them. Understanding, when it comes, is a powerful thing.

The more eloquent Straddlers are the ones you have met in this book. While each chapter looks at different aspects of being in limbo, I made sure to include many of the same people throughout. These main characters offer a kind of continuity and help illustrate the Straddlers' total experience. By way of balance, I introduced a new Straddler in each chapter.

Along with Straddlers and experts (sometimes, a person was both), the book includes a few friends and family members of the limbo folk. What follows is a list of many of the people I interviewed: Gregg Andrews, Nick Artim, Rebecca Beckingham, Suzanne Bilello, Susan Borrego, Bob Carroll, Yonna Carroll, Samme Chittum, Renny Christopher, Peter

Ciotta, Marianne Costantinou, Veronica De Vivar, Nancy Dean, Laurene
Finley, Mary Lou Finn, Patrick Finn, Maria Fosco, Tom Fricke, Larry
Gabriel, John Garcia, Fred Gardaphé, Tom Gariepy, Dennis George, Peter
Giangiulio, Dennis Gilbert, Dana Gioia, Rita Giordano, Paul Groncki, Ed
Haldeman, Elizabeth Higgenbotham, Michael Hout, Sandy Hunt,
Barbara Jensen, George Kanelos, Signe Kastberg, Angela Kulp, Annette
Lareau, Eils Lotozo, Anthony Lukas, Christine Lunardini, Don
McNeeley, Mike Moronczyk, Tim Moronczyk, Stephen Musick, Mark
Natale, James Neal, Dot Newton, Ken Oldfield, Jeffrey Orridge, Sal
Paolantonio, Barbara Peters, Patsy Pope, Amy Reed, Gillian Richardson,
Richard Rodriguez, Douglas Russell, Homer Russell, Zelma Russell, Jake
Ryan, Charles Sackrey, Anthony Salerno, Isabel Sawhill, Cheryl Shell, Art
Shostak, Loretta Stec, Michelle Tokarczyk, Joe Terry, Andrea Todd,
Helen Tom, Leticia Vega, Mo Wortman, Janet Zandy.

Generally, the chapters contain details from my life as well as the
lives of the Straddlers, as gleaned from interviews. Synopses of those
interviews follow.

INTRODUCTION

I have thought about class since my undergraduate days, when my
father and I shared a campus. I began speaking with Charles Sackrey
and Jake Ryan about class in 1988, a conversation that's continued, on
and off, through the years. Jack Metzgar, Sherry Linkon, Barbara
Jensen, and others were among the many people I met at the State
University of New York at Stony Brook, which sponsored a working-
class studies seminar last year. For years, the center of the working-
class studies movement has been at Youngstown State University, Ohio,
under the direction of Linkon and John Russo.

CHAPTER ONE

Much of the chapter is memoir and a discussion of class influence in my
life. As for the interviews: Sackrey chimes in; he has a way of boiling the
heavy-duty scholarship down to its essence, and he does so here,
explaining the key points of cultural capital. He provides a working

metaphor for mobility—a move into a new neighborhood. Isabel Saw-hill explains the influence of family on class. Two anonymous Straddlers recall important moments in their lives.

Straddlers Peter Ciotta, James Neal, and Samme Chittum talk about the differences between themselves and the middle-class-born. Straddler and academic Janet Zandy introduces the notion of the heritage of struggle, a basic part of blue-collar existence. Jeffrey Orridge and Andrea Todd discuss their parents' desires and sacrifices for their kids. Nancy Dean talks about the sometimes harsh blue-collar edicts with which we grew up.

Sociologist Dennis Gilbert says that people born to the working class (roughly 60 percent of the population) don't have the same life chances as those born to the middle class (around 30 percent of the population). He and others add, by the way, that things are only getting tougher. Working-class salaries stagnate as upper-class compensation rises, and blue-collar people have seen a decline in living standards over the last 25 years or so, Gilbert says. The tools that helped generations of blue-collar people to be class-mobile—including well-functioning public schools, as well as the expansion of public higher education and the explosion of grants and scholarships in the 1960s and 1970s—are not available for today's blue-collar kids, Michael Hout and others assert. Gilbert goes on to explain the working-class penchant to stress obedience over curiosity. Temple University's Annette Lareau discusses her study demonstrating the differences in the way working- and middle-class children are raised. In dealing with the outside world, middle-class kids, like their parents, are not intimidated by institutions. They are taught to speak up among adults and assert themselves. Chauffeured by their parents from one enriching activity to the next, middle-class kids come to the logical conclusion that they are special and worthy of having adults devote much of their time to making sure they are fulfilled. This develops a sense of entitlement in the kids, Lareau says. Patrick Finn, a Straddler and an expert on class and education, discusses the role of language in the home. Hout explains broad mobility trends.

Jensen, Gilbert, Art Shostak of Drexel University, and others offer "flash cards"—handy descriptions of class differences that are difficult to prove but widely held.

CHAPTER TWO

Jensen relates a personal story about her mother's objection to Jensen's attending college merely "to learn." An anonymous Straddler bitterly regrets a lack of parental support. Dot Newton and Maria Fusco share important aspects of their difficult upbringings, and their respective fights to educate themselves, despite parental opposition. Mary Lou Finn recalls her own fight for education. Father and son Tim and Michael Moronczyk each gives his side on the family decision to allow Michael to attend college.

CHAPTER THREE

Gregg Andrews warns freshmen about education's destabilizing influence in the home. Ryan discusses how education fosters distance in a family. Richard Rodriguez explains the scholarship boy, who must withdraw from the family to be educated and must learn to live with "lonely reason." Dennis George gives an account of an epiphany in the street, the very moment he realizes he has to move out of the working class. Finn explains how schools reinforce class. Rita Giordano discusses the growing differences between herself and her friends growing up. Loretta Stec remembers a disastrous encounter with an old flame from the working class.

Todd explains how her education could grate on her father. "Michael" talks about escaping the coal mines and old-time religion of the working class. Marianne Costantinou recounts the story of family class differences at her wedding. "Donna" recalls how relatives were upset that she would believe she was better than others in the family because of her college degree. Dean describes a similar reaction from her aunts. Sociologist Barbara Peters explains her family's mixed emotions about her education. Anthony Lukas tells me about the difficulties in becoming white collar from blue-collar Philadelphia. Gillian Richardson talks about her family's inability to understand her white-collar life. Larry Gabriel discusses the differences between himself and his brother. Psychologist Laurene Finley brings up the question of what children owe their parents, and Straddler Rebecca Beckingham illustrates that quandary with a story from her own life.

CHAPTER FOUR

Straddler Joe Terry talks about his first encounter with middle- and upper-class people and Jensen's so-called cashmere kids, as do Shell, Peters, Dana Gioia, Signe Kastberg, and Tom Fricke. Paul Groncki talks about his unfulfilled wish to join a fraternity. Susan Borrego and Richardson lament the lack of know-how among blue-collar types. Michelle Tokarczyk, working-class studies academic and Straddler, describes Straddlers' difficulties in school. Christine Lunardini reveals a fear of being "found out" because she's blue collar. Yonna Carroll and "Tina" talk about their problems with the middle class. Mo Wortman says he has felt class-superior as a blue-collar guy.

Peter Giangiulio, who grew up as a rich blue-collar kid, confesses his dislike of his prep-school friends. Orridge talks about the extremes in his life: his blue-collar upbringing and his prep-school background. Don McNeeley and Eils Lotozo discuss experiencing culture shock at a young age. Suzanne Bilello offers a case study in ambition, recounting her formative days among the well-to-do of Westchester County, and her desire to better herself. Eighteen-year-old University of Pennsylvania freshmen Angela Kulp, Mark Natale, and Stephen Musick prove that class differences hold their shape and form, and have resonance even among the young.

CHAPTER FIVE

I follow two limbo men as they return to the blue-collar hometowns they left years ago. Doug Russell talks about never fitting in. His parents, Zelma and Homer, explain how they tried all they could to help their son, but felt ill-equipped to give him what he needed. Doug's friend Sandy Hunter explains his decision to stay in town. Fred Gardaphé talks about why leaving town saved his life. Friends Anthony, Patsy, and George reminisce about the old days and revel in the realization that they all still feel close.

CHAPTER SIX

Kastberg says she cannot be tactful. Finley explains how many of the blue-collar-born do not fit into the workplace because it's a middle-class space. Straddlers unaware of how to be white collar in the white-collar world get "slam-dunked," she says. An anonymous Straddler confesses she wishes she hadn't fought so hard in the office. Bob Carroll talks about how his blue-collar frankness held him back at work. Gioia talks about corporate wimpishness. An anonymous Straddler talks about a suppressed need to tell off a colleague in middle-class meetings. [Mary Lou] Finn realizes she cannot communicate with a middle-class-born boss. Giangiulio explains how he prefers his one-man office to working with white-collar people. Veronica De Vivar says she's too honest at work. Wortman says his blue-collar brashness among doctor colleagues would get him voted off the island. Nick Artim talks about taking on a Supreme Court justice in his blue-collar pique. Giordano describes a blue-collar person's inability to shmooze correctly. Groncki talks about yes-men. Jensen, Kastberg, Chittum, and [Patrick] Finn explain their reluctance to play the white-collar game, especially networking. John Garcia won't play golf, and pays a price. Amy Reed reports feeling uncomfortable bowling with colleagues. Tokarczyk does not promote her career with dinner parties at home.

Lukas believes his city, Philadelphia, is too class-conscious. Sal Paolantonio recalls a problem a coworker had with his Italian name. Giordano talks about being class-ostracized at work. "Donna" talks about the strains and difficulties of working in a nearly all-middle- and upper-class workplace. Todd discusses the difficult life of a working-class kid in the world of women's magazines. Russell returns with talk about how he learned to network. Elizabeth Higgenbotham explains that it is important for a person to be class-mobile for his or her race. Renny Christopher talks about a "humiliating" ability to shmooze, and Dean says she's learned to play the corporate game as well. Terry talks about his technique of keeping quiet and listening. Don McNeeley explains why he'd hire a blue-collar-born person 100 out of 100 times. Ed Haldeman explains why it's important for working-class people to not think of him as a Harvard snob. Gioia talks about Jell-O and other blue-collar foods.

CHAPTER SEVEN

Jensen talks about class warfare in marriage. [Patrick] Finn and Reed discuss how the classes differ in terms of use of language and handling money. Terry explains how his middle-class girlfriend didn't understand what he went through to pay for a date. Andrews talks about sad

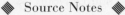

class-based encounters with young women. Wortman and Gioia discuss the pluses and minuses of flirtations with the upper classes. Dean and an anonymous Straddler remember being surprised by middle-class posers pretending to be down-to-earth. Christopher discusses being "rehabbed" by an ex. De Vivar explains her discomfort with a working-class beau.

Richardson talks about her entitled child. Gabriel worries that his daughter won't understand what the working class is. Terry is on guard for signs of entitlement in his kids. Leticia Vega believes a parent cannot instill values in children if they simply give them things. Haldeman and McNeeley talk about trying to teach their rich children about values. Helen Tom eschews affluence, for fear of its negative influence on her kids. Beckingham marvels at the enriched lives her fiancé's children lead. Christopher compares her blue-collar upbringing with that of her stepdaughter.

CHAPTER EIGHT

Zandy says a working-class person in the middle class will never belong there. Richardson talks about the difficulty of never fitting in—of feeling in constant limbo. Carlos Figueroa talks about never forgetting his time working on an assembly line. Metzgar, Rodriguez, and Groncki address ambivalence in limbo lives. Stec confesses that she must convince herself that she's good enough to be a professor, because of a sense of blue-collar inferiority. Christopher talks about her inability to reconcile the two halves of herself. Costantinou says she'll never change her working-class attitude, but she still craves validation from the middle class.

Kastberg says her Scandinavian background makes her seem more white collar. Lukas says he uses his blue-collar swagger to gain advantage. Straddlers like Milton Sommerfeld find they can live in both worlds easily. Orridge and Bilello say the same thing. Borrego, George, and [Mary Lou] Finn talk about reunions and trying to revisit their blue-collar pasts. Gabriel talks about the Detroit newspaper strike and his sense of duality. De Vivar tries to reconcile her needs with her family's. Wortman and Giangiulio say they're drawn to Straddlers. Rodriguez discusses his duality with some sadness. McNeeley and Artim worry that they not seem above it all to family. Terry and Borrego work hard to maintain relationships with kin.

Acknowledgments

I thank the Straddlers.

There simply could not have been a book without them. They entrusted a stranger with their stories, handing over parts of themselves to me. I remain stunned, honored, and grateful for their generosity.

Special thanks go to Charles Sackrey and Jake Ryan, the rowdy old heads of the still-young field of working-class studies. They pulled double duty, talking about their own former blue-collar lives, while patiently explaining the scholarship of class to me, at night, on weekends, or whenever I asked. They gave me private tutorials since I began writing about class in 1988, first for the Cleveland *Plain Dealer*, then for *GQ* magazine, and after that, for the *Philadelphia Inquirer*. Barbara Jensen also granted me many hours of her time and knowledge, both as an insightful working-class studies psychologist and as a Straddler with important memories to impart. I need her to know I appreciate that.

I would also like to thank Richard Rodriguez for interrupting a tiring and overwhelming schedule to make sure I got the nuances right. He helped me understand that feeling ambivalent about my limbo status is okay. In fact, it's how I should feel. Thanks also to my talented pal, Rita Giordano. I must acknowledge the kind patience and indulgences of Loretta Stec, Renny Christopher, Elizabeth Higgenbotham, Doug Russell, Laurene Finley, Andrea Todd, Marianne Costantinou, Samme Chittum, Sherry Linkon, and Tanya Barrientos. Thanks, also, to my old friend Ellen Kadin for good counsel. My gratitude goes out also to Denise Boal, for research help, and to Joan Fairman Kanes, for literary assistance. I should also acknowledge sharp-eyed Virginia Carroll for her hard work.

My thanks also to my editor at Wiley, Airié Stuart, who was gratifyingly enthusiastic from the start, and never wavered in her convictions. A book like this needs an advocate, and she has been that and more. In that vein, I thank my agent David Vigliano, who braved Amtrak and came all the way down to Philadelphia to tell me that I had an idea worth exploring, instilling in me the confidence I needed through the months.

My cousin, Ann Lubrano (Ph.D., I'm proud to say), steadied me at the uncertain start of this project, urging me to move ahead and write it as I saw it.

My brother, Christopher, offered insights into our childhoods and consistently on-target assessments of a working-class man's place in the white-collar life. Plus, he can make me laugh like no one else can.

I would be remiss if I did not thank my editors at the *Inquirer*, specifically Michael Rozansky and Nancy Cooney, who rearranged their lives to make mine easier. I also thank my boss Anne Gordon, who made sure I had the time to write, and who encouraged my work. Special, belated thanks to Eliot Kaplan, for recognizing the story the first time.

As for the people to whom this book is dedicated:

I've read that parents quake when there's a writer in the family, fearful of some awful filial revenge. My parents have only ever acted out of love, and I hope they see that reflected back at them in this book.

And I remain in awe of the scary gifts of my wife, Linda: She could tame the balky computer, critique Chapter 4 like the lit major she was, and repeat the words "Of course, you can" with the same patient conviction each of the 400 times I needed to hear them. The greatest piece of luck in my life was our chance meeting at a California earthquake. It has made all the difference.

Index